Strange Survivals

Some Chapters in the History of Man

S. Baring-Gould

Alpha Editions

This edition published in 2024

ISBN : 9789362991638

Design and Setting By
Alpha Editions
www.alphaedis.com
Email - info@alphaedis.com

As per information held with us this book is in Public Domain.
This book is a reproduction of an important historical work. Alpha Editions uses the best technology to reproduce historical work in the same manner it was first published to preserve its original nature. Any marks or number seen are left intentionally to preserve its true form.

Contents

I. On Foundations..- 1 -

II. On Gables...- 20 -

III. Ovens..- 39 -

IV. Beds..- 53 -

V. Striking a Light...- 68 -

VI. Umbrellas..- 80 -

VII. Dolls..- 85 -

VIII. Revivals..- 92 -

IX. Broadside Ballads...................................- 108 -

X. Riddles..- 134 -

XI. The Gallows...- 145 -

XII. Holes..- 154 -

XIII. Raising the Hat....................................- 176 -

NOTES..- 180 -

I.
On Foundations.

When the writer was a parson in Yorkshire, he had in his parish a blacksmith blessed, or afflicted—which shall we say?—with seven daughters and not a son. Now the parish was a newly constituted one, and it had a temporary licensed service room; but during the week before the newly erected church was to be consecrated, the blacksmith's wife presented her husband with a boy—his first boy. Then the blacksmith came to the parson, and the following conversation ensued:—

Blacksmith: "Please, sir, I've gotten a little lad at last, and I want to have him baptised on Sunday."

Parson: "Why, Joseph, put it off till Thursday, when the new church will be consecrated; then your little man will be the first child christened in the new font in the new church."

Blacksmith (shuffling with his feet, hitching his shoulders, looking down): "Please, sir, folks say that t' fust child as is baptised i' a new church is bound to dee (die). T' old un (the devil) claims it. Now, sir, I've seven little lasses, and but one lad. If this were a lass again 'twouldn't 'a' mattered; but as it's a lad—well, sir, I won't risk it."

A curious instance this of a very widespread and very ancient superstition, the origin of which we shall arrive at presently.

In the first place, let us see the several forms it takes.

All over the north of Europe the greatest aversion is felt to be the first to enter a new building, or to go over a newly erected bridge. If to do this is not everywhere and in all cases thought to entail death, it is considered supremely unlucky. Several German legends are connected with this superstition. The reader, if he has been to Aix-la-Chapelle, has doubtless had the rift in the great door pointed out to him, and has been told how it came there. The devil and the architect made a compact that the first should draw the plans, and the second gain the *Kudos*; and the devil's wage was to be that he should receive the first who crossed the threshold of the church when completed. When the building was finished, the architect's conscience smote him, and he confessed the compact to the bishop. "We'll do him," said the prelate; that is to say, he said something to this effect in terms more appropriate to the century in which he lived, and to his high ecclesiastical office.

When the procession formed to enter the minster for the consecration, the devil lurked in ambush behind a pillar, and fixed his wicked eye on a fine fat and succulent little chorister as his destined prey. But alas for his hopes! this fat little boy had been given his instructions, and, as he neared the great door, loosed the chain of a wolf and sent it through. The evil one uttered a howl of rage, snatched up the wolf and rushed away, giving the door a kick, as he passed it, that split the solid oak.

The castle of Gleichberg, near Rönskild, was erected by the devil in one night. The Baron of Gleichberg was threatened by his foes, and he promised to give the devil his daughter if he erected the castle before cockcrow. The nurse overheard the compact, and, just as the castle was finished, set fire to a stack of corn. The cock, seeing the light, thought morning had come, and crowed before the last stone was added to the walls. The devil in a rage carried off the old baron—and served him right—instead of the maiden. We shall see presently how this story works into our subject.

At Frankfort may be seen, on the Sachsenhäuser Bridge, an iron rod with a gilt cock on the top. This is the reason: An architect undertook to build the bridge within a fixed time, but three days before that on which he had contracted to complete it, the bridge was only half finished. In his distress he invoked the devil, who undertook the job if he might receive the first who crossed the bridge. The work was done by the appointed day, and then the architect drove a cock over the bridge. The devil, who had reckoned on getting a human being, was furious; he tore the poor cock in two, and flung it with such violence at the bridge that he knocked two holes in it, which to the present day cannot be closed, for if stones are put in by day they are torn out by night. In memorial of the event, the image of the cock was set up on the bridge.

Sometimes the owner of a house or barn calls in the devil, and forfeits his life or his soul by so doing, which falls to the devil when the building is complete.

And now, without further quotation of examples, what do they mean? They mean this—that in remote times a sacrifice of some sort was offered at the completion of a building; but not only at the completion—the foundation of a house, a castle, a bridge, a town, even of a church, was laid in blood. In heathen times a sacrifice was offered to the god under whose protection the building was placed; in Christian times, wherever much of old Paganism lingered on, the sacrifice continued, but was given another signification. It was said that no edifice would stand firmly unless the foundations were laid in blood. Some animal was placed under the corner-stone—a dog, a sow, a wolf, a black cock, a goat, sometimes the body of a malefactor who had been executed for his crimes.

Here is a ghastly story, given by Thiele in his "Danish Folk-tales." Many years ago, when the ramparts were being raised round Copenhagen, the wall always sank, so that it was not possible to get it to stand firm. They, therefore, took a little innocent girl, placed her in a chair by a table, and gave her playthings and sweetmeats. While she thus sat enjoying herself, twelve masons built an arch over her, which, when completed, they covered with earth to the sound of drums and trumpets. By this process the walls were made solid.

When, a few years ago, the Bridge Gate of the Bremen city walls was demolished, the skeleton of a child was actually found embedded in the foundations.

Heinrich Heine says on this subject: "In the Middle Ages the opinion prevailed that when any building was to be erected something living must be killed, in the blood of which the foundation had to be laid, by which process the building would be secured from falling; and in ballads and traditions the remembrance is still preserved how children and animals were slaughtered for the purpose of strengthening large buildings with their blood."

The story of the walls of Copenhagen comes to us only as a tradition, but the horrible truth must be told that in all probability it is no invention of the fancy, but a fact.

Throughout Norway, Sweden, Denmark, and North Germany, tradition associates some animal with every church, and it goes by the name of Kirk-Grim. These Kirk-Grims are the goblin apparitions of the beasts that were buried under the foundation-stones of the churches. It is the same in Devonshire—the writer will not say at the present day, but certainly forty or fifty years ago. Indeed, when he was a boy he drew up a list of the Kirk-Grims that haunted all the neighbouring parishes. To the church of the parish in which he lived, belonged two white sows yoked together with a silver chain; to another, a black dog; to a third, a ghostly calf; to a fourth, a white lamb.

Afzelius, in his collection of Swedish folk-tales, says: "Heathen superstition did not fail to show itself in the construction of Christian churches. In laying the foundations, the people retained something of their former religion, and sacrificed to their old deities, whom they could not forget, some animal, which they buried alive, either under the foundation or without the wall. The spectre of this animal is said to wander about the churchyard at night, and is called the Kirk-Grim. A tradition has also been preserved that under the altar of the first Christian churches, a lamb was usually buried, which imparted security and duration to the edifice. This is an emblem of the true Church Lamb—the Saviour, who is the Corner-Stone of His Church. When anyone enters a church at a time when there is no service, he may chance to see a little lamb spring across the quire and vanish. This is the church-lamb. When it appears to a person in the churchyard, particularly to the grave-digger, it is said to forbode the death of a child."

Thiele, in his "Danish Folk-tales," says much the same of the churches in Denmark. He assures us that every church there has its Kirk-Grim, which dwells either in the tower, or in some other place of concealment.

What lies at the base of all stories of haunted houses is the same idea. All old mansions had their foundations laid in blood. This fact is, indeed, forgotten, but it is not forgotten that a ghostly guard watches the house, who is accounted for in various ways, and very often a crime is attributed to one of the former inhabitants to account for the walking of the ghost. By no means infrequently the crime, which, in the popular mind, accounts for the ghost, can be demonstrated historically not to have taken place. Again, in a great number of cases, the spectre attached to a building is not that of a human being at all, but of some animal, and then tradition is completely at a loss to explain this phenomenon.

The proverb says that there is a skeleton in every man's house, and the proverb is a statement of what at one time was a fact. Every house had its skeleton, and every house was intended to have its skeleton; and what was more, every house was designed to have not only its skeleton, but its ghost.

We are going back to heathen times, when we say that at the foundation-stone laying of every house, castle, or bridge, provision was made to give to each its presiding, haunting, protecting spirit. The idea, indeed, of providing every building with its spectre, as its spiritual guard, was not the primary idea, it grew later, out of the original one, the characteristically Pagan idea, of a sacrifice associated with the beginning of every work of importance.

When the primeval savage lived in a hut of poles over which he stretched skins, he thought little of his house, which could be carried from place to place with ease, but directly he began to build of stone, or raise earthworks as fortifications, he considered himself engaged on a serious undertaking. He was disturbing the face of Mother Earth, he was securing to himself in permanency a portion of that surface which had been given by her to all her children in common. Partly with the notion of offering a propitiatory sacrifice to the earth, and partly also with the idea of securing to himself for ever a portion of soil by some sacramental act, the old Pagan laid the foundations of his house and fortress in blood.

Every great work was initiated with sacrifice. If a man started on a journey, he first made an offering. A warlike expedition was not undertaken till an oblation had been made, and the recollection of this lingered on in an altered form of superstition, *viz.*, that that side would win the day which was the first to shed blood, a belief alluded to in the "Lady of the Lake." A ship could not be launched without a sacrifice, and the baptism of a vessel nowadays with a bottle of wine is a relic of the breaking of the neck of a human victim and the suffusion of the prow with blood, just as the burial of a bottle with coins at the present day under a foundation stone is the faded reminiscence of the immuring of a human victim.

Building, in early ages, was not so lightly taken in hand as at present, and the principles of architectural construction were ill understood. If the walls showed tokens of settlement, the reason supposed was that the earth had not been sufficiently propitiated, and that she refused to bear the superimposed burden.

Plutarch says that when Romulus was about to found the Eternal City, by the advice of Etruscan Augurs, he opened a deep pit, and cast into it the "first fruits of everything that is reckoned good by use, or necessary by nature," and before it was closed by a great stone, Faustulus and Quinctilius were killed and laid under it. This place was the Comitium, and from it as a centre, Romulus described the circuit of the walls.[1] The legend of Romulus slaying Remus because he leaned over the low walls is probably a confused recollection of the sacrifice of the brothers who were laid under the bounding wall. According to Pomponius Mela, the brothers Philæni were buried alive at the Carthaginian frontier. A dispute having arisen between the Carthaginians and Cyrenæans about their boundaries, it was agreed that deputies should start at a fixed time from each of the cities, and that the place of their meeting should thenceforth form the limit of demarcation. The Philæni departed from Carthage, and advanced much farther than the Cyrenæans. The latter accused them of having set out before the time agreed upon, but at length consented to accept the spot which they had reached as a boundary line, if the Philæni would submit to be buried alive there. To this the brothers consented. Here the story is astray of the truth. Really, the Philæni were buried at the confines of the Punic territory, to be the ghostly guardians of the frontier. There can be little doubt that elsewhere burials took place at boundaries, and it is possible that the whipping of boys on gang-days or Rogations may have been a mediæval and Christian mitigation of an old sacrifice. Certainly there are many legends of spectres that haunt and watch frontiers, and these legends point to some such practice. But let us return to foundations.

In the ballad of the "Cout of Keeldar," in the minstrelsy of the Border, it is said,

> "And here beside the mountain flood
> A massy castle frowned,
> Since first the Pictish race in blood
> The haunted pile did found."

In a note, Sir Walter Scott alludes to the tradition that the foundation stones of Pictish raths were bathed in human gore.

A curious incident occurs in the legend of St. Columba, founder of Iona, which shows how deep a hold the old custom had taken. The original idea of a sacrifice to propitiate the earth was gone, but the idea that appropriation of a site was not possible without one took its place. The Saint is said to have buried one of his monks, Oran by name, alive, under the foundations of his new abbey, because, as fast as he built, the spirits of the soil demolished by night what he raised by day. In the life of the Saint by O'Donnell (Trias Thaumat.) the horrible truth is disguised. The story is told thus:—On arriving at Hy (Iona), St. Columba said, that whoever willed to die first would ratify the right of the community to the island by taking corporal possession of it. Then, for the good of the community, Oran consented to die. That is all told, the dismal sequel, the immuring of the living monk, is passed over. More recent legend, unable to understand the burial alive of a monk, explains it in another way. Columba interred him because he denied the resurrection.

It is certain that the usage remained in practice long after Europe had become nominally Christian; how late it continued we shall be able to show presently.

Grimm, in his "German Mythology," says: "It was often considered necessary to build living animals, even human beings, into the foundations on which any edifice was reared, as an oblation to the earth to induce her to bear the superincumbent weight it was proposed to lay on her. By this horrible practice it was supposed that the stability of the structure was assured, as well as other advantages gained." Good weather is still thought, in parts of Germany, to be secured by building a live cock into a wall, and cattle are prevented from straying by burying a living blind dog under the threshold of a stable. The animal is, of course, a substitute for a human victim, just as the bottle and coins are the modern substitute for the live beast.

In France, among the peasantry, a new farmhouse is not entered on till a cock has been killed, and its blood sprinkled in the rooms. In Poitou, the explanation given is that if the living are to dwell in the house, the dead must have first passed through it. And in Germany, after the interment of a living being under a foundation was abandoned, it was customary till comparatively recently to place an empty coffin under the foundations of a house.

This custom was by no means confined to Pagan Europe. We find traces of it elsewhere. It is alluded to by Joshua in his curse on Jericho which he had destroyed, "Cursed be the man before the Lord, that riseth up, and buildeth this city Jericho: *he shall lay the foundation thereof in his firstborn*, and in his youngest son shall he set up the gates of it." (Josh. vi. 26.)

The idea of a sacrifice faded out with the spread of Christianity, and when tenure of soil and of buildings became fixed and usual, the notion of securing it by blood disappeared; but in its place rose the notion of securing a spiritual protector to a building, sacred or profane, and until quite late, the belief remained that weak foundations could be strengthened and be made to stand by burying a living being, generally human, under them. The thought of a sacrifice to the Earth goddess was quite lost, but not the conviction that by a sacrifice the cracking walls could be secured.

The vast bulk of the clergy in the early Middle Ages were imbued with the superstitions of the race and age to which they belonged. They were of the people. They were not reared in seminaries, and so cut off from the influences of ignorant and superstitious surroundings. They were a little ahead of their fellows in culture, but only a little. The mediæval priest allowed the old Pagan customs to continue unrebuked, he half believed in them himself. One curious and profane incident of the close of the fifteenth century may be quoted to show to how late a date heathenism lingered mixed up with Christian ideas. An Italian contemporary historian says, that when Sessa was besieged by the King of Naples, and ran short of water, the inhabitants put a consecrated host in the mouth of an ass, and buried the ass alive in the porch of the church. Scarcely was this horrible ceremony completed, before the windows of heaven were opened, and the rain poured down.[2]

In 1885, Holsworthy parish church was restored, and in the course of restoration the south-west angle wall of the church was taken down. In it, embedded in the mortar and stone, was found a skeleton. The wall of this portion of the church was faulty, and had settled. According to the account given by the masons who found the ghastly remains, there was no trace of a tomb, but every appearance of the person having been buried alive, and hurriedly. A mass of mortar was over the mouth, and the stones were huddled about the corpse as though hastily heaped about it, then the wall was leisurely proceeded with.

The parish church of Kirkcudbright was partially taken down in 1838, when, in removing the lintel of the west doorhead, a skull of a man was found built into the wall above the doorway. This parish church was only erected in 1730, so that this seems to show a dim reminiscence, at a comparatively recent date, of the obligation to place some relic of a man in the wall to insure its stability.

In the walls of the ancient castle of Henneberg, the seat of a line of powerful counts, is a relieving arch, and the story goes that a mason engaged on the castle was induced by the offer of a sum of money to yield his child to be built into it. The child was given a cake, and the father stood on a ladder superintending the building. When the last stone was put in, the child screamed in the wall, and the man, overwhelmed with self-reproach, lost his hold, fell from the ladder, and broke his neck. A similar story is told of the castle of Liebenstein. A mother sold her child for the purpose. As the wall rose about the little creature, it cried out, "Mother, I still see you!" then, later, "Mother, I can hardly see you!" and lastly, "Mother, I see you no more!" In the castle of Reichenfels, also, a child was immured, and the superstitious conviction of the neighbourhood is, that were the stones that enclose it removed, the castle would fall.

In the Eifel district, rising out of a gorge is a ridge on which stand the ruins of two extensive castles, Ober and Nieder Manderscheid. According to popular tradition, a young damsel was built into the wall of Nieder Manderscheid, yet with an opening left, through which she was fed as long as she was able to eat. In 1844 the wall at this point was broken through, and a cavity was discovered in the depth of the wall, in which a human skeleton actually was discovered.

The Baron of Winneburg, in the Eifel, ordered a master mason to erect a strong tower whilst he was absent. On his return he found that the tower had not been built, and he threatened to dismiss the mason. That night someone came to the man and said to him: "I will help you to complete the tower in a few days, if you will build your little daughter into the foundations." The master consented, and at midnight the child was laid in the wall, and the stones built over her. That is why the tower of Winneburg is so strong that it cannot be overthrown.

When the church of Blex, in Oldenburg, was building, the foundations gave way, being laid in sand. Accordingly, the authorities of the village crossed the Weser, and bought a child from a poor mother at Bremerleke, and built it alive into the foundations. Two children were thus immured in the basement of the wall of Sandel, one in that of Ganderkesee. At Butjadeirgen, a portion of the dyke gave way, therefore a boy named Hugo was sunk alive in the foundations of the dam. In 1615 Count Anthony Günther of Oldenburg, on visiting a dyke in process of construction, found the workmen about to bury an infant under it. The count interfered, saved the child, reprimanded the dam-builders, and imprisoned the mother who had sold her babe for the purpose. Singularly enough, this same count is declared by tradition to have buried a living child in the foundations of his castle at Oldenburg.

When Detinetz was built on the Danube, the Slavonic settlers sent out into the neighbourhood to capture the first child encountered. A boy was taken, and walled into the foundations of their town. Thence the city takes its name, *dijete* is the Slavonic for boy.

In the life of Merlin, as given by Nennius and by Geoffrey of Monmouth, we are told that Vortigern tried to build a castle, but that the walls gave way as fast as he erected them. He consulted the wise men, and they told him that his foundations could only be made to stand if smeared with the blood of a fatherless boy. Thus we get the same superstition among Celts, Slaves, Teutons, and Northmen.

Count Floris III. of Holland, who married Ada, daughter of Henry, the son of David, King of Scotland, visited the island of Walcheren in 1157, to receive the homage of the islanders. On his return to Holland he despatched a number of experienced workmen to repair the sea-walls which were in a dilapidated condition. In one place where the dam crossed a quicksand, they were unable to make it stand till they had sunk a live dog in the quicksand. The dyke is called Hontsdamm to this day. Usually a live horse was buried in such places, and this horse haunts the sea-walls; if an incautious person mounts it, the spectre beast plunges into the sea and dissolves into foam.

The dog or horse is the substitute for a child. A few centuries earlier the dyke builders would have reared it over an infant buried alive. The trace of the substitution remains in some folk-tales. An architect promises the devil the soul of the first person who crosses the threshold of the house, or church, or goes over the bridge he has built with the devil's aid. The evil one expects a human victim, and is put off with a wolf, or a dog, or a cock. At Aix-la-Chapelle, as we have seen, a wolf took the place of a human victim: at Frankfort a cock.

In Yorkshire, the Kirk-Grim is usually a huge black dog with eyes like saucers, and is called a padfoot. It generally frequents the church lanes; and he who sees it knows that he must die within the year. And now—to somewhat relieve this ghastly subject—I may tell an odd incident connected with it, to which the writer contributed something.

On a stormy night in November, he was out holding over his head a big umbrella, that had a handle of white bone. A sudden gust—and the umbrella was whisked out of his hand, and carried away into infinite darkness and mist of rain.

That same night a friend of his was walking down a very lonely church lane, between hedges and fields, without a house near. In the loneliest, most haunted portion of this lane, his feet, his pulsation and his breath were suddenly arrested by the sight of a great black creature, occupying the middle of the way, shaking itself impatiently, moving forward, then bounding on one side, then running to the other. No saucer eyes, it is true, were visible, but it had a white nose that, to the horrified traveller, seemed lit with a supernatural phosphoric radiance. Being a man of intelligence, he would not admit to himself that he was confronted by the padfoot; he argued with himself that what he saw was a huge Newfoundland dog. So he addressed it in broad Yorkshire: "Sith'ere, lass, don't be troublesome. There's a bonny dog, let me pass. I've no stick. I wi'nt hurt thee. Come, lass, come, let me by."

At that moment a blast rushed along the lane. The black dog, monster, padfoot, made a leap upon the terrified man, who screamed with fear. He felt claws in him, and he grasped—an umbrella. Mine!

That this idea of human victims being required to ensure the stability of a structure is by no means extinct, and that it constitutes a difficulty that has to be met and overcome in the East, will be seen from the following interesting extract from a recent number of the *London and China Telegraph*. The writer says:—"Ever and anon the idea gets abroad that a certain number of human bodies are wanted, in connection with laying the foundation of some building that is in progress; and a senseless panic ensues, and everyone fears to venture out after nightfall. The fact that not only is no proof forthcoming of anyone having been kidnapped, but that, on the contrary, the circle of friends and acquaintances is complete, quite fails to allay it. But is there ever any reasoning with superstition? The idea has somehow got started; it is a familiar one, and it finds ready credence. Nor is the belief confined either to race, creed, or locality. We find it cropping up in India and Korea, in China and Malaysia, and we have a strong impression of having read somewhere of its appearance in Persia. Like the notions of celibacy and retreat in religion, it is common property—the outcome, apparently, of a certain course of thought rather than of any peculiar surroundings. The description of the island of Solovetsk in Mr. Hepworth Dixon's 'Free Russia' might serve, *mutatis mutandis*, for a description of Pootoo; and so a report of one of these building scares in China would serve equally well for the Straits. When the last mail left, an idea had got abroad among the Coolie population that a number of heads were required in laying the foundations of some Government works at Singapore; and so there was a general fear of venturing out after nightfall, lest the adventurer should be pounced on and decapitated. One might have thought the ways of the Singapore Government were better understood! That such ideas should get abroad about the requirements of Government even in China or Annam is curious enough; but the British Government of the Straits above all others! Yet there it is; the natives had got it into their heads that the Government stood in need of 960 human heads to ensure the safe completion of certain public works, and that 480 of the number were still wanting. Old residents in Shanghai will remember the outbreak of a very similar panic at Shanghai, in connection with the building of the cathedral. The idea got abroad that the Municipal Council wanted a certain number of human bodies to bury beneath the foundation of that edifice, and a general dread of venturing out after nightfall—especially of going past the cathedral compound—prevailed for weeks, with all kinds of variations and details. A similar notion was said to be at the bottom of the riots which broke out last autumn at Söul. Foreigners—the missionaries for choice—were accused of wanting children for some mysterious purpose, and the mob seized and decapitated in the public streets nine Korean officials who were said to have been parties to kidnapping victims to supply the want. This, however, seems more akin to the curious desire for infantile victims which was charged against missionaries in the famous Honan proclamation which preceded the Tientsin massacre, and which was one of the items in the indictment against the Roman Catholics on the occasion of that outbreak. Sometimes children's brains are wanted for medicine, sometimes their eyes are wanted to compound material for photography. But these, although cognate, are not precisely similar superstitions to the one which now has bestirred the population of Singapore. A case came to us, however, last autumn, from Calcutta, which is so exactly on all fours with this latest manifestation, that it would almost seem as if the idea had travelled like an epidemic and broken out afresh in a congenial atmosphere. Four villagers of the Dinagepore district were convicted, last September, of causing the death of two Cabulis and injuring a third, for the precise reason that they had been kidnapping children to be sacrificed in connection with the building of a railway bridge over the Mahanuddi. A rumour had got abroad that such proceedings were in contemplation, and when these Cabulis came to trade with the villagers they were denounced as kidnappers and mobbed. Two were killed outright, their bodies being flung into the river; while the third, after being severely handled, escaped by hiding himself. We are not aware whether the origin of this curious fancy has ever been investigated and explained, for it may be taken for granted that, like other superstitions, it has its origin in some forgotten custom or faded belief of which a burlesque tradition only remains. This is not the place to go into a disquisition on the origin of human sacrifice; but it is not difficult to believe that, to people who believe in its efficacy, the idea of offering up human beings to propitiate the deity, when laying the foundations of a public edifice, would be natural enough. Whether the notion which crops up now and again, all over Asia, really represents the tradition of a practice—whether certain monarchs ever did bury human bodies, as we bury newspapers and coins, beneath the foundations of their palaces and temples, is a question we must leave others to answer. It is conceivable that they may have done so, as an extravagant form of sacrifice; and it is also conceivable that the abounding capacity of man for distorting superstitious imagery, may have come to transmute the idea of sacrificing human beings as a measure of propitiation, into that of employing human bodies as actual elements in the foundation itself. It is possible that the inhabitants of Dinagepore conserve the more ideal and spiritual view, which the practical Chinese mind has materialised, as in the recent instance at Singapore. Anyhow, the idea is sufficiently wide-spread and curious to deserve a word of examination as well as of passing record."

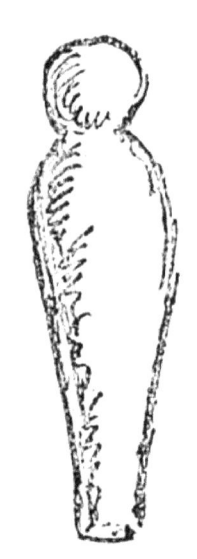

Fig. 1.—FIGURE FOUND UNDER THE FOUNDATIONS AT STINVEZAND.

When the north wall of the parish church of Chulmleigh in North Devon was taken down a few years ago—a wall of Perpendicular date—in it was found laid a very early carved figure of Christ crucified to a vine, or interlacing tree, such as is seen in so-called Runic monuments. The north wall having been falling in the fifteenth century, had been re-erected, and this figure was laid in it, and the wall erected over it, just as, in the same county, about the same time, the wall of Holsworthy Church was built over a human being. At Chulmleigh there was an advance in civilisation. The image was laid over the wall in place of the living victim.

When, in 1842, the remains of a Romano-Batavian temple were explored at Stinvezand, near Rysbergen, a singular mummy-like object was found under the foundation. This was doubtless a substitute for the human victim.

The stubborn prejudice which still exists in all parts against a first burial in a new cemetery or churchyard is due to the fact that in Pagan times the first to be buried was the victim, and in mediæval times was held to be the perquisite of the devil, who stepped into the place of the Pagan deity.

Every so-called Devil's Bridge has some story associated with it pointing to sacrifice, and sometimes to the substitution of an animal for the human victim. The almost invariable story is that the devil had been invoked and promised his aid, if given the first life that passed over the bridge. On the completion of the structure a goat, or a dog, or a rabbit is driven over, and is torn to pieces by the devil. At Pont-la-Ville, near Courbières, is a four-arched Devil's Bridge, where six mice, then six rats, and lastly six cats, were driven across, according to the popular story, in place of the eighteen human souls demanded by the Evil One.

At Cahors, in Ouercy, is a singularly fine bridge over the Lot, with three towers on it. The lower side of the middle tower could never be finished, it always gave way at one angle. The story goes that the devil was defrauded of his due—the soul of the architect—when he helped to build the bridge, and so declared that the bridge never should be finished. Of late years the tower has been completed, and in token that modern skill has triumphed, the Evil One has been represented on the angle, carved in stone. The legend shows that the vulgar thought that the bridge should have been laid in blood, and as it was not so, concluded that the faulty tower was due to the neglect of the Pagan usage.

The black dog that haunts Peel Castle, and the bloodhound of Launceston Castle, are the spectres of the animals buried under their walls, and so the White Ladies and luminous children, who are rumoured to appear in certain old mansions, are the faded recollections of the unfortunate sacrifices offered when these houses were first reared, not, perhaps, the present buildings, but the original manor-halls before the Conquest.

At Coatham, in Yorkshire, is a house where a little child is seen occasionally—it vanishes when pursued. In some German castles the apparition of a child is called the "Still child;" it is deadly pale, white-clothed, with a wreath on the head. At Falkenstein, near Erfurth, the appearance is that of a little maiden of ten, white as a sheet, with long double plaits of hair. A white baby haunts Lünisberg, near Aerzen. I have heard of a house in the West of England, where on a pane of glass, every cold morning, is found the scribbling of little fingers. However often the glass be cleaned, the marks of the ghostly fingers return. The Cauld Lad of Hilton Castle in the valley of Wear is well known. He is said to wail at night:

> "Wae's me, wae's me,
> The acorn's not yet
> Fallen from the tree
> That's to grow the wood,
> That's to make the cradle,
> That's to rock the bairn,
> That's to grow to a man,
> That's to lay me."

At Guilsland, in Cumberland, is another Cauld Lad; he is deadly white, and appears ever shivering with cold, and his teeth chattering.

An allied apparition is that of the Radiant Boy. Lord Castlereagh is said to have seen one, a spectre, which the owner of the castle where he saw it admitted had been visible to many others. Dr. Kerner mentions a very similar story, wherein an advocate and his wife were awakened by a noise and a light, and saw a beautiful child enveloped in a sort of glory. I have heard of a similar appearance in a Lincolnshire house. A story was told me, second-hand, the other day, of a house where such a child was seen, which always disappeared at the hearth, and sometimes, instead of the child, little white hands were observed held up appealingly above the hearthstone. The stone was taken up, quite recently, and some bones found under it, which were submitted to an eminent comparative anatomist, who pronounced them to be those of a child.

Mrs. Crowe, in her "Night Side of Nature," gives an account of such an apparition from an eye-witness, dated 1824. "Soon after we went to bed, we fell asleep: it might be between one and two in the morning when I awoke. I observed that the fire was totally extinguished; but, although that was the case, and we had no light, I saw a glimmer in the centre of the room, which suddenly increased to a bright flame. I looked out, apprehending that something had caught fire, when, to my amazement, I beheld a beautiful boy standing by my bedside, in which position he remained some minutes, fixing his eyes upon me with a mild and benevolent expression. He then glided gently away towards the side of the chimney, where it is obvious there is no possible egress, and entirely disappeared. I found myself in total darkness, and all remained quiet until the usual hour of rising. I declare this to be a true account of what I saw at C—— Castle, upon my word as a clergyman."

When we consider that the hearth is the centre and sacred spot of a house, and that the chimney above it is the highest portion built, and the most difficult to rear, it is by no means improbable that the victim was buried under the hearthstone or jamb of the chimney. The case already mentioned of a child's bones having been found in this position is by no means an isolated one.

It would be impossible to give a tithe of the stories of White Ladies and Black Ladies and Brown Ladies who haunt old houses and castles.

The latest instance of a human being having been immured alive, of which a record remains and which is well authenticated, is that of Geronimo of Oran, in the wall of the fort near the gate Bab-el-oved, of Algiers, in 1569. The fort is composed of blocks of *pise*, a concrete made of stones, lime, and sand, mixed in certain proportions, trodden down and rammed hard into a mould, and exposed to dry in the sun. When thoroughly baked and solid it is turned out of the mould, and is then ready for use. Geronimo was a Christian, who had served in a Spanish regiment; he was taken by pirates and made over to the Dey of Algiers. When the fort was in construction, Geronimo was put into one of the moulds, and the concrete rammed round him (18th Sept., 1569), and then the block was put into the walls.

Don Diego de Haedo, the contemporary author of the "Topography of Algiers," says, "On examining with attention the blocks of pise which form the walls of the fort, a block will be observed in the north wall of which the surface has sunk in, and looks as if it had been disturbed; for the body in decaying left a hollow in the block, which has caused the sinkage."

On December 27, 1853, the block was extracted. The old fort was demolished to make room for the modern "Fort des vingt-quatre-heures," under the direction of Captain Susoni, when a petard which had been placed beneath two or three courses of pise near the ground, exploded, and exposed a cavity containing a human skeleton, the whole of which was visible, from the neck to the knees, in a perfect state of preservation. The remains, the cast of the head, and the broken block of pise, are now in the Cathedral of Algiers.

The walls of Scutari are said also to contain the body of a victim; in this case of a woman, who was built in, but an opening was left through which her infant might be passed in to be suckled by her as long as life remained in the poor creature, after which the hole was closed.

At Arta also, in the vilajet of Janina, a woman was walled into the foundation of the bridge. The gravelly soil gave way, and it was decided that the only means by which the substructure could be solidified was by a human life. One of the mason's wives brought her husband a bowl with his dinner, when he dropped his ring into the hole dug for the pier, and asked her to search for it. When she descended into the pit, the masons threw in lime and stones upon her, and buried her.

The following story is told of several churches in Europe. The masons could not get the walls to stand, and they resolved among themselves to bury under them the first woman or child that came to their works. They took oath to this effect. The first to arrive was the wife of the master-mason, who came with the dinner. The men at once fell on her and walled her into the foundations. One version of the story is less gruesome. The masons had provided meat for their work, and the wife of the master had dealt so carelessly with the provision, that it ran out before the building was much advanced. She accordingly put the remaining bones into a cauldron, and made a soup of vegetables. When she brought it to the mason, he flew into a rage, and built the cauldron and bones into the wall, as a perpetual caution to improvident wives. This is the story told of the church of Notre Dame at Bruges, where the cauldron and bones are supposed to be still seen in the wall. At Tuckebrande are two basins built into the wall, and various legends not agreeing with one another are told to account for their presence. Perhaps these cauldrons contained the blood of victims of some sort immured to secure the stability of the edifice.[3]

A very curious usage prevails in Roumania and Transylvania to the present day, which is a reminiscence of the old interment in the foundations of a house. When masons are engaged on the erection of a new dwelling, they endeavour to catch the shadow of a stranger passing by and wall it in, and throw in stones and mortar whilst his shadow rests on the walls. If no one goes by to cast his shade on the stones, the masons go in quest of a woman or child, who does not belong to the place, and, unperceived by the person, apply a reed to the shadow, and this reed is then immured; and it is believed that when this is done, the woman or child thus measured will languish and die, but luck attaches to the house. In this we see the survival of the old confusion between soul and shade. The Manes are the shadows of the dead. In some places it is said that a man who has sold his soul to the devil is shadowless, because soul and shadow are one. But there are other instances of substitution hardly less curious. In Holland have been found immured in foundations curious objects like ninepins, but which are really rude imitations of babes in their swaddling-bands. When it became unlawful to bury a child, an image representing it was laid in the wall in its place. Another usage was to immure an egg. The egg had in it life, but undeveloped life, so that by walling it in the principle of sacrificing a life was maintained without any shock to human feelings. Another form of substitution was that of a candle. From an early period the candle was burnt in place of the sacrifice of a human victim. At Heliopolis, till the reign of Amasis, three men were daily sacrificed; but when Amasis expelled the Hyksos kings, he abolished these human offerings, and ordered that in their place three candles should be burned daily on the altar. In Italy, wax figures, sometimes figures of straw, were burnt in the place of the former bloody sacrifices.

In the classic tale, at the birth of Meleager, the three fates were present; Atropos foretold that he would live as long as the brand then burning on the hearth remained unconsumed; thereupon his mother, Althæa, snatched it from the fire, and concealed it in a chest. When, in after years, Meleager slew one of his mother's brothers, she, in a paroxysm of rage and vengeance, drew forth the brand, and burnt it, whereupon Meleager died.

In Norse mythology a similar tale is found. The Norns wandered over the earth, and were one night given shelter by the father of Nornagest; the child lay in a cradle, with two candles burning at the head. The first two of the Norns bestowed luck and wealth on the child; but the third and youngest, having been thrust from her stool in the crush, uttered the curse, "The child shall live no longer than these candles burn." Instantly the eldest of the fateful sisters snatched the candles up, extinguished them, and gave them to the mother, with a warning to take good heed of them.

A story found in Ireland, and Cornwall, and elsewhere, is to this effect. A man has sold himself to the devil. When the time comes for him to die, he is in great alarm; then his wife, or a priest, persuades the devil to let him live as long as a candle is unconsumed. At once the candle is extinguished, and hidden where it can never be found. It is said that a candle is immured in the chancel wall of Bridgerule Church, no one knows exactly where. A few years ago, in a tower of St. Osyth's Priory, Essex, a tallow candle was discovered built in.

As the ancients associated shadow and soul, so does the superstitious mind nowadays connect soul with flame. The corpse-candle which comes from a churchyard and goes to the house where one is to die, and hovers on the doorstep, is one form of this idea. In a family in the West of England the elder of two children had died. On the night of the funeral the parents saw a little flame come in through the key-hole and run up to the side of the cradle where the baby lay. It hovered about it, and presently two little flames went back through the key-hole. The baby was then found to be dead.

In the Arabic metaphysical romance of "Yokkdan," the hero, who is brought up by a she-goat on a solitary island, seeks to discover the principle of life. He finds that the soul is a whitish luminous vapour in one of the cavities of the heart, and it burns his finger when he touches it.

In the German household tale of "Godfather Death," a daring man enters a cave, where he finds a number of candles burning; each represents a man, and when the light expires, that man whom it represents dies. "Jack o' lanterns" are the spirits of men who have removed landmarks. One of Hebel's charming Allemanic poems has reference to this superstition.

The extinguished torch represents the departed life, and in Yorkshire it was at one time customary to bury a candle in a coffin, the modern explanation being that the deceased needed it to light him on his road to Paradise; but in reality it represented an extinguished life, and probably was a substitute for the human sacrifice which in Pagan times accompanied a burial. In almost all the old vaults opened in Woodbury Church, Devon, candles have been found affixed to the walls. The lamps set in graves in Italy and Greece were due to the same idea. The candle took the place of a life, as a dog or sow in other places was killed instead of a child.

It is curious and significant that great works of art and architecture should be associated with tragedies. The Roslyn pillar, the Amiens rose window, the Strassburg clock, many spires, and churches. The architect of Cologne sold himself to the devil to obtain the plan. A master and an apprentice carve pillars or construct windows, and because the apprentice's work is best, his master murders him. The mechanician of a clock is blinded, some say killed, to prevent him from making another like it. Perdix, for inventing the compass, was cast down a tower by Daedalus.

It will be remembered that the architect of Cologne Cathedral, according to the legend, sold himself to the devil for the plan, and forfeited his life when the building was in progress. This really means that the man voluntarily gave himself up to death, probably to be laid under the tower or at the foundation of the choir, to ensure the stability of the enormous superstructure, which he supposed could not be held up in any other way.

An inspector of dams on the Elbe, in 1813, in his "Praxis," relates that, as he was engaged on a peculiarly difficult dyke, an old peasant advised him to get a child, and sink it under the foundations.

As an instance of even later date to which the belief in the necessity of a sacrifice lingered, I may mention that, in 1843, a new bridge was about to be built at Halle, in Germany. The people insisted to the architect and masons that their attempt to make the piers secure was useless, unless they first immured a living child in the basement. We may be very confident that if only fifty years ago people could be found so ignorant and so superstitious as to desire to commit such an atrocious crime, they would not have been restrained in the Middle Ages from carrying their purpose into execution.

I have already said that originally the sacrifice was offered to the Earth goddess, to propitiate her, and obtain her consent to the appropriation of the soil and to bearing the burden imposed on it. But the sacrifice had a further meaning. The world itself, the universe, was a vast fabric, and in almost all cosmogonies the foundations of the world are laid in blood. Creation rises out of death. The Norsemen held that the giant Ymir was slain, that out of his body the world might be built up. His bones formed the rocks, his flesh the soil, his blood the rivers, and his hair the trees and herbage. So among the Greeks Dionysos Zagreus was the Earth deity, slain by the Titans, and from his torn flesh sprang corn and the vine, the grapes were inflated with his blood, and the earth, his flesh, transubstantiated into bread. In India, Brahma gave himself to form the universe. "Purusha is this All; his head is heaven, the sun is fashioned out of his eyes, the moon out of his heart, fire comes from his mouth, the winds are his breath, from his navel is the atmosphere, from his ears the quarters of the world, and the earth is trodden out of his feet" ("Rig. Veda" viii. c. 4, hymn 17-19).

So, in Persia, the Divine Ox, Ahidad, was slain that the world might be fashioned out of him; and the Mithraic figures represent this myth. If we put ourselves back in thought to the period when the Gospel was proclaimed, we shall understand better some of its allusions; with this notion of sacrifice underlying all great undertakings, all *constructive* work, we shall see how some of the illustrations used by the first preachers would come home to those who heard them. We can see exactly how suitable was the description given of Christ as the Lamb that was slain from the foundation of the world. As the World-Lamb, He was the sustainer of the great building, He secured its stability; and just as the sacrifice haunts the building reared on it, so was the idea of Christ to enter into and haunt all history, all mythology, all religion.

We see, moreover, the appropriateness of the symbol of Christ as the chief Corner-stone, and of the Apostles as foundation stones of the Church; they are, as it were, the pise blocks, living stones, on whom the whole superstructure of the spiritual city is reared.

With extraordinary vividness, moreover, does the full significance of the old ecclesiastical hymn for the Dedication of a Church come out when we remember this wide-spread, deeply-rooted, almost ineradicable belief.

> "Blessèd city, heavenly Salem,
> Vision dear of peace and love,
> Who *of living stones* upbuilded,
> Art the joy of heaven above.

> Many a blow and biting sculpture
> Polished well those stones elect,
> In their places now compacted
> By the heavenly Architect.

> Christ is made the sure foundation
> And the precious corner-stone,
> Who, the twofold walls uniting,
> Binds them closely into one."

II.
On Gables.

The tourist on the Rhine, as a matter of duty, visits in Cologne three points of interest, in addition to providing himself with a little box of the world-famous *Eau*, at the real original Maria Farina's factory. After he has "done" the Cathedral, and the bones of the Eleven Thousand Virgins, he feels it incumbent on him to pay a visit to the horses' heads in the market-place, looking out of an attic window.

Fig. 2.—THE HORSES' HEADS, COLOGNE.

Myths attach equally to the Minster, the Ursuline relics, and to the horses' heads. The devil is said to have prophesied that the cathedral would never be completed, yet lo! it is finished to the last stone of the spires! The bones of the eleven thousand virgins have been proved to have come from an old neglected cemetery, broken into when the mediæval walls of Cologne were erected. It will be shown that the heads of the two grey mares near the Church of the Apostles have a very curious and instructive history attaching to them, and that, though the story that accounts for their presence on top of a house is fabulous, their presence is of extreme interest to the antiquary.

The legend told of these particular heads is shortly this:[4] Richmod of Adocht was a wealthy citizen's wife at Cologne. She died in 1357, and was buried with her jewelry about her. At night the sexton opened her grave, and, because he could not remove the rings, cut her finger. The blood began to flow, and she awoke from her cataleptic fit. The sexton fled panic-stricken. She then walked home, and knocked at her door, and called up the apprentice, who, without admitting her, ran upstairs to his master, to tell him that his wife stood without. "Pshaw!" said the widower, "as well make me believe that my pair of greys are looking out of the attic window." Hardly were the words spoken, than, tramp—tramp—and his horses ascended the staircase, passed his door, and entered the garret. Next day every passer-by saw their heads peering from the window. The greatest difficulty was experienced in getting the brutes downstairs again. As a remembrance of this marvel, the horses were stuffed, and placed where they are now to be seen.

Such is the story as we take it from an account published in 1816. I had an opportunity a little while ago of examining the heads. They are of painted wood.

The story of the resuscitation of the lady is a very common one, and we are not concerned with this part of the myth. That which occupies us is the presence of the horses' heads in the window. Now, singularly enough, precisely the same story is told of other horses' heads occupying precisely similar positions in other parts of Germany. We know of at least a dozen.[5] It seems therefore probable that the story is of later origin, and grew up to account for the presence of the heads, which the popular mind could not otherwise explain. This conjecture becomes a certainty when we find that pairs of horses' heads were at one time a very general adornment of gable ends, and that they are so still in many places.

Fig. 3.—GABLE OF A FARM-HOUSE IN MECKLENBURG.

In Mecklenburg, Pomerania, Luneburg, Holstein, it is still customary to affix carved wooden horse-heads to the apex of the principal gable of the house. There are usually two of these, back to back, the heads pointed in opposite directions. In Tyrol, the heads of chamois occupy similar positions. The writer of this article was recently in Silesia, and sketched similar heads on the gables of wooden houses of modern construction in the "Giant Mountains." They are also found in Russia.

Fig. 4.—ANCIENT GERMAN HOUSE.

Originally, in Germany, Norway, Sweden, Denmark, and indeed England, all houses were built of timber, and those which were not of circular form, with bee-hive roofs, had gables. Unfortunately, we have but one very early representation of a Teutonic village, and that is on the Antonine column at Rome. One of the bas-reliefs there shows us the attack by Romans on a German village. The houses are figured as built of wattled sides, and thatched over. Most are of bee-hive shape, but one, that of the chief, is oblong and gabled. The soldiers are applying torches to the roofs, and, provokingly enough, we cannot see the gable of the quadrangular house, because it is obscured by the figure of a German warrior who is being killed by a Roman soldier. Though this representation does not help us much, still there is abundance of evidence to show that the old German houses—at least, those of the chiefs—were like the dwellings of the Scandinavian Bonders, with oblong walls with gables, and with but a single main front and gable a-piece. The Icelandic farmhouses perpetuate the type to the present day, with some modifications. These dwellings have lateral walls of stone and turf scarcely six feet high, and from six to ten feet thick, to bank out the cold. On these low parallel walls rest the principals of the roof, which is turf-covered. The face of the house is to the south, it is the only face that shows; the back is banked up like the sides, so that from every quarter but one a house looks like a grassy mound. The front consists of two or more wooden gables, and is all of wood, often painted red. Originally, we know, there was but a single gable. At present the subsidiary gable is low, comparatively insignificant, and contains the door. Now the old Anglo-Saxon, Norse, and German houses of the chiefs were all originally constructed on the same principle, and the timber and plaster gable fronts of our old houses, the splendid stone and brick-gabled faces of the halls of the trade guilds in the market-place at Brussels, and the wonderful stepped and convoluted house-fronts throughout Holland and Germany, are direct descendants of the old rude oblong house of our common forefathers.

We come now to another point, the gable apex. A gable, of course, is and must be an inverted v, $\wedge$; but there are just three ways in which the apex can be treated. When the principals are first erected they form an x, $\times$, the upper limbs shorter than the lower. Sometimes they are so left. But sometimes they are sawn off, and are held together by mortices into an upright piece of timber. Then the gable represents an inverted $\curlywedge$. If the ends are sawn off, and there be no such upright, then there remains an inverted v, but, to prevent the rotting of the ends at the apex, a *crease* like a small v is put over the juncture, $\hat{\wedge}$. These are the only three variations conceivable. The last is the latest, and dates from the introduction of lead, or of tile ridges. By far the earliest type is the simplest, the leaving of the protruding ends of the principals forming $\times$. Then, to protect these ends from the weather, to prevent the water from entering the grain, and rotting them, they were covered with horse-skulls, and thus two horse-skulls looking in opposite directions became an usual ornament of the gable of a house. Precisely the same thing was done with the tie-beams that protruded under the eaves. These also were exposed with the grain to the weather, though not to the same extent as the principals. They also were protected by skulls being fastened over their ends, and these skulls at the end of the tie-beams are the prototypes of the corbel-heads round old Norman churches.

Among the Anglo-Saxons the $\times$ gable was soon displaced by that shaped like $\curlywedge$, if we may judge by early illustrations, but the more archaic and simple construction prevailed in North Germany and in Scandinavia. To the present day the carved heads are affixed to the ends of the principals, and these heads take the place of the original skulls. The gable of the Horn Church in Essex has got an ox's head with horns on it.

HORNED HEAD ON CHURCH
GABLE OF CHURCH, HORN-CHURCH.—*Fig. 5*.

In one Anglo-Saxon miniature representing a nobleman's house, a stag's head is at the apex. The old Norwegian wooden church of Wang of the twelfth century, which was bought and transported to the flanks of the Schnee-Koppe in Silesia by Frederick William IV. in 1842, is adorned with two heads of sea-snakes or dragons, one at each end of the gable. In the Rhætian Alps the gables of old timber houses have on them the fore-parts of horses, carved out of the ends of the intersecting principals.

But the horse's head, sometimes even a human skull, was also affixed to the upright leg of the inverted *y*—the hipknob,[6] as architects term it—partly, no doubt, as a protection of the cross-cut end from rain and rotting. But though there was a practical reason for putting skulls on these exposed timber-ends, their use was not only practical, they were there affixed for religious reasons also, and indeed principally for these.

As a sacrifice was offered when the foundations of a house were laid, so was a sacrifice offered when the roof was completed. The roof was especially subject to the assaults of the wind, and the wind was among the Northmen and Germans, Odin, Woden, or Wuotan. Moreover, in high buildings, there was a liability to their being struck by lightning, and the thunder-god Thorr had to be propitiated to stave off a fire. The farmhouses in the Black Forest to the present day are protected from lightning by poles with bunches of flowers and leaves on the top, that have been carried to church on Palm Sunday, and are then taken home and affixed to the gable, where they stand throughout the year. The bunch represents the old oblation offered annually to the God of the Storm.[7] Horses were especially regarded as sacred animals by the Germans, the Norsemen, and by the Slaves. Tacitus tells us that white horses were kept by the ancient Germans in groves sacred to the gods; and gave auguries by neighing. The Icelandic sagas contain many allusions to the old dedication of horses to the gods. Among the Slaves, horses were likewise esteemed sacred animals; swords were planted in the ground, and a horse was led over them. Auguries were taken by the way in which he went, whether avoiding or touching the blades. In like manner the fate of prisoners was determined by the actions of an oracular horse. When a horse was killed at a sacrifice, its flesh was eaten. St. Jerome speaks of the Vandals and other Germanic races as horse-eaters, and St. Boniface forbade his Thuringian converts to eat horse-flesh.

The eating of this sort of meat was a sacramental token of allegiance to Odin. When Hakon, Athelstan's foster-son, who had been baptised in England, refused to partake of the sacrificial banquet of horse-flesh at the annual Council in Norway, the Bonders threatened to kill him. A compromise was arrived at, so odd that it deserves giving in the words of the saga: "The Bonders pressed the King strongly to eat horse-flesh; and as he would not do so, they wanted him to drink the soup; as he declined, they insisted that he should taste the gravy; and on his refusal, were about to lay hands on him. Earl Sigurd made peace by inducing the King to hold his mouth over the handle of the kettle upon which the fat steam of the boiled horse-flesh had settled; and the King laid a linen cloth over the handle, and then gaped above it, and so returned to his throne; but neither party was satisfied with this." This was at the harvest gathering. At Yule, discontent became so threatening, that King Hakon was forced to appease the ferment by eating some bits of horse's liver.

Giraldus Cambrensis says of the Irish that in Ulster a king is thus created: "A white mare is led into the midst of the people, is killed, cut to pieces and boiled; then a bath is prepared of the broth. Into this the King gets, and sitting in it, he eats of the flesh, the people also standing round partake of it. He is also required to drink of the broth in which he has bathed, lapping it with his mouth." ("Topography of Ireland," c. xxv.) This is, perhaps, the origin of the Irish expression, "a broth of a boy."

Tacitus tells us that after a defeat of the Chatti, their conquerors sacrificed horses, ate their flesh, and hung up their heads in trees, or affixed them to poles, as offerings to Wuotan. So, after the defeat of Varus and his legions, when Cæcina visited the scene of the disaster, he found the heads of the horses affixed to the branches and trunks of the trees. Gregory the Great, in a letter to Queen Brunehild, exhorted her not to suffer the Franks thus to expose the heads of animals offered in sacrifice. At the beginning of the fifth century, St. Germanus, who was addicted to the chase before he was made Bishop of Auxerre, was wont to hang up the heads and antlers of the game killed in hunting in a huge pear-tree in the midst of Auxerre, as an oblation to Odin, regardless of the reproof of his bishop, Amator, who, to put an end to this continuance of a heathenish ceremony, cut down the tree.

Adam of Bremen tells of the custom of hanging men, horses, and dogs at Upsala; and a Christian who visited the place counted seventy-two bodies. In Zeeland, in the eleventh century, every ninth year, men, horses, dogs, and cocks were thus sacrificed, as Dietmar (Bishop of Merseburg) tells us. Saxo, the grammarian, at the end of the twelfth century, describes how horses' heads were set up on poles, with pieces of wood stuck in their jaws to keep them open. The object was to produce terror in the minds of enemies, and to drive away evil spirits and the pestilence. For this reason it was, in addition to the practical one already adduced, that the heads of horses, men, and other creatures which had been sacrificed to Odin were fastened to the gables of houses. The creature offered to the god became, so to speak, incorporate in the god, partook of the Divine power, and its skull acted as a protection to the house, because that skull in some sort represented the god.

In the Egil's saga, an old Icelandic chief is said to have taken a post, fixed a horse's head on the top, and to have recited an incantation over it which carried a curse on Norway and the King and Queen; when he turned the head inland, it made all the guardian spirits of the land to fly. This post he fixed into the side of a mountain, with the open jaws turned towards Norway.[8] Another Icelander took a pole, carved a human head at the top, then killed a mare, slit up the body, inserted the post and set it up with the head looking towards the residence of an enemy.[9]

These figures were called Nith-stangs, and their original force and significance became obscured. The nith-stang primarily was the head of the victim offered in sacrifice, lifted up with an invocation to the god to look on the sacrifice, and in return carry evil to the houses of all those who wished ill to the sacrificer. The figure-head of a war-ship was designed in like manner, to strike terror into the opponents, and scare away their guardian spirits. The last trace of the nith-stang as a vehicle of doing ill was at Basle, where the inhabitants of Great and Little Basle set up figures at their several ends of the bridge over the Rhine to outrage each other.

Fig. 6.—A GABLE, GUILDFORD.

In Ireland we meet with similar ideas. On the death of Laeghaire (King Lear), his body was carried to Tara and interred with his arms and cuirass, and with his face turned towards his enemies, as if still threatening them. Eoghan, King of Connaught, was so buried in Sligo, and as long as his dead head looked towards Ulster, the Connaught men were victorious; so the Ulster men disinterred him and buried him face downwards, and then gained the victory. According to Welsh tradition, the head of Bran was buried with the face to France, so that no invasion could come from thence. A Welsh story says that the son of Lear bade his companions cut off his head, take it to the White Hill in London, and bury it there, with the face directed towards France. The head of man and beast, when cut off, was thought to be gifted with oracular powers, and the piping of the wind in the skulls over the house gables was interpreted—as he who consulted it desired.

In an account we have of the Wends in the fifteenth century, we are told that they set up the heads of horses and cows on stakes above their stables to drive away disease from their cattle, and they put the skull of a horse under the fodder in the manger to scare away the hobgoblins who ride horses at night. In Holland, horses' heads are hung up over pigstyes, and in Mecklenburg they are placed under the pillows of the sick to drive away fever. It must be remembered that pest or fever was formerly, and is still among the superstitious Slaves, held to be a female deity or spirit of evil.

Now we can understand whence came the headless horses, so common in superstition, as premonitions of death. Sometimes a horse is heard galloping along a road or through a street. It is seen to be headless. It stops before a door, or it strikes the door with its hoof. That is a sure death token. The reader may recall Albert Dürer's engraving of the white horse at a door, waiting for the dead soul to mount it, that it may bear him away to the doleful realms of Hæla. In Denmark and North Germany the "Hell-horse" is well known. It has three legs, and is not necessarily headless. It looks in at a window and neighs for a soul to mount it. The image of Death on the Pale Horse in the Apocalypse was not unfamiliar to the Norse and German races. They knew all about Odin's white horse that conveyed souls to the drear abode.

Properly, every village, every house had its own hell-horse. Indeed, it was not unusual to bury a live horse in a churchyard, to serve the purpose of conveying souls. A vault was recently opened in a church at Görlitz, which was found to contain a skeleton of a horse only, and this church and yard had long been believed to be haunted by a hell-horse. The horse whose head was set up over the gable of a house was the domestic spirit of the family, retained to carry the souls away.

The child's hobby-horse is the degraded hell-horse. The grey or white hobby was one of the essential performers in old May Day mummings, and this represents the pale horse of Odin, as Robin Hood represents Odin himself.[10] We see in the hobby-horse the long beam of the principal with the head at the end. It was copied therefrom, and the copy remains long after the original has disappeared from among us.

A man was on his way at night from Oldenburg to Heiligenhafen. When he came near the gallows-hill he saw a white horse standing under it. He was tired, and jumped on its back. The horse went on with him, but became larger and larger at every step, and whither that ghostly beast would have carried him no one can say; but, fortunately, the man flung himself off the back. In Sweden the village of Hästveda is said to take its name from häst-hvith, a white horse which haunts the churchyard and village.

In Bürger's ballad of Leonore, the dead lover comes riding at night to the door of the maiden, and persuades her to mount behind him. Then the horse dashes off.

> "How fast, how fast, fly darting past
> Hill, mountain, tree, and bower;
> Right, left, and right, they fly like light,
> Hamlet, and town, and tower.
> 'Fear'st thou, my love? The moon shines bright.

Hurrah! the dead ride fast by night,
　　And dost thou dread the silent dead?'"

They dash past a graveyard in which is a mourning train with a coffin. But the funeral is interrupted; the dead man must follow horse and rider.

Fig. 7.—OLD TEMPLE BAR, WITH TRAITORS' HEADS.

They pass a gallows, round which a ghostly crew are hovering. The hanging men and the spectral dance must follow.
The rider carries his bride to a churchyard, and plunges down with her into a vault.
Bürger has utilised for his ballad a tradition of Woden as the God of the Dead, carrying off the souls on his hell-horse. The story is found in many places; amongst others in Iceland, and variously modified.
The nightmare is the same horse coming in and trampling on the sleeper's chest. The reader will remember Fuseli's picture of the head of the spectre horse peering in at the sleeper between the curtains of her bed, whilst an imp sits on and oppresses her bosom.
But the horse is not always ridden. Modern ideas, modern luxury, have invaded the phantom world, and now—we hear of death-coaches drawn by headless horses. These are black, like mourning carriages, and the horses are sable; a driver sits on the box; he is in black, but he has no weeper to his hat, because he has not a hat. He has not a hat, because he is without a head. The death-coach is sometimes not seen, but heard. At others it is seen, not heard. It rolls silently as a shadow along the road.
But, indeed, Woden had a black horse as well as one that was white. Rime-locks (Hrimfaxi) was his sable steed, and Shining-locks (Skinfaxi) his white

one. The first is the night horse, from whose mane falls the dew; the second is the day horse, whose mane is the morning light. One of the legends of St. Nicholas refers to these two horses, which have been transferred to him when Woden was displaced. The saint was travelling with a black and a white steed, when some evil-minded man cut off their heads at an inn where they were spending the night. When St. Nicholas heard what had been done, he sent his servant to put on the heads again. This the man did; but so hurriedly and carelessly, that he put the black head on the white trunk, and *vice versâ*. In the morning St. Nicholas saw, when too late, what had been done. The horses were alive and running. This legend refers to the morning and the evening twilights, part night and part day. The morning twilight has the body dark and the head light; and the evening twilight has the white trunk and the black head.

St. Nicholas has taken Odin's place in other ways. As Saint Klaus he appears to children at Yule. The very name is a predicate of the god of the dead. He is represented as the patron of ships; indeed, St. Nicholas is a puzzle to ecclesiastical historians—his history and his symbols and cult have so little in common. The reason is, that he has taken to him the symbols, and myths, and functions of the Northern god. His ship is Odin's death-ship, constructed out of dead men's finger and toe-nails.

Fig. 8.—A GABLE, CHARTRES.

In Denmark, a shovelful of oats is thrown out at Yule for Saint Klaus's horse; if this be neglected, death enters the house and claims a soul. When a person is convalescent after a dangerous illness, he is said to have "given a feed to Death's Horse." The identification is complete. Formerly, the last bundle of oats in a field was cast into the air by the reapers "for Odin at Yule to feed his horse." And in the writer's recollection it was customary in Devon for the last sheaf to be raised in the air with the cry, "A neck Weeday!" That is to "Nickar Woden."

The sheaf of corn, which is fastened in Norway and Denmark to the gable of a house, is now supposed to be an offering to the birds; originally, it was a feed for the pale horse of the death-god Woden. And now we see the origin of the bush which is set up when a roof is completed, and also of the floral hip-knobs of Gothic buildings. Both are relics of the oblation affixed to the gable made to the horse of Woden,—corn, or hay, or grass; and this is also the origin of the "palms," poles with bouquets at the top, erected in the Black Forest to keep off lightning.

A little while ago the writer was at Pilsen in Bohemia, and was struck with the gables in the great square. Each terminated in a vase of flowers or fruit, or some floral ornament, except only the Town Hall, which had three gables, each surmounted by spikes of iron, and spikes stood between each gable, and each spike transfixed a ball. The floral representations are far-away remembrances of the bunch of corn and hay offered to Woden's horse, but the balls on the spikes recall the human skulls set up to his honour. That the skulls were offerings to a god was forgotten, and those set up were the heads of criminals. The Rath-Haus had them, not the private houses, because only the town council had a right to execute.

Throughout the Middle Ages, among ourselves down to the end of last century, heads of traitors and criminals were thus stuck up on spikes over city gates, and town halls, and castles. Those executed by justice were treated according to immemorial and heathen custom. A new meaning was given to the loathsome exhibition. It deterred from treason and crime. Nevertheless, our Christian mediæval rulers simply carried out the old custom of offering the heads to Odin, by setting them up above the gables. Skulls and decaying heads came to be so thoroughly regarded as a part—an integral ornament of a gate or a gable—that when architects built renaissance houses and gateways, they set up stone balls on them as substitutes for the heads which were no more available. A lord with power of life and death put heads over his gate; it was the sign that he enjoyed capital rights. The stone balls on lodge gates are their lineal descendants. Some manors were without capital jurisdiction, and the lords of these had no right to set up heads, or sham heads, or stone balls. If they did so they were like the modern *parvenu* who assumes armorial bearings to which he has no heraldic right.

When the writer was a boy, he lived for some years in a town of the south of France, where was a house that had been built by one of the executioners in the Reign of Terror. This man had adorned the pediment of his house with stone balls, and the popular belief was that each ball represented a human head that he had guillotined. Whether it was so or not, we cannot say. It was, perhaps, an unfounded belief, but the people were right in holding that the stone balls used as architectural adornments were the representatives of human heads.

Fig. 9.—RIDGE-TILE, TOTNES.

In the Pilsen market-place, it was remarkable that only the Town Hall had balls on it, and balls in the place where there had previously been spiked heads. No private citizen ventured to assume the cognisance of right of life and death.

At Chartres all the pinnacles of the cathedral are surmounted by carved human heads.

In the farmhouse of Tresmarrow in Cornwall, in a niche, is preserved a human skull. *Why* it is there, no one knows. It has been several times buried, but, whenever buried, noises ensue which disturb the household, and the skull is disinterred and replaced in its niche. Formerly it occupied the gable head.

As already said, these heads were regarded as oracular. In one of Grimm's "Folk-Tales" a King marries a chamber-maid by mistake for her mistress, a princess, who is obliged to keep geese. The princess's horse is killed, and its head set up over the city gate. When the princess drives her geese out of the town she addresses the head, and the head answers and counsels her. So in Norse mythology Odin had a human head embalmed, and had recourse to it for advice when in any doubt. In the tale of the Greek King and Douban, the Physician, in the Arabian Nights' Tales, the physician's head, when he is decapitated, is set on a vase, where it rebukes the King. Friar Bacon's brazen head whereby he conjured is a reminiscence of these oracular heads.

Fig. 10.—RIDGE-TILE, TOTNES.

In one of the Icelandic Sagas, the gable ends whistle in the wind, and give oracles according to the tone or manner in which they pipe.

The busts that occupy niches in Italian buildings are far-off remembrances of the real human heads which adorned the fronts of the wigwams of our savage ancestors. So, also, as already said, are the head corbels of Norman buildings.

On old Devonshire houses, the first ridge-tile on the main gable was very commonly moulded to represent a horse and his rider. The popular explanation is that these tiles were put up over the houses where Charles I. slept; but this is a mistake; they are found where Charles I. never was.

At one time they were pretty common. Now some remain, but only a few, at Plymouth, Exeter, Totnes, Tavistock, and at East Looe, and Padstow, in Cornwall. One at Truro represents a horse bearing skins on the back, and is so contrived as to whistle in the wind. None are earlier than the seventeenth century, yet they certainly take the place of more ancient figures, and they carry us back in thought to the period when the horse or horse-head was the ornament proper to every gable. These little tile-horses and men are of divine ancestry. They trace back to Wuotan and his hell-horse.[11]

The historical existence of the leaders Hengest and Horsa, who led the Anglo-Saxons to the conquest of Britain, has long been disputed. There probably never were such personages. What is more likely is that they were the horse-headed beams of the chief's house of the invading tribe. Both names indicate horses. When the Norsemen moved their quarters, they took the main beams of their dwellings with them, and they took omens from these beams, when they warped or whistled in wet and wind. The first settlers in Iceland threw their house-beams into the sea off Norway, and colonised at the spot where they were washed ashore on the black volcanic sands of Iceland.

Fig. 11.—RIDGE-TILE, WEST LOOE.

The white horse in the arms of Kent, the white horse on the Hanovarian coat, the white horses on the chalk downs throughout Wessex, have all reference to Woden and his grey hell-horse. The greatest respect was paid to the main principals of the roof with their horse-heads. We can understand how that when the old house in the market-place at Cologne was rebuilt, the old heads were retained; and when the original skulls decayed, they were replaced with painted wooden imitations; just as in the Norman churches the skull-like corbels of stone, and in Gothic churches the monstrous gaping gurgoyles, and on our Elizabethan mansions the stone balls, also the figure-heads on ships, all trace back to real heads of sacrificed beasts and men.

In 1877 it was found necessary to pull down the spire terminating the bell-turret surmounting the western gable of St. Cuthbert's Church, Elsdon, Northumberland. In the spire, immediately over the bell, was discovered a small chamber, without any opening to it, and within this, nearly filling the cavity, were three horse-heads, or rather skulls, piled in a triangular form, the jaws uppermost. The receptacle had been made for them with some care, and then they had been walled up in it.[12]

Fig. 12.—RIDGE-TILE, EXETER.

On the tower of the Church of Sorau in Lusatia are two heads, one is that of a woman, the other that of a horse. The story told to account for them is this. A girl was drawing water at the fountain in the market-place, when a horse, filled with madness, rushed at her. She fled round the market-place pursued by the horse, which was gaining on her, when, seeing the door into the tower open, she ran in, and up the winding stair. Arrived at the top, she stopped to breathe, when, to her dismay, she heard the clatter of the horse's hoofs on the steps; the creature was pursuing her up the tower. In her terror she leaped from the bell window, and the horse leaped after her. Both were dashed to pieces on the pavement. The heads were set up on stone as a memorial of the event.

In 1429 the town of Budissin was besieged by the Hussites. The town notary, Peter Prichwitz, promised to open the gates to the investing forces, but his treachery was discovered in time, and the traitor was executed on December 6th, in the market-place, and when he had been drawn and quartered, his quarters were set up over the bastions, and his head carved in stone above the city gate, and this remains to the present day.

Here we have two instances, and many more could be adduced, of these carved heads being made to represent the heads of certain persons who have died violent deaths.

The first instance is peculiarly interesting. The story, however, as little explains the figures as does that of Richmod of Adocht at Cologne. There is a great deal of evidence to show that till a late period, when a lofty tower or spire was erected, human or animal victims were cast from the top, to ensure the erection from being struck by lightning. The woman and the horse at Sorau had been thus offered. We know that this was a mode of sacrifice to Odin. Victims to him were flung down precipices.

In North Germany, at the close of the last century, on St. James's day, it was customary to throw a goat with gilt horns and adorned with ribbons from the top of a church or town hall tower. At Ypres, on the second Wednesday in Lent, cats were flung down from the tower. Abraham à Santa Clara says that three illustrious Italian families, those of Torelli, Pieschi, and Gonzaga, have white ladies who appear before death; these are the spirits of three damsels who were falsely accused of incontinence, and were precipitated from the topmost battlements of the towers belonging to these three families. Now it is clear that Abraham à Santa Clara has got his story wrong. The coincidence would be extraordinary in all three families. The real explanation is, that when the several castles of these families were erected, from the highest tower of each a virgin was cast down as a superstitious insurance against lightning, actually—though this was forgotten—because from immemorial times such a sacrifice had been offered.

Fig. 13.—TOP OF SPIRE, ASSIER.

In 1514 the spire of the Cathedral Church of Copenhagen was erected. A carpenter's assistant had an altercation with his master, as to which had the steadiest brain. Then the master ran a beam out from the top of the tower, took an axe in his hand, walked out on the beam, and struck the axe into the end of it. "There," said he to his man, on his return, "go out and recover the axe."

The assistant instantly obeyed. He walked out; but when he was stooping to take hold of the axe it seemed to him that it was double. Then he asked, "Master, *which* of them?"

The master saw that he had lost his head, and that it was all up with the man, so he said, "God be with your soul!" At the same moment the man fell, and was dashed to pieces in the market-place at the foot of the tower.

It is possible that this may be the true version of the story; but it is much more likely that the man was flung down by his master, with deliberate purpose, to secure by his death the stability of the spire he had erected.

A very similar story is told of the tower of Assier Church in the Department of Lot. This singular renaissance church was erected by Galiot de Ginouillac, Grand Master of Artillery under Francis I. On the roof of the central tower are three wooden pinnacles. The story goes that De Ginouillac ascended with his son to the top of the tower, and bade the boy affix the cross. The lad walked along the ledge and exclaimed, "Father, which of the pinnacles is in the middle?" When the father heard that, he knew his son had lost his head. Next moment the boy fell and was dashed to pieces. Popular superstition held that so high a tower, with so steep a roof, must be consecrated by the sacrifice of a life.

Countless stories remain concerning spires and towers indicating similar tragedies; but we are not further concerned with them than to point out that the heads carved on towers may, and in some cases certainly do, refer to a life sacrificed to secure the tower's stability.

An ancestor of the writer in the seventeenth century visited China, and brought home a puzzle which became an heirloom in the family. The puzzle, fast locked, remains; but the secret how to open it is forgotten. Many a puzzling custom and usage comes down to us from the remote past; the clue to interpret it has been lost, and wrong keys have been applied to unlock the mystery, but the patience and research of the comparative mythologist and the ethnologist are bringing about their results, and one by one the secrets are discovered and the locks fly open.

III.
Ovens.

When Tristram and Ysonde were driven from the Court of Mark, King of Cornwall, they fled to a forest of "holts and hills," and there found and inhabited an "erthe house" which "etenes, bi old dayse had wrought;" that is to say, a house constructed by the giants of old. King Mark came that way one day when hunting, and looking in saw Ysonde asleep, with a patch of sunlight about to fall on her closed eyes through the tiny orifice which alone served as chimney and window to the "erthe house;" and, very considerately, he stuffed his glove into the hole, so as to prevent her sleep being broken.[13]

That earth house built by the vanished race of the giants was, there can be little question, a bee-hive hut such as are to be found over the Cornish moors. When Thomas of Erceldoune wrote in the thirteenth century, the origin of these bee-hive huts was already lost in fable.

Of these bee-hive huts there remain thousands—nay, tens of thousands—in more or less ruinous condition, on the Cornish moors and on Dartmoor. They are found also in Wales, Ireland, and Scotland. The structure of the bee-hive hut is this:—

A circle was described in the grass, in diameter from 6 feet to 9 feet. Then a second circle, concentric, 3 feet beyond the first, that is to say, with a diameter 12 feet to 15 feet. Stones were set up on end in the ground where these circles had been described, and walls of horizontal slabs were laid between and on these uprights, their interstices filled in with moss and turf. After the walls had been carried to the height of four feet, the horizontal courses were drawn together inwards, so as to form a dome of overlapping slabs, and in the centre an opening was left to admit light and to serve as a smoke-hole, but sufficiently small to be easily closed with a stone or a wad of turf. On the south side of this bee-hive habitation a door was contrived by planting two jambs in the soil at right angles to the walls, standing about 2 feet 6 inches high, and placing over these a broad flat slab as lintel, on which the structure of the dome could be continued, and could rest.

There are several of these huts still in existence as perfect as when first made. One is on the Erme on Dartmoor; it is almost buried in heather, and might be passed without observation as a mere mound. The door remains, and it will serve the pedestrian, as it has served many a shepherd, as a place of refuge from a shower. There are three or four under and on Brown Willy, the highest peak of the Cornish moors. Connected with one of these is a smaller hut of similar structure that served apparently as a store chamber.

Comparatively few are perfect. The vast majority have fallen in. All were not originally domed over with stones, some—the majority—were roofed over by planting sticks in the walls and gathering them together in the centre, and then thatching them with reed, or packing turf round the beams. This we judge from the ruins. Some give evidence of having been domed, by the amount of stone that has fallen within the circle of the foundations; others, on the other hand, are deep in turf and peat, and show no fallen stones within the ring.

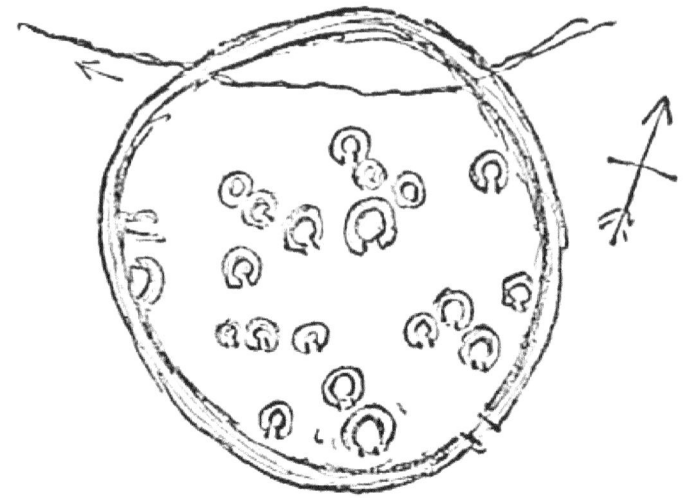

Fig. 14.—GRIMSPOUND, DARTMOOR.

Very often clusters of these circular hovels are enclosed within a circular wall of defence. The villages were, in a word, defended against assault. At Grimspound on Dartmoor is such a walled village. The pound contains four acres; a stream is ingeniously diverted from its course and brought within the enclosure. There remain the ruins of about twenty-five huts, but there are scattered heaps that indicate the former existence of other habitations which have been destroyed. Near Post Bridge, in the heart of Dartmoor, are the remains of something like fourteen village enclosures, whereof one contains about forty of these huts.[14] An account of a very numerous and remarkable group within fortifications, near Holyhead, was published by the Hon. W. O. Stanley in 1871. He explored the settlement with the spade.

Who inhabited these bee-hive huts? Certainly the tin-workers. Mr. Stanley satisfied himself that the dwellers in the bee-hive huts of Holyhead were metal-workers. He found their tools, fused metal, and scoria. The villages in

Cornwall and on Dartmoor have unaccountably been left unexplored, but there is some evidence to show that they were occupied by those who "streamed" for tin.

It is remarkable how folk-tradition has preserved some reminiscence of a large and of a small race as existing in Northern Europe before the Keltic wave, and also before the Scandinavian wave rolled west. The smallest race is generally associated in tradition with the rude stone monuments. The dolmens are *cabannes des fées*, or caves of dwarfs; whereas the giants are spoken of as inhabiting natural caverns. The early mythical sagas of the Norse are full of such mention, and the pedigrees give us evidence of the intermarriage between the newly-arrived Scandinavians and the people they found in the land before them. It is certainly a remarkable coincidence that the cave men, as revealed to us by the skeletons of the Vézère, of Solutrè, and Mentone, should have been men of about seven feet high. When the Cymri and Gaels invaded our isles, a population of blended blood was subjugated, and became vassal to the Kelt, worked for it in the mines, and tended the flocks on the wolds, and the swine in the oak woods for the new masters. The Kelt knew the use of iron. He had not come from the East in quite the same way as the people of rude stone monuments. He came along the shores of the Black Sea, passed up the Danube, and, crossing the Rhine, poured over the Jura and the Vosges into the plains of Gaul. He met the stone monument builder at the head waters of the Seine, and drove him back; he stopped his passage of the Rhine; and it is possible that it was this arrest which forced the polished-stone man to cross the Pyrenees and people the Iberian peninsula.

Fig. 15.—BEE-HIVE HUT, FENNACRE, CORNWALL.

We have strayed from our subject—the bee-hive hut. On no part of Dartmoor have the miners worked so vigorously and so continuously as on the East Webber, at Vitifer. Here, on a slope, is to be found a collection of bee-hive hut foundations. The ground below, above, and along one side has been turned up to the depth of fourteen to twenty feet; but the tin searchers have avoided the little settlement, leaving the huts on a sort of peninsula of unworked gravel, a clear evidence that the workers were those who occupied these huts. When we come to the date of these habitations we are unable to arrive at any very satisfactory conclusion. Some of these settlements certainly date back from the age of the rude stone monument builders, and to that of the polished stone weapons.

It is noticeable in Cornwall and on Dartmoor that the clusters of hut circles are generally associated on the one hand with tin stream works, and on the other with avenues and circles of upright stones, and that the heights of the hills near them are topped with cairns that contain kistvaens, or graves of rude stones, set on end and capped with large granite coverers. It may be taken as almost certain that where there is a large cluster of these dwellings, there will be found some megalithic monument hard by, or if not, that the enclosures, or the moor, will bear some name, such as Ninestones, or The Twelve Men (Maen = a stone), that testifies to there having been a circle there, which has been destroyed. With tin works the circles of hut foundations are invariably associated. In Holyhead, where is the cluster of bee-hive huts examined by Mr. Stanley, there also are to be found the Meinihirion, long stones, two stones standing ten feet apart, rising eleven feet above the soil, and originally surrounded by a circle of upright stones, now removed to serve as gate posts, or to form fences. There is sufficient evidence to show that the first builders of the bee-hive huts were the men of that race which erected the rude stone monuments in our island, and who also worked the tin. But what race was that? It was not Keltic. It was in our island before the Britons arrived. We can trace its course of migration from the steppes of Asia by the monuments it erected. This mysterious people came to the Baltic and followed its shores, some crossed into what was afterwards Scandinavia, but the main tide rolled along the sea-shore. They have left their huge stone monuments in Pomerania, in Hanover. They crossed the Rhine, and from Calais saw the white cliffs of Albion and one large branch of the stream invaded and colonised the British Isles. Another, still hugging the sea, passed along the coast of Gaul to Brittany, thence descended the shores of the Bay of Biscay, sent settlers up the Seine, the Loire, and the Dordogne, swept on into the Iberian peninsula, crossed into Africa, and after setting up circles and dolmens in Algeria, disappeared. They never penetrated to the centre of Germany; the Oder, and the Elbe, and the Rhine offered them no attractions. They were a people of rocks and stones, and they were not attracted by the vast plains of Lower Germany; they never saw, never set up a stone in the highlands, in the Black Forest, or the Alps. But it was otherwise with the great rivers of Gaul; with the sole exception of the Rhone they followed them up. Their monuments are numerous on the Loire; they are as dense in the upper waters of the Lot and Tarn as they are among the islets and on the headlands of Brittany. It is doubtful if they ever set foot in Italy. Such was the course taken by the great people which migrated to Europe. But another branch had separated at the Caspian, and had turned South. It passed over the Tigris and Euphrates, and occupied both Palestine and Arabia. The Palestine exploration has led to the discovery of numerous remains in that land, identical in character with those found everywhere else where this people sojourned. And Mr. Palgrave was startled to find that Arabia had its Stonehenges precisely like that which figures on the Wiltshire Downs.

The researches of French antiquaries have led to the conclusion that the men who set up these great stone monuments were those who used weapons of polished flint and chert. Precisely the same conclusion has been reached by the archæologists of Scotland. Bronze was indeed employed, but at a later period; and then bronze and polished stone were used together.

In the tumuli of Great Britain and of Gaul, two distinct types of heads are found. These are the long and the round bullet skull. In France, before the dawn of history, there seems to have been as great a mixture of races as there is at present. It is not possible for us in England to determine the succession of peoples and civilisations as nicely as can be done in France, for we have not such deposits of the remains of successive populations superposed as they have in Perigord. Under the overhanging limestone cliffs on the Vézère, men lived in succession one age on another to the present day, from the first who set foot on the soil, and by digging through these beds to the depth of forty feet, we obtain the remains of these men in their order—

    Modern men.

    Mediæval.

    Gallo-Roman (coins).

    Gauls (iron weapons).

    Neolithic men | bronze.
                     | polished stone.

    [Gap. This gap questioned.]

    Palæolithic men | of ivory and bone weapons.
                      | of delicately-worked flint blades.

| of rudely-worked flint weapons. | Moustier. Chelles.[15] |

The Palæolithic men were the great reindeer and horse hunters, and the development of their civilisation may be followed in their remains. What became of them we know not. Perhaps they migrated north after the reindeer.

The Neolithic men erected the rude stone monuments, the circles of upright stones. They were the men of Stonehenge and of Carnac. But this race was not pure. Its skulls exhibit a great mixture of character and kind, and it is probable that it took up into it other peoples subjugated on its way west and south. Perhaps it also was conquered. We cannot tell; but it seems from certain indications that it was so, and that by the metal-working race.

When the Gaels and Cymri invaded our isles, they found them peopled, and peopled by various races, and these they in turn subjugated.

We know but very little of the primitive populations of our isles and of Europe; and a good deal of what we think we know is due to guesswork based on a few observations.

As far as we can judge, the dwellers in bee-hive huts were the same as those who erected the rude stone monuments, but it does not follow that the Megalithic monument builders did not impose their customs on the race they conquered; and indeed it is possible, even probable, that a people conquering them may have adopted their religious ideas and their methods of interment.

It is curious to note how that in legend the subjugated people are supposed to live in earth mounds. No story is more common than that of a man passing a mound at night and seeing it open, and finding that merriment and drinking are going on within. Sometimes children are snatched away, and are brought up in these mounds. He who desires to have a sword of perfect temper goes to one of the mounds, taps, and bargains with the mound-dweller to make him a sword. The name now given to the race—not a pure, but a mixed one—that occupied the land before the dawn of history, is Ivernian. It was a dark-haired and sallow-complexioned race. The Kelt was fair; and if in Ireland, and in Cornwall, and in France so much dark hair and dusky skin is found, this is due to the self-assertion of the primitive race that was subjugated by the blue-eyed, fair-haired conquerors from the Black Sea and the Danube.

What was the conquered race? "What," asks the author of "Chaldæa," in the "Story of the Nations," "What is this great race which we find everywhere at the very roots of history, so that not only ancient tradition calls them 'the oldest of men,' but modern science more and more inclines to the same opinion? Whence came it?" And the answer Mme. Ragozin gives to the question is—that this was the yellow Turanian people which overflowed from the steppes of Northern Asia, which carried with it thence acquaintance with the metals, and through this acquaintance established itself as masters wherever it went. That may be, but before this Ivernian race arrived in the west, whatever it was, it found that man had been on the soil before it—aye, and for ages on ages—occupying caves, hunting the reindeer and the horse, ignorant of the art of the potter, and yet in some particulars his superior in intellectual power.[16]

Although the bee-hive hut may have originated with the dark-haired Ivernian metal-worker, it by no means follows that it was not in use long after, to a comparatively recent period. As we have seen, Tristan and Ysonde took refuge in one. The bee-hive hut is still in employ in the Hebrides. I will quote a most interesting account of one by Dr. A. Mitchell. "I turn now to a more remarkable form of dwelling which is still tenanted, but is just passing into complete disuse. Nearly all the specimens of it remaining in Scotland are to be found in the Lewis and Harris, or other islands of the outer Hebrides. There are probably only from twenty to thirty now in occupation, and although some old ones may yet be repaired, it is not likely that a new one will ever again be built. The newest we know of is not yet a century old. It was still occupied in 1866, and was built by the grandfather of a gentleman who died a few years ago in Liverpool.

Fig. 16.—BO'H IN THE HEBRIDES.
(*From Mitchell: The Past and the Present.*)

"My first visit to one of these houses was paid in 1866, in the company of Captain Thomas. They are commonly spoken of as bee-hive houses, but their Gaelic name is *bo'h* or *bothay*. They are now only used as temporary residences or shealings by those who herd the cattle at their summer pasturage; but at a time not very remote they are believed to have been the permanent dwellings of the people.

"We had good guides, and were not long in reaching Larach Tigh Dhubhstail. As we had been led to expect, we found one of these bee-hive houses actually tenanted, and the family happened to be at home. It consisted of three young women. It was Sunday, and they had made their toilette with care at the burn, and had put on their printed calico gowns. None of them could speak English; but they were not illiterate, for one of them was reading a Gaelic Bible. They showed no alarm at our coming, but invited us into the *bo'h*, and hospitably treated us to milk. They were courteously dignified, neither feeling nor affecting to feel embarrassment. There was no evidence of any understanding on their part that we should experience surprise at their surroundings. I confess, however, to having shown, as well as felt, the effects of the wine of astonishment. I do not think I ever came upon a scene which more surprised me, and scarcely know where and how to begin my description of it.

"By the side of a burn which flowed through a little grassy glen, we saw two small round hive-like hillocks, not much higher than a man, joined together, and covered with grass and weeds. Out of the top of one of them a column of smoke slowly rose, and at its base there was a hole about three feet high and two feet wide, which seemed to lead into the interior of the hillock—its hollowness, and the possibility of its having a human creature within it being thus suggested. There was no one, however, actually in the *bo'h*, the three girls, when we came in sight, being seated on a knoll by the burnside, but it was really in the inside of these two green hillocks that they slept, and cooked their food, and carried on their work, and—dwelt, in short.

"The dwelling consisted of two apartments opening into each other. Though externally the two blocks looked round in their outline, and were in fact nearly so, internally the one apartment might be described as irregularly round, and the other as irregularly square. The rounder of the two was the larger and was the dwelling-room. The squarish and smaller one was the store-room for the milk and food. The floor space of this last was about six feet in its shorter and nine feet in its longer diameter. The greatest height of the living room—in its centre, that is—was scarcely six feet. In no part of the dairy was it possible to stand erect. The door of communication between the two rooms was so small that we could get through it only by creeping. The great thickness of the walls, six to eight feet, gave this door, or passage of communication, the look of a tunnel, and made the creeping through it very real. The creeping was only a little less real in getting through the equally tunnel-like, though somewhat wider and loftier passage which led from the open air into the first, or dwelling-room.

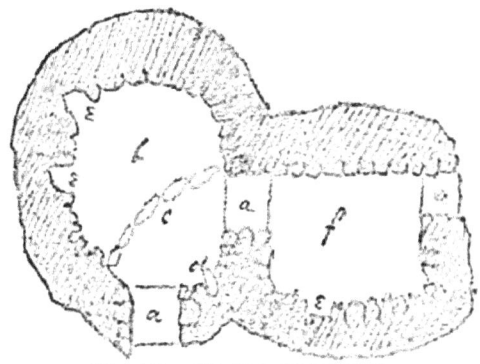

Fig. 17.—PLAN OF BO'H.
a a a. Entrances; *b.* Sleeping platform; *c.* Range of cobble stones; *d.* Hearth; *e e e.* Lockers; *f.* Dairy.

"At the right hand side on entering there was the fireplace. The smoke escaped at a small opening at the apex of the dome. The floor was divided into two spaces by a row of curb-stones eight or nine inches high. These served as seats, the only seats in the house; but they at the same time cut off the part of the floor on which the inmates slept, the bed, in short—the whole space behind the row of stones being covered with hay and rushes. In the part of the wall bounding the bed there were three niches or presses, in which, among other things, we observed a hair-comb and some newly-made cheeses. The walls of these bee-hive huts are built of rough, undressed stones gathered from the moor, which are of fair size, but not larger than one or two men could easily lift and put into position. The dome shape, or bee-hive form, is given by making the successive courses of stone overlap each other, till at length they approach so closely all round as to leave nothing but a small hole, which can be either closed by a large sod, or left open for the escape of smoke or the admission of light. I need scarcely say that no cement is used. The principle of the arch is ignored, and the mode of construction is that of the oldest known masonry. Though the stone walls are very thick, they are soon covered on the outside with turf, which soon becomes grassy like the land round about, and thus secures perfect wind and water tightness."[17]

Now, this extremely interesting account shows us two things. First, that we can not safely conclude from the structure of a bee-hive hut that it belongs to a pre-historic date. We are only justified in so asserting when we find it in connection with megalithic monuments, or when the spade in exploring it reveals implements of bronze or stone. Secondly, we see how man clings to tradition, how that actually at the present day men will occupy habitations on precisely the model of those erected by the population of Great Britain ages before the Roman set foot on our land.

It may be said, and with some justice, that there is no certainty that the bee-hive hut was not a mode of construction adopted by many different races. This is true. The huts in the vineyards on the river Lot in France are of precisely the same construction. In the south of Africa the Kaffir, at the sources of the Nile the Niams, build themselves circular huts of clay and wattles. Nevertheless, when we find this sort of hut identical in structure to the smallest particular, as far apart as the Desert of Beersheba, and the dunes of Brittany, the Hebrides, the Cornish peninsula, and the Pyrenees,[18] and very generally associated with megalithic monuments, we may safely conclude that they are the remains of one primitive people, and if in later ages similar habitations have been raised, it is because that with the blood, the traditions of that race have been continued.

Fig. 18.—HUTS IN THE VINEYARDS, CAHORS.

How striking is this passage from Dr. Geikie's "Holy Land and the Bible." He says, "In the Wilderness of Beersheba are bee-hive huts of stone, conjectured to be ancient native houses of the Amalekites. They are from seven to eight ft. in diameter, with a small door of two uprights and a lintel, about two ft. square. In one dwelling a flint arrowhead and some shells were found. *Close by are some circles of upright stones.* The whole country was at one time inhabited. Nearly every hill has ancient dwellings on the top and stone circles, also great cairns. The extraordinary resemblance, the identity in every point so struck Professor Palmer, who discovered this settlement, that in his 'Desert of Exodus' he engraved a Cornish bee-hive hut to show how it was a counterpart to the huts of Beersheba."

Fig. 19.—OVEN AT NOUGARET, DEP. OF LOT.
(*Dog Kennel under Shelf.*)

But these bee-hive huts are themselves a reproduction in stone of the tents with which the primeval race wandered on the steppes of the Altai before ever they reached Palestine on the one hand and Europe on the other. The Nomad made his tent of skins stretched on poles. It was circular, and the smoke escaped through a hole in the top. When he ceased to ramble, he constructed his habitation on the same principle exactly as his tent, circular and domed. On the Siberian tundras and in Lapland there are still in use two sorts of huts; one, the smoke-hut, is precisely like a bee-hive habitation. It is, however, too small to allow of a fire being kept burning in the centre, and it is heated in this way—a fire is kindled and then allowed to go out. When extinct, the chimney hole at the top is closed, and the owner retires into his hut, which retains the heat for a great many hours. Sometimes, however, like the *bo'h* in the Hebrides, the fire is at the side, but owing to the smallness of the hovel, must be kept low. Castrén, in his travels among the Samojeds and Ostjaks, was sometimes obliged to spend months in one of these huts. At first he was obliged to go outside in all weathers, climb up the side of the hut and plug his chimney to keep in the warmth; but after a while he rigged up a bundle of old cloth attached to a pulley, and he was able by this means to block the opening from within, by pulling a string.

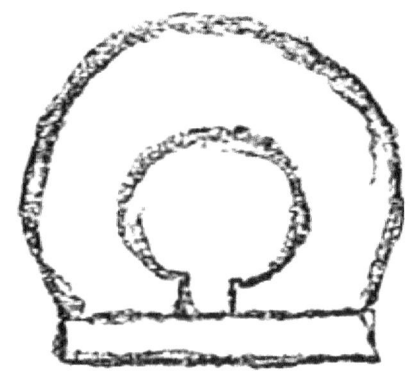

Fig. 20.—PLAN OF OVEN AT NOUGARET.

A very similar hut is still in use among the Finns, but no longer as a habitation. It is employed for bathing purposes. A fire is lighted in it, and stones are heated in the fire red hot, then plunged in a vessel of water. This generates steam, and the bather enters the bee-hive hut, shuts the door, and is parboiled in the steam. Now, the inconvenience of these bee-hive huts was obvious. Intense heat could be generated in them, but owing to their smallness, a whole family could not live in one. In the Fostbraethra Saga, an Icelandic account of transactions in the eleventh century, that comes to us in a twelfth century form, is an account of how one Thormod went to Greenland. Having committed a murder there, he took refuge with an old woman in her hut. When his foes came to seek him, she lit a fire on the hearth, and filled the hut with smoke, so that they could not see who was in it. But one man climbed on the roof and pulled the plug out of the chimney hole, whereupon the atmosphere within cleared. In time the long house with four corners to it was discovered or adopted. This was an immense advance in comfort. But, at the same time, the peculiar advantage of the bee-hive hut was not lost sight of. If human beings had been baked and boiled therein—why not their bread and their meat? They saw that a bee-hive hut was a hot-air chamber retaining the heat for an extraordinary length of time. So the next step in civilisation was to build the bee-hive hut on a smaller scale for the sake of boiling and stewing. In the year 1891 I exhumed on the edge of Trewortha Marsh, on the Cornish moors, an ancient settlement. The houses were all oblong. The principal house consisted of two great halls. The upper hall was divided by stone screens into stalls, and in front of each stall had been formerly a hearth. In each stall a family had lived, each family had enjoyed its own fire, burning on the ground. But such an open fire would not bake. The inmates had knowledge of corn, for we found a hand quern for grinding it. In order to bake, they had erected independent huts, with bee-hive ovens in the walls, identical in structure with the old bee-hive huts, and the reddened stones showed that fires had been lighted in these for baking purposes. But that was not all, we found heaps of burnt pebbles about the size of a goose-egg. These had been employed for throwing into vessels of water either to boil them, or to generate steam for baking purposes.

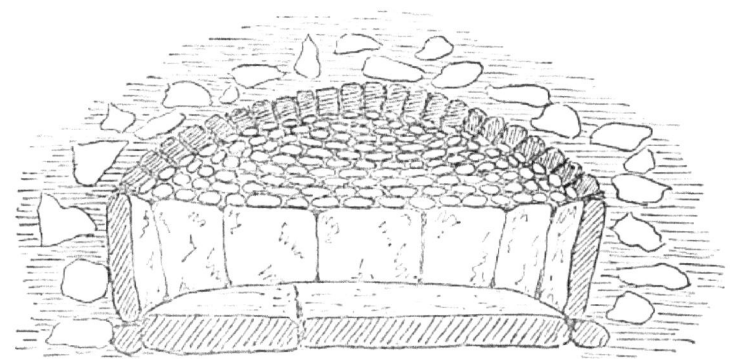

Fig. 21.—SECTION OF GRANITE OVEN, ALTARNON, CORNWALL. *Date, 16th century.*

A common English word has completely lost its primitive signification. That word is *stove*. The stove is the Norse word *stofa*, and the German *stube*. It does not mean a heating apparatus, but a warm chamber.

There is a curious old book, "The Gardener's Dictionary," by Philip Miller, the fourth edition of which was published in 1754. He gives an account of greenhouses and conservatories as places usually unheated. "I suppose," says he, "many people will be surprised to see me direct the making of flues under a greenhouse; but though perhaps it may happen that there will be no necessity to make any fires in them for two or three years together, yet in very hard winters they will prove extremely useful." But when the author comes to hothouses, he describes them under the name of "*stoves.*"

Fig. 22.—EARTHENWARE OVEN AS IN USE AT PRESENT.

The stove is a hot chamber, heated maybe by an oven, but we have turned the name about, and we apply it mistakenly to the heating apparatus.

In Germany the room that is heated is the *stube*, but the heater is the *ofen*. The *ofen* is, however, itself a reproduction in small of the hot chamber. The oven is employed to radiate outwards in heating a room; it radiates inwards when employed for baking.

The German *ofen*, or, as we would term it, stove, is an earthenware vessel in a room. A fire is lighted in it, till it is thoroughly heated. Then the fire is allowed to expire, and the damper is turned, effectually closing the flue. Thenceforth all the heat within and in the earthenware walls radiates into the apartment, and keeps it warm for eight or nine hours. In the ancient oven, as in the bee-hive huts at Trewortha, every precaution was adopted to retain the heat. The outside was banked up with peat, and the heat gathered within baked bread or meat.

The bee-hive oven of courses of stone was not all that could be desired. The fire acted on the granite or limestone or slate, and split or crumbled it, and when one or two stones gave way, the whole dome collapsed.

After a while a further advance was made. The bee-hive hut was constructed of earthenware, of clay baked hard, so as to resist fire for an indefinite number of years. Now in the West of England in every cottage may be seen one of these "cloam" ovens. It is in structure a bee-hive hut precisely. The old tradition hangs on, is followed from century to century and year to year, and he who looks at these ovens may think of the story they tell—of the ages unnumbered that have passed since the type was fixed by the tent of the wanderer on the Siberian steppes, of the changes that type has gone through, of the stone bee-hive hut supplanting the tent of skins, of the bee-hive hut abandoned for the house with four corners, and the old hut converted into a baking oven, and then finally of the adoption of the oven of "cloam." In another ten or fifteen years that also will have passed away, to be replaced by the iron square oven, and then one of the links that attach us to that remote past, to that mysterious race that Mme. Ragotzin says "lies at the roots of all history," a race which has marked its course by gigantic structures, but has left behind it no history—then, I say, one of the last links will be broken.

IV.
Beds.

I had let my house. Two days after, I received the following letter:—
"Friday.
"My Dear Sir,
"In the best bedroom is a four-post bed. Mrs. C. assures me that it will be quite impossible for her to invite any friend to stay with her unless the four-poster be removed, and its place occupied by a brass or iron double-tester. Four-posters are entirely exploded articles. I will trouble you to see to this at your earliest convenience this week.
"Yours faithfully,
"C. C."

Of course I complied. Two years ago I went to a sale. As I was not very well I did not remain, but left word with my agent to buy certain articles for me. Next day a waggon arrived with my purchases, and among them—a mahogany four-post bed. "Why, good gracious! I do not want *that*." "It was going so cheap, and is of solid mahogany," answered my agent, "so I thought you ought to have it." That four-poster has never been put together. It lies now in an outhouse with a chaff-cutter, empty cement barrels, and much rubbish. It probably never will be used, except by boring woodworms.

I saw some little while ago in one of the illustrated papers a recommendation how to make use of old carved four-post beds—that is to say, of the carved four posts. Let them be sawn through, and converted into massive picture frames or ornamental chimney-pieces.
I am sorry that the four-poster is doomed to extinction, for it has a history, and it attaches us to our Scandinavian ancestry.
The Greeks and Romans had nothing of the sort. Their beds were not closed in on all sides; it is a little doubtful whether these beds were very comfortable. In great houses they were richly ornamented, the legs enriched with ivory, and were sometimes even of precious metal. They were covered with silk and tissues of interwoven gold; but somehow in classic literature we do not come upon much that speaks of the luxurious comfort of a bed. In the charming passage on Sleep in the first Ode of the Second Book, Horace makes no allusion to the bed as having any relation to sleep, does not hang upon it tenderly as something to be fond of. The bedroom of a Roman house was a mere closet. The Roman flung himself on a bed

because he was obliged to take some rest, not because he loved to sink among feathers, and enjoy repose.

The modern Italian bed is descended by direct filiation from the classic *lectus*, and what an uncomfortable article it is! There are plenty of representations of ancient beds on tombstones and on vases; they are not attractive; they look very hard, unpleasantly deficient in soft mattresses.

The Roman noble had his *lectica*—a litter enclosed within curtains—in which he was carried about. One of bronze, inlaid with silver, is preserved in the Palace of the Conservators at Rome. Now and then mosquito curtains were used round a bed, and Horace represents the rout of the forces of Antony at Actium as due to the disgust entertained by the Roman legionaries at seeing their general employ mosquito curtains to his bed at night. The couches on which guests and host reclined at dinner were, in fact, beds, and they had curtains or a sort of a canopy over them. Great fun is made by Fundanius in his account to Horace of a banquet in the house of a *nouveau-riche*, of the fall of the canopy on the table during dinner, covering all the meats and dishes, and filling the goblets with a cloud of black dust.[19]

But the true four-poster derives from the north. The Briton had it not when invaded by the Romans, and the Roman did not teach the Briton to construct it.

The Saxon did not bring his four-poster with him, nor did the Jute or the Angle, for the four-poster was unknown to these Teutonic peoples. It came to us with the "hardy Norseman."

Fig. 23.—INTERIOR OF A SCANDINAVIAN HALL.
A The fire in the midst. On great occasions goes the whole length of the hall.
B The principal bench and its footstool F. D The second bench and its footstool F.
C The high seat of honour. E The seat of secondary consideration.
G The beds. On high occasions curtains hung before them.
H Steps into the beds.
I The lokrekkjur or lokhvilur, closed beds, bolted from within. M Windows.

Let us see what was the construction of a Scandinavian house. The house consisted of one great hall that served most purposes (*skali*). In it men and women ate and drank, the dinner was cooked, work was done when the weather was bad, and there also were the beds. In addition to the hall, there was in the greatest houses a ladies' bower (*badstòfa*), but with that we need not concern ourselves. The hall consisted of a nave and side aisles. The walls of the aisles were of stone, banked up with turf, but the roof was of timber throughout. Down the centre of the hall ran a trough, paved with stone, in which fires burnt, and parallel with this long hearth were benches. It was not always that fires were maintained through the whole length of the hall; one alone was in general use in the centre, and here was the principal seat—that occupied by the master of the house, and opposite him, beyond the fire, was the second seat of honour. The roof was sustained by a row of beams, or pillars, and the space of the aisles was occupied by beds. At an entertainment, curtains were hung along the sides from post to post, concealing the beds, but some of the bed compartments were boxed in, both at back, foot, and front, between the pillars, and had in front doors by which admission was obtained to them, and a man who retired to rest in one of these *lokrekkjur*, or *lokhvilur*, as they were called, fastened himself in. The object of these press beds was protection. When, as among the Norsemen, every man revenged himself with his own hand for a wrong done, it was necessary for each man who was sensible that he had enemies, to provide that he was not fallen upon in his sleep. In the Icelandic Saga of Gisli Sursson, relating to incidents in the tenth century, is a story that illustrates this. As this saga is exceedingly curious, I venture here to give the substance:—

In Hawkdale in Iceland lived two brothers, Thorkel and Gisli. "Sons of Whey," they were called, because, when their father's house had been set on fire, they and he had extinguished the flames with vats of curds and whey. Thorkel had to wife a woman named Asgerda, and Gisli was married to Auda, sister of his intimate friend Vestein. Their sister Thordisa was married to a certain Thorgrim. The brothers and brothers-in-law were great merchants, and went trafficking to Norway and Denmark. Gisli and Vestein were partners in one vessel, and went one way; Thorkel and Thorgrim were in partnership, and went their way. But the brothers were very good friends; they and their wives lived together in one house, and managed the farm in common. Thorkel, however, was a proud man, and would not put his hand to farm work, whereas Gisli was always ready to do what was needed by night or by day. Things prospered, and it occurred to Gisli that if they took an oath of close brotherhood, they would each stand by the other, and would be too strong to meet with opposition in their quarter of the island. Accordingly the four men proceeded to a headland, cut a piece of turf so that it remained attached to the soil at both ends, raised it on a spear, and passing under it, opened their veins and dropped their mingled blood into the mould from which the strip of turf had been cut. Then they were to join hands, and swear eternal fellowship. But at this moment Thorgrim drew back his hand—he was ready to be brother to Thorkel and Gisli, but not to Gisli's brother-in-law, Vestein. Thereat Gisli withdrew his hand, and declared that he would not pledge eternal brotherhood with a man who would not be friends with Vestein.

One day Gisli went to his forge and broke a coin there with the hammer in two parts, and gave one half to Vestein, and bade him preserve it. At any time, when one desired to communicate with the other in a matter of supreme importance, he was to send to the other the broken token.

On one of his voyages, Gisli was a winter at Viborg, in Denmark, and he there picked up just so much Christianity that he resolved never again to sacrifice to Thor and Freya.

He returned to Iceland in the same week as did his brother Thorkel; and as it was hay weather, at once turned up his sleeves, and went forth with all his house churls, haymaking. Thorkel, on the other hand, flung himself on a bench in the hall, and went to sleep. When he awoke, he heard voices, and dreamily listened to the gossip of his wife and sister-in-law, who were cutting out garments in the ladies' bower. "I wish," said Asgerda, "that you would cut me out a shirt for my husband Thorkel." "I am no better hand at cutting out than you are," answered Auda. "I am sure of one thing, if it were anything that was wanted doing for my brother, Vestein, you would not ask for my help or for anyone else to assist you." "Maybe," said Asgerda, "I always did admire Vestein, and I have heard it said that Thorgrim was sweet on you before Gisli snapped you away." "This is idle talk," said Auda.

Then up stood Thorkel, and striding in at the door, said, "This is dangerous talk, and it is talk that will draw blood."

The women stood aghast.

Soon after this Thorkel told his brother that he wished to divide the inheritance with him. Gisli regretted this, and endeavoured to dissuade him, but in vain. They cast lots, and the movable goods fell to Thorkel, the farm to Gisli. Thereupon Thorkel departed to Thorgrim, his brother-in-law.

Sometime after this came the season of the autumn sacrifice. Gisli would not sacrifice, but he was ready to entertain all his friends, and invited to a great feast. Just before this, he heard that Vestein had arrived in Iceland in his merchant vessel, and had put into a fiord some way off. He immediately sent him the half-token by a servant, who was to ride as hard as he could, and stop him from coming to Hawkdale. The servant rode, but part of his way lay along a lava chasm, and as ill fate would have it, he took the way above the rift at the very time that Vestein was riding in the opposite direction through the bottom. So he missed him, and on reaching the ship, learned that he had done so. He turned at once, and rode in pursuit till his horse fell under him just as he had caught sight of the merchant. He ran after him shouting. Vestein turned and received the message and the token that was to assure him the message that accompanied it was serious.

"I have come more than half way," said he. "All the streams are running one way—towards my brother-in-law's vale—and I will follow them."

"I warn you," said the servant, "be on your guard." Vestein had to cross a river. As he was being put across, the boatman said, "Be on your guard. You are running into danger." As he rode near Thorgrim's farm, he was seen by a serf who belonged to Thorkel. The serf recognised him, and bade him be on his guard. Just then, out came the serf's wife, Rannveig, and called to her husband to tell her who that was in a blue cloak, and carrying a spear. The serf went in, and Thorgrim, who was in the hall, inquired who had passed the garth. The woman said it was Vestein, spear in hand, wearing a blue cloak, and seated in a rich saddle. "Pshaw," said her husband, "the woman can not see aright. It was a fellow named Ogjorl, and he was wearing a borrowed cloak, a borrowed saddle, and carrying a harpoon tipped with horn."

"One or other of you is telling lies," said Thorgrim. "Run, Rannveig, to Hol, Gisli's house, and ascertain the truth."

When Vestein arrived at his brother-in-law's, Gisli received him, and again cautioned him. Vestein opened his saddlebags, and produced some beautiful Oriental stuffs interwoven with gold, and some basins, also inlaid with gold—presents for Gisli, for his sister Auda, and for Thorkel. Next day Gisli went to Thorgrim's house, carrying one of these beautiful bowls, and offered it to his brother as a present from Vestein; but Thorkel refused to receive it. Gisli sighed. "I see how matters tend," said he.

One night shortly after, a gale driving over the house, tore the thatch off the hall, and the rain poured in through the roof. Everyone woke, and Gisli summoned all to help. The wind had abated, but not the rain; they must go to the stackyard and re-cover the roof as best they might. Vestein volunteered his help, but Gisli refused it. He bade him remain within. Vestein pulled his bed away from the locked compartment where the water leaked in, drew it near the fire in the open hall, and fell asleep on it. Then softly someone entered the hall, stole up to his bedside, and transfixed him to the bed with a spear. Vestein cried out, and was dead. Auda, his sister, woke, and seeing what had taken place, call to a thrall, Witless Thord, to pull out the weapon. Thord was too frightened to do so. He stood quaking with open mouth. Then in came Gisli, and, seeing what had been done, drew out the weapon, and cast it, all bloody, into a chest. Now according to Scandinavian ideas, not only was Gisli solemnly bound to avenge Vestein's death, as knit to him by oath of brotherhood, but also by the fact of his having withdrawn the weapon from the wound. He at once called his sister to him, and said, "Run to Thorgrim's house, and bring me word what you see there." She went, and found the whole house up, and armed.

"What news? what news?" shouted Thorgrim. The woman told him that Vestein had been murdered.

"An honourable man," said Thorgrim. "Tell Gisli we will attend the funeral, and let the wake be kept as Vestein deserves."

Gisli prepared for the burying of his brother-in-law according to the custom of the times. The body was placed where a great cairn was to be heaped over it. Then first Thorgrim stepped forward. "The death-shoes must be made fast," said he, and he shod the feet of the dead man with a pair of shoes, in which he might walk safely the ways of Hela. "There now," said he, "I have bound the hell-shoes so fast they will never come off."

The summer passed, and winter drew on, then Thorgrim resolved on a great sacrifice to Frey at the Solstice, and on a mighty feast, to which a hundred guests were invited. Gisli would not hold a sacrifice, but he sent out invitations to a banquet.

Whilst Thorgrim and Thorkel were preparing to receive their guests, it occurred to one of them that Vestein had given splendid curtains to Gisli and his sister for hanging along the sides of the hall. "I wonder whether he would lend them?" asked Thorgrim. "For a banquet, everyone is ready to lend anything," answered Thorkel. Then Thorgrim called to him the same thrall who had endeavoured to deceive him relative to the passing by of Vestein, and bade him go to Gisli, and ask for the curtains. "I don't relish the job," answered the man. Thorgrim knocked him down, and bade him go as he was bid. The man's name was Geirmund. Geirmund went to Hol, and found Gisli and his wife engaged in hanging up the very curtains in preparation for their feast. The serf proffered his request. Gisli looked at his wife, and said, "What answer shall we make to this?"

Then an idea struck him, and taking Geirmund by the arm, he led him outside the hall, and said, "One good turn deserves another. If I let you carry off the curtains, will you leave the hall door ajar to-night?" Geirmund hesitated, looked steadily at Gisli, and said, "No harm is intended against my master, your brother, Thorkel?" "None in the least." "Then," said Geirmund, "I will do it."

The snow fell thick that night, and the frost was keen. A hundred men roystered in the hall of Thorgrim. Gisli entertained but sixty men. In the night, when all had retired to their beds round the hall, and were snoring, Gisli said to his wife, "Keep up one of the fires. I must go out." Then he drew from the chest the weapon wherewith Vestein had been murdered, and stepped forth into the night. There was a little brook ran down the vale, and he walked up the bed of the stream till he came to the well-trodden way leading to the mansion of Thorgrim. He went to that, and found, as he anticipated, that the door was not locked. He entered the hall. Three fires were burning in the midst. No one was stirring. He stood still and listened. Then he took the rushes up from the floor, wove them together, and threw them as a mat on one of the fires, and covered it. He waited a minute. No one stirred, so he went on to the second fire, and treated it in the same manner. The third was but smouldering, but there was a lamp burning. He saw a young man's hand thrust forth from a bed to the lamp, draw it to him, and extinguish it. Then he knew that all slept save Geirmund, who had left the door ajar.

On tiptoe Gisli stepped to the closed bed-recess of Thorgrim, and found that it was not fastened from within. Thorgrim had not dreamed of danger, with a hundred guests and all his servants about him. Gisli put his hand into the bed, and touched a bosom. It was that of his sister, the wife of Thorgrim, who slept on the outside. The icy touch roused her, and she said, "Husband! how cold your hand is." "Is it so?" answered Thorgrim, half roused, and turned in bed. Then with one hand Gisli sharply drew down the coverlet, and with the other drove the spear—still stained with Vestein's blood—through the heart of his murderer. Thordisa woke with a cry, started up and screamed, "Wake, and up all! my husband has been killed!" In the dark, Gisli escaped, and returned home by the same way he had come.

Next morning very early, Thorkel and the nephews of Thorgrim came to Hol. Thorkel led the way into the hall, and walked direct to the closed bed of his brother. As he came to it, his quick eye detected Gisli's shoes frozen and covered with snow, and he hastily kicked them under the stool lest the nephews should see them, and conclude who had murdered their uncle.

"What news?" said Gisli, rousing and sitting up in bed.

"News serious and bad," answered Thorkel. "Thorgrim, my brother-in-law, is murdered."

"Let him be buried as he deserves," said Gisli. "I will attend and greet him on his way."

Now, at the funeral, Thorgrim was laid in a ship that was placed on a hill-top, and all prepared to heap a cairn over the dead man. Then Gisli heaved a mighty stone, and flung it into the ship of the dead, so that the beams brake, and he said, "Let none say I cannot anchor a death-ship, for I have anchored this that it will sail no more." And all who heard him remembered the words of Thorgrim when he bound the hell-shoes on the feet of Vestein.

There are a good many passages in the sagas that refer to the press-beds. In the saga of the Droplauga-sons we read—"It was anciently the custom not to use the *badstòfa* (the heated room); men had instead great fires, at which they sat to heat themselves, for at that time there was plenty of fuel in the country. The houses were so constructed that one hall served all purposes for banqueting and sleeping, and the men could lie under the tables and sleep, or each in his own room, some of the bed places being enclosed, and in these lay the most honourable men."

In the saga of Gunnlaug with the Serpent's Tongue, we are told how that "One morning Gunnlaug woke, and everyone was on foot except himself. He lay dozing in his press-bed behind the high seat. Then in came a dozen armed men into the hall," etc.

The Droplauga-sons saga tells us how one Helgi, Asbjorn's son, slept with his wife in one of these closed-in beds for fear of his mortal enemies. One day a friend came to his house. In the evening Helgi said to his wife, "Where have you put Ketilorm to sleep?" "I have made him up a bed—a good one—out on the long bench in the hall." Then Helgi said, "When I go to Ketilorm's house, he always turns out of his press-bed and gives it up to me, so you and I must to-night lie in the hall, and give up our close-bed to him." They did so, and that night the murderer came, and Helgi died through his hospitality.

In the saga of Egill Skallagrim's son is a story that shows us how that some of the closed bedchambers contained more than one sleeping place. Egill, who lived in Iceland, had lost his son Bödvar, who was drowned. The grief of the old man was excessive. He retired to his locked-up bedchamber, fastened himself in, and, lying down, refused food. After three days had elapsed, his wife, in serious concern, sent for his married daughter, Thorgerthr, who, on entering the house, said loud enough to be heard, "I intend not to touch food till I reach the halls of Freya. I can do naught better than follow my father's example." Then she knocked at the opening into the *lokhvila*, and called, "Father, open, I desire to travel the same road with you."
The old man let her in, and she laid herself down on another bed in the same enclosed place.
After some hours had passed in silence, Egill said, "Daughter, you are munching something."
"Yes, father. It is sol (*alga saccharina*). It shortens life. Will you have some?"
"If it does that, I will."
Then she gave him some of the seaweed. He chewed it, and naturally both became very thirsty.
Presently Thorgerthr said she must taste a drop of water. She rose, went to the door, and called for water. Her mother brought a drinking horn. Thorgerthr took a slender draught, and offered the horn to her father.
"Certainly," said he, "that weed has parched my throat with thirst." So he lifted the horn with both hands, and drained it.
"Father," said Thorgerthr, "we have both been deceived; we have been drinking milk." As she spoke, the old man clenched his teeth in the horn, and tore a great shred from it, then flung the vessel wrathfully on the ground.
"Our scheme has failed," said Thorgerthr, "and we cannot now continue it. I have a better plan to propose. Compose a death-lay on your son, Bödvar, and I will carve it in runes on oaken staves."
Then the spirit of song came on the old man, and he composed the long Wake-song of Bödvar that goes by the name of the Sonartorrek, and in singing it his grief was assuaged.

The invasion of the Northmen, of Dane and Viking of Norway, that made the Saxons tremble, was an invasion of something more than marauders—it was one of four-post beds. They did not, indeed, bring their press beds with them in their "Long Serpents," but no sooner did they establish themselves in the land—Ragnar Lodbrog's sons in Northumbria, and King Knut in England—than they set up their four-posters, and made themselves both secure and comfortable. They shut themselves in for the night, pulled the bolt, and were safe till next morning. We do not half understand the horrors of St. Brice's Day, 1002, when the Danes were massacred throughout the dominions of Æthelred, unless we introduce these closed beds into the picture. We must imagine the Saxons storming the closed and bolted boxes, and the Danes within, unable to escape, as the axes and crowbars crashed against the oak doors and hinges of their *lokhvilur*. They could but muffle themselves in their feather beds, and endeavour to burst forth when the entrance was forced.

The cairn, or tumulus, that covered a dead Norseman was heaped over a sort of wooden or stone bed made after the fashion of a *lokhvila*. In the Grettis saga we have the story of the hero breaking into the cairn of an old king, and he found him enclosed in a box of boards—stout oak planks—very much as he had been shut in every night when he retired to sleep. The *kistvaens* of stone, oblong boxes of stones set on end, and covered over with great slabs, to contain the dead, are nothing other than stone four-posters. And the modern coffin is nought else but the wooden enclosed *lokhvila*—the Scandinavian close bed reduced to the smallest possible dimensions. There is no particular sense in the coffin, but it is a reminiscence of what the beds of our Scandinavian forefathers were, and will continue to be used long after the four-poster is banished from our bedrooms.

In the Völsunga saga is a ghastly story of two men buried alive in a kistvaen. Sigmund was the sole surviving son of King Völsung, who had been killed by King Siggeir of Gothland. Siggeir was married to Signy, the sister of Sigmund. The duty to revenge the death of Völsung lay on Sigmund, and Signy was by no means indisposed to further this vengeance-taking. Sigmund and his son Sinfjotli came secretly to the hall of King Siggeir, and concealed themselves in full harness in an outhouse behind a cask of ale. The two boys of the king, running out, saw them hiding there, and raised the alarm, whereupon Sigmund and Sinfjotli cut them down. King Siggeir called together his men, and they closed round Sigmund and his son and took them alive. Then the King of Gothland declared he would bury them alive. Accordingly he ordered his men to erect large stones set on end, and to cover them over with flat stones, and then he placed the two men, Sigmund and Sinfjotli, in the chamber thus formed, and heaped over them a cairn of earth and small stones. Now, just before the last stone coverer was placed on this living grave, Signy, the queen, flung in a big bundle. When the cairn was raised the two men who were entombed alive felt the bundle, and discovered that it consisted of a stout rope wrapped round the sword of Sigmund. That gave to them hope. With the blade they dug at the bases of the upright stones, and, raking out the small stuff between them, managed to pass the rope round them, and drew them down. By the fall of these stones a gap was made, the top of the cairn ran in, and the two entombed men crawled out. They at once went to the hall of the king, heaped wood about it, and set it on fire. As it flared, Signy came out, kissed her brother, and his son, refused life, and went back into the flames to die with her husband and his men.

The Völsunga saga is valuable, as it carries us back to the pre-Christian condition of life in the semi-mythical period. The Völsungs are kings of the land of the Huns: they are not Huns themselves, but belong to the Odin-born conquering race. The historic Huns have the rude stone monuments attributed to them in Hanover, Pomerania, and Mecklenburg, but they had nothing to do with their erection. These monuments belong to a far earlier race.

When King Harold Fairhair converted Norway into a single monarchy, many of the old chiefs fled the land rather than submit; but one, Herlaugi, in Naumudal, went alive with twelve of his men into a cairn that contained a kist, and had it closed upon him.

In the saga of Egil and Asmund is a queer story of two men who swore brotherhood with each other, that he who survived the other should spend three nights in the cairn with his dead brother, "and then depart *if he liked*." The saga goes on to tell how that one of these, Aran, was slain, then his fellow, Asmund, "threw up a cairn, and placed by the dead man his horse, with saddle and bridle, and all his harness and his banner, his hawk, also, and his hound; Aran sat in the high stool in full armour. Then Asmund had his chair brought into the cairn and sat there, and the cairn was closed on them. In the first night Aran rose from his stool and killed hawk and hound, and ate them both. In the second night Aran stood up and slew his horse, and tore it in pieces, rending it with his teeth, and he ate the horse, the blood running over his jaws. And he invited Asmund to eat with him. The third night Asmund felt heavy with sleep, and he snoozed off, and was not aware before the dead man had gripped him by both ears and had torn them off his head. Asmund then drew his sword, hewed off the head of Aran, took fire, and burned him to ashes. Then he went to the rope and was drawn up, and the cairn was closed. But Asmund carried away with him all the treasure it contained."[20]

The Norsemen were buried seated in their chairs or in their boats, but the builders of the megalithic monuments were interred lying on their sides, with their hands folded, as though in sleep. Their great dolmens and covered avenues were family cemeteries. The slab at the east end was movable, so as to allow of admission into the tomb on each fresh death in the family. A hole in the stone at the foot is very usual. Of that elsewhere. The latest interments in a dolmen are always nearest the opening; sometimes the more ancient dead have been removed farther back in the monument to make room for the new-comers. There is an allusion in Snorn's Heimskringla to these holes in the kists containing the dead: "Freyr fell sick and his men raised a great mound, in which they placed a door with three holes in it. Now when Freyr was dead they conveyed him secretly into the mound, but told the Swedes he was alive; and they kept watch over him for three years. They brought all the taxes into the mound—through one hole they thrust in the gold, through another they put in the silver, and through the third the copper money that was paid."[21]

It is probable that the Scandinavians followed to some extent the usage of the race that preceded them, and used their megalithic monuments, much as we know that tumuli were employed for later interments, and by races different from that which raised the tumuli. That the idea of sleep was connected with death in many cases of burials, is certain, from the position given to the corpse, the hands are folded and the knees drawn up.

We cannot say for certain that the dolmens, as the French call the monuments which we term cromlechs, were reproductions in stone of the closed beds of the men of the polished-stone age, but it is probable. The great family dolmens were cemeterial big Beds of Ware to accommodate a number, and the small kistvaens were single beds for old bachelors. Some of the largest dolmens contain as many as forty sleepers. Under Brown Willy, the highest point of the Cornish moors, is one long kistvaen, and beside it a tiny one for a baby—the mother's bed and the cradle, side by side, for the long night of death.

Fig. 24.—DOLMEN, GABAUDET, NEAR GRAMAT. DEP. DE LOT.

It has been supposed that the cromlechs, or dolmens, and the kistvaens, represent the ancient dwellings of the neolithic men. I do not think so. The position of the bodies shows that they were intended, not as dwellings, but as beds. If they resembled anything used in life, it was the bed-compartments in the huts, not the huts themselves. These bed-compartments were backed, walled, and roofed with stone.

I was once offered in Antwerp a very beautifully carved oak bed; it was but an oblong box, with an opening on one side only, which could be closed with a curtain, and very much like a berth in an old-fashioned steam-packet. The reader will remember the graphic description, in "Wuthering Heights," of a very similar close-bed of boards as used in Yorkshire. That Yorkshire bed was a lineal descendant from the *lokhvila* of the Scandinavian colonists of Northumbria.

When danger of assassination in bed ceased, men began to sleep easier, breathe freer, and dispensed with the door and its bolts. They shut themselves in with curtains instead; and as there were practical inconveniences in making beds, where the bed maker could not go round to the wall side, cautiously and with hesitation suffered the bed to be pulled out, so that it might stand free on all sides save the head. Then head and top alone remained of board, two sides and foot were left open, or partially open; they could be closed with curtains, and the sleeper could and did convert his bed into a sort of box when he retired to rest.

So beds remained throughout the Middle Ages and to last century. Some ancient beds had gabled roofs over them, and many remained fixed in on all sides save one. But at the same time there was the truckle-bed for the servant; even the iron bedstead without tester, precisely like those turned out by every ironmonger. Viollet le Duc gives an engraving of one such in his "Dictionnaire du Mobilier Français," from a miniature of the tenth century. He gives also a representation of an iron bed thrust under a roof-like covering, with curtains, and ventilating windows, on which Solomon is shown asleep, from a MS. of the twelfth century. It would almost seem that in the Middle Ages a contest raged between the four-poster and the bed without tester, and in the MS. from which the illustration just mentioned is taken the wisdom of Solomon is represented as combining both fashions.

Anyone who has taken lodgings in Germany is aware of the alcove-bed; the curtains are let fall that conceal a recess, and, lo! the chamber has ceased to be a bedroom and has become a reception-room. This is another adaptation of the Northern conception of a bed. In the London houses of Gower Street, and of streets built at the same period, the same idea is carried out in a somewhat pretentious form. In front, looking out on the street, is the sitting-room, opposite the window are folding doors, and behind them the bedroom. The little back room behind these doors is the *lokhvila* somewhat enlarged.

Fig. 25.—HUT, TREWORTHA MARSH, WITH STONE BED.
(By *kind permission of "The Daily Graphic."*)

Indeed, the two ideas of bed, the open and the closed, go back a long way. I have mentioned in the preceding article the exploration of an ancient settlement—date early but unfixed—on the Cornish moors. One hut had in it both types of bed. We saw in the article on "Ovens" how that in the Hebrides, in the bee-hive huts to this day, a portion of the floor is marked off by curb stones, and this portion is converted into a bed at night and a seat by day. So was it in one of the stone huts on Trewortha Marsh. A set of granite blocks in a curve parted one portion of the earth floor from the rest. That was the bed according to the Keltic ideal. But, and this was curious, in the depth of the wall at the farther end of the hut, was a hole seven feet deep in the thickness of the wall, with a great slab of granite at the bottom smoothed to serve as mattress. It was about 2 feet 3 inches wide at the foot, as much at the head, but widened to 3 feet 4 inches in the middle. The height above the floor was 4 inches. It adjoined the oven—it was a bed according to Scandinavian ideas, with this sole difference, that access to it was obtained at the foot, which alone was open, and not at the side.

Fig. 26.—A RUINED HUT, TREWORTHA.
a. Chamber, 11½ ft. × 10 ft.; *b.* Bed; *c.* Locker; *d.* Entrance, 2 ft. 3 in. high; *e.* Sunkenway leading to the door and beyond to water.

Do those two types of bed in one hovel 10 feet square signify that men of two nationalities occupied it, each with his bed-ideal, which he would not abandon? We cannot say; probably it means no more than this, the confluence of two streams of tradition.

The wooden coffin is neither more nor less than the wooden four-poster or rather closed bed reduced to the smallest possible dimensions. Among the megalithic people the stone grave was gradually reduced in dimensions from the mighty dolmen to the small kistvaen. The great tumulus or cairn is now represented by the little green mound in the churchyard, and the menhir or long stone, rude and uninscribed, has its modern counterpart much altered in the headstone. The enclosed box-like stone tombs that were erected during last century were survivals of the kistvaen, as were also the sarcophagi of the ancients. The wooden coffin is but in small the wooden chamber of the dead of our Norse ancestors, which was itself but a reproduction of the closed bedchamber.

For myself, when I think how much that is great and vigorous and noble comes to us through our Norse ancestry, I regret that by the abandonment of the four-poster we are casting aside one of its most cherished traditions, and yet there remains matter of consolation in the thought that, for the last sleep of all, we revert to the fashion of bed *a la Scandinave*.

V.
Striking a Light.

"Please, sir, the rats be a rampagin' in the lumber-room as makes the blood curl!"

For fifty years I had never been into that lumber-room. It is situated up a steep flight of steps in the back kitchen, and had once been inhabited by a button-boy. Here is an extract from my grandmother's account-book for the year 1803:—

Footman   £14

Page   4

Cook   12

Housemaid   7

Verily prices have risen since 1803.

However, to return to the four-pounder. He inhabited this room some ninety years ago: then it was abandoned, finally locked up, and the key lost. About fifty years ago, as a boy, I did explore the place, through the window, after nests. My grandfather died. Then my father succeeded, and the room remained unopened during his reign. My father died, and I succeeded to the old house. I had been in it some years, when the other day the kitchen-maid complained that the rats in this lumber-room over the back kitchen made her blood "curl," by which she meant, presumably, "curdle;" till then I had never thought of an exploration.

To abate the nuisance, however, I broke open the door and entered the long-abandoned room. Since the four-pounder had occupied it, for some years that room must have been employed as a place for lumber, because it proved to contain a quantity of old, disused articles in iron and tin, and amongst these were two stands for rushlights, a tinder-box, and a glass phosphorus bottle.

Such a find carried one back, as few other things could, to early days, and showed one the enormous advance we have made in this century in the comforts of life.

Some of us can remember the rushlight, a few the phosphorus bottle, fewer the tinder-box.

Of the rushlights I found, one was familiar to me; the other, probably an earlier type, I had never seen. The former consisted of a cylinder of sheet-iron, perforated with round holes, the cylinder about two feet high. This contained the rushlight. At the bottom was a basin for a little water, that the sparks, as they fell, might be extinguished.

Well do I recall such rushlight lamps! One always burned at night in my father's bedroom, and when I was ill I was accommodated with one as well. The feeble, flickering light issued through the perforations and capered in fantastic forms over the walls and furniture.

The other rushlight lamp was of a different construction. It consisted of a long spiral of iron wire, and was probably discarded for the newer and safer invention of the lamp with perforated holes. The spiral coil would prevent the lanky rushlight from falling over and out of the lamp, but not the red-hot dock from spluttering on to the carpet or boards of the floor.

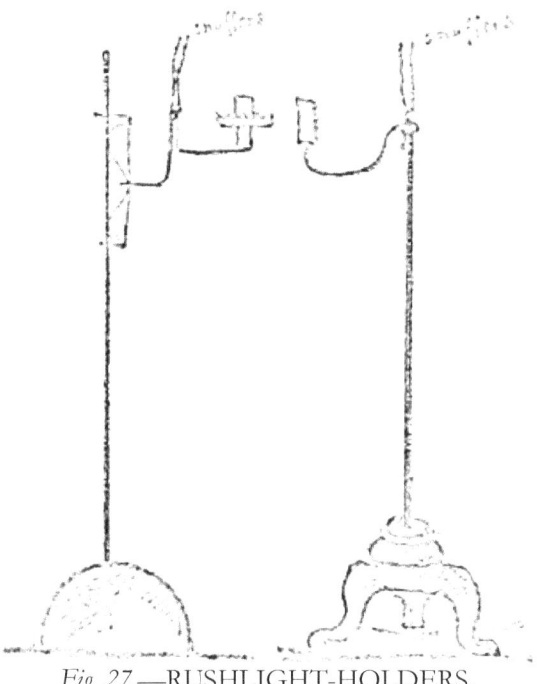

Fig. 27.—RUSHLIGHT-HOLDERS.

There was in use, formerly, in England another sort of rushlight-holder. It consisted of an iron rod planted in a socket of wood that stood on the floor. To this rod, which was round, was affixed a sliding contrivance that upheld a socket for the rushlight, which might be raised or lowered as suited convenience. Connected with the holder was the snuffer. The candle had to be taken *out* of its socket to have its wick pinched between the upright unremovable snuffers. Conceive the inconvenience! The drip of tallow about fingers and floor! We have indeed advanced since such candle-holders were in use. They stood about four feet from the floor.

It was necessary in former times for a light to be kept burning all night in one room, for to strike a light was a long and laborious operation. There were little silver boxes that contained amadou, the spongy texture of a puff-ball, and some matches dipped in sulphur, also a flint. One side of the box was armed with a steel. In striking a light the holder put the amadou in position to receive the sparks from the steel as he struck the flint, then, when the amadou glowed, he touched it with the brimstone end of the match and ignited that—a matter of five to ten minutes. Why, a burglar could clear off with the plate before the roused master of the house could strike a light and kindle his candle to look for him.

The tinder-box employed commonly in kitchens and cottages was a different application of the same principle. It consisted of a circular tin or iron box, with the socket for a candle soldered on to the top. This box contained a removable bottom. When opened it displayed a steel and a lump of flint. These were taken out and the removable bottom lifted up, when below was disclosed a mass of black tinder. The manufacture of this tinder was one of the accomplishments of our forefathers, or rather foremothers. It was made of linen rag burned in a close vessel, completely charred, without being set on fire, and the manufacture of tinder had to take place weekly, and consumed a considerable amount of linen.

In the morning early, before dawn, the first sounds heard in a small house were the click, click, click of the kitchen-maid, striking flint and steel over the tinder in the box. When the tinder was ignited, the maid blew upon it till it glowed sufficiently to enable her to kindle a match made of a bit of stick dipped in brimstone. The cover was then returned to the box, and the weight of the flint and steel pressing it down extinguished the sparks in the carbon. The operation was not, however, always successful; the tinder or the matches might be damp, the flint blunt, and the steel worn; or, on a cold, dark morning, the operator would not infrequently strike her knuckles instead of the steel; a match, too, might be often long in kindling, and it was not pleasant to keep blowing into the tinder-box, and on pausing a moment to take breath, to inhale sulphurous acid gas, and a peculiar odour which the tinder-box always exhaled.

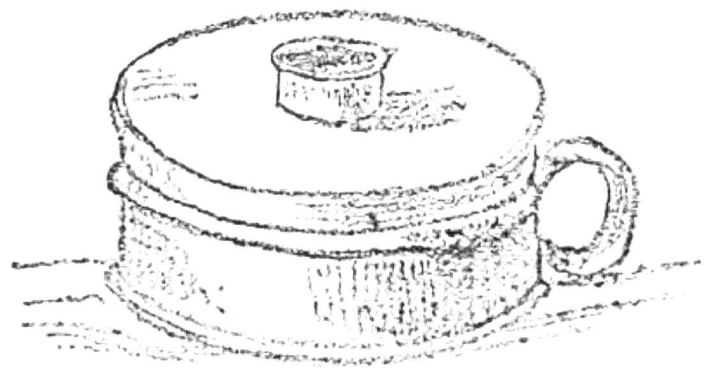

Fig. 28.—A TINDERBOX.

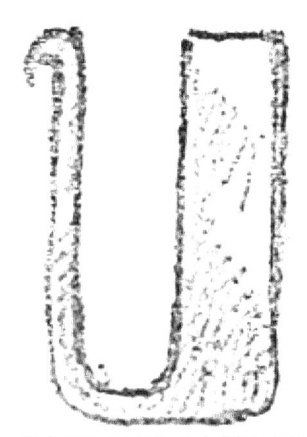

Fig. 29.—STEEL FROM A TINDERBOX.

Here is a curious passage from an article on "The Production of Fire," in the *Penny Magazine* for 26th July, 1834:—"The flint and steel, with the tinder and match of some kind or other, have long been the instruments of getting a light in the civilised world.... Within the present century the aid of chemistry has been called in, ... and instantaneous lights have become quite common, under the various names of Promethians, Lucifers, etc., although, from its superior cheapness, *the tinder-box will probably always keep its place in domestic use.*" This article was published in the very year in which I was born, and now it is extremely difficult to obtain an old tinder-box. I have sought in the cottages and farmhouses in my own parish and those adjoining, and have been unsuccessful in discovering more than one. A generation has grown up that has never even heard of the tinder-box.

In or about 1673 phosphorus was discovered, and its easy ignition by mere friction made known, and this opened the prospect of more easy means of obtaining a light. But phosphorus was costly, and a century and a half elapsed before the phosphorus match came into use. Phosphoric tapers were employed; these were small wax tapers, the wicks of which were coated with phosphorus; they were enclosed in glass tubes hermetically sealed, and when a light was required, one end of the tube was removed with a file, when the taper became ignited by exposure to the air.

The plan was, however, clumsy, besides being dangerous and costly, and never took hold of public estimation. The next attempt was to put a piece of phosphorus into a small phial, and dissolve it at a moderate heat, then keep the phial corked. The bottle was about the size of one of smelling salts, and was kept at the head of the bed. When a light was required, the glass stopper was removed, and a match coated with sulphur was dipped into it, and worked about till a flame was produced, when the match was withdrawn, and the phial hastily corked. Another method was to rub the match, after dipping it in the bottle, against a piece of cork or soft wood, the friction more certainly or less dangerously promoting the combination of the sulphur and phosphorus, and the consequent production of flame.

Another method of kindling a match was by means of Homberg's phosphorus, or fire-bearer. It was a black powder compound of flour, sugar, and alum, which took fire on exposure to the air. But it never came into general use. It remained in the hands of the curious. None of these inventions displaced the old tinder-box, which maintained itself to within the memory of many of us who are over fifty years.

Of all the ingenious attempts to get rid of the tinder-box, the oxymuriate matches were the most successful. From them our present lucifers are lineally descended. The oxymuriate matches were composed of chlorate of potash and sugar coating a strip of wood. The match was dipped into a bottle containing a piece of asbestos soaked in oil of vitriol. The bottle and a number of these matches, with tipped ends downwards, were put into a neat little case, and this was called the "phosphorus box." On their first introduction, these boxes sold as high as 15s. each; they gradually fell to 10s., then 5s., but never went below half-a-crown. But they were not altogether successful. The oil of vitriol lost its force after a while, owing to the readiness with which it absorbed moisture from the air, and then the matches smouldered instead of bursting into flame.

The next advance was the lucifer-match, with phosphorus and sulphur combined at the end. But this was dangerous, and frightful accidents attended the manufacture. I spent some winters at Pau, in the south of France, and near our house were the cottages of poor people who worked at match-making. The pans of melted phosphorus into which the heads of the matches were dipped would explode suddenly, and scatter their flaming contents over the match-girls. My mother, as an angel of goodness, was wont to visit and minister to many and many a poor little burnt girl, who had thus been set fire to.

But the phosphorus match-making had another objection to it, besides the accidents produced in the melting of phosphorus. It brought on a frightful disease in the jaw. The bone was attacked, and rotted away. In the "Dublin Quarterly Journal of Medical Science" for 1852, the nature of the disease is thus described:—"An affection ensues which is so insidious in its nature that it is at first supposed to be common toothache, and a most serious disease of the jaw is produced before the patient is aware of his condition. The disease gradually creeps on until the sufferer becomes a miserable and loathsome object, spending the best period of his life in the wards of a public hospital. Many patients have died of the disease; many unable to open their jaws have lingered with carious and necrosed bones; others have suffered dreadful mutilations from surgical operations, considering themselves happy to escape with the loss of the greater portion of the lower jaw. In the Museum of the Manchester Infirmary is the lower jaw of a young woman who is now at work. Her face is much disfigured by the loss of her chin, and, on looking into her mouth, the root of the tongue is seen connected with her under lip, the space formerly occupied by the jaw being obliterated by the contraction of the cheek."

Thus, in the advance of civilisation, great agonies have been gone through. Our present conveniences have been purchased at the cost of throes and tears in the past. We should not forget that civilisation has had its martyrs.

Lastly came the match made without phosphorus. When we think of the toil and trouble that the lighting of a fire occasioned, we can understand what store was set on never letting a fire on the hearth go out. An old woman on Dartmoor, recently dead, boasted on her death-bed: "I be sure I'se goin' to glory; for sixty-three years have I been married, and never in all them years once let the hearth-fire go out." But there the fire was of peat, which will smoulder on untouched for many hours.

There was a stage of civilisation before the tinder-box came in, and that was a stage when fire had to be kept in, and if it went out, borrowed from a neighbour. In the earliest age, fire was obtained by friction; a piece of wood with a hole in it was placed on the ground between the feet. Then a man held a piece shaped like the letter T in his hands, and rapidly twirled this about, with the long end inserted in the hole of the piece he held between his feet, till by friction the upright was ignited. The pieces of wood must be very dry, and requisite dryness was not easily procurable in our moist northern climes, consequently the labour of kindling a flame was proportionately great. Sometimes a wheel was employed, and the axle turned in that to produce a flame. It has been thought that the *fylfot* , the crook-legged cross found on so many monuments of antiquity, the *Svastika* of India, represents an instrument for the production of fire by friction. But owing to the great difficulty in producing fire by this means, the greatest possible care was taken of the household fire, lest it should become extinguished. This originated the worship of Vesta. The flame once procured was guarded against extinction in some central spot by the unmarried women of the house, and when villages and towns were formed, a central circular hut was erected in which a common fire was maintained, and watched continuously. From this central hearth all the hearths of the settlement were supplied. Ovid tells us that the first temple of Vesta at Rome was constructed of wattled walls, and roofed with thatch like the primitive huts of the inhabitants. It was little other than a circular, covered fireplace, and was tended by the unmarried girls of the infant community. It served as the public hearth of Rome, and on it glowed, unextinguished throughout the year, the sacred fire, which was supposed to have been brought from Troy, and the continuance of which was thought to be linked with the fortunes of the city. The name Vesta is believed to be derived from the same root as the Sanscrit *vas*, which means "to dwell, to inhabit," and shows that she was the goddess of home, and home had the hearth as its focus. A town, a state, is but a large family, and what the domestic hearth was to the house, that the temple of the perpetual fire became to the city. Every town had its Vesta, or common hearth, and the colonies derived their fire from the mother hearth. Should a vestal maiden allow the sacred fire to become extinguished, she was beaten by the Grand Pontiff till her blood flowed, and the new fire was solemnly rekindled by rubbing together dry wood, or by focussing the sun's rays. It might not be borrowed from a strange place. The circular form and domed roof of the Temples of Vesta were survivals of the prehistoric huts of the aborigines.

Among the legends of the early Celtic saints nothing is more common than the story of the saint being sent to borrow fire, and carrying it in his lap without the fire injuring his garment.

In Ireland, before St. Patrick introduced Christianity, there was a temple at Tara where fire burned ever, and was on no account suffered to go out.

When Christianity became dominant, it was necessary to dissociate the ideas of the people from the central fire as mixed up with the old gods; at the same time some central fire was an absolute need. Accordingly the Church was converted into the sacred depository of the perpetual fire, and a lamp was kept in it ever burning, not only that the candles might be ignited from it for the services, without recourse had to friction or tinder flint and steel, but also that the parish, the village, the town, might obtain thence their fire.

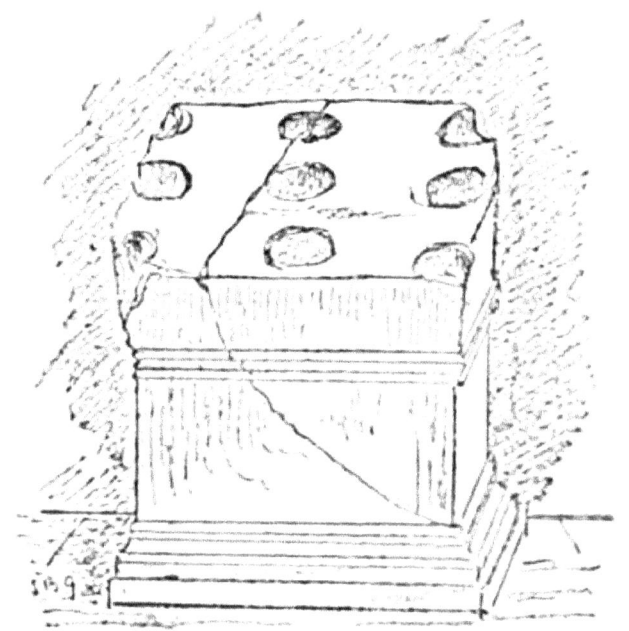

Fig. 30.—CRESSET-STONE, ST. AMBROGIO, MILAN.

Fig. 31.—CRESSET-STONE, LEWANNICK.

There exist still a few—a very few—contrivances for this perpetual fire in our churches; they go by the name of cresset-stones. The earliest I know is not in England, but is in the atrium outside the remarkable church of St. Ambrogio at Milan. It is a block of white marble on a moulded base, it is now broken, but banded together with iron. It stands 3 feet 10 inches high, and is 2 feet 6 inches in diameter at top. It consists of a flat surface in which are depressed nine cuplike hollows. These were originally filled with oil, and wicks were placed in them and ignited. In England one is still *in situ*, in the church of Lewannick, in Cornwall. There it is not far from the door. It consists of a circular block containing on its flat upper surface, which is twenty-two inches across, seven cuplike hollows, four and a half inches deep. The stone stands on a rudely moulded base, octagonal, and is in all about 2 feet 6 inches high. In Furness Abbey, among the ruins, has been found another, with five cups in it; at Calder Abbey another, with sixteen such cups for oil and wicks. At York is another with six such fire-cups, and at Stockholm another with the same number, in a square stone table. At Wool Church, Dorset, is again another example built into the south wall of a small chapel on the north side of the chancel. It is a block of Purbeck marble, and has in the top five cup-shaped cavities quite blackened with the oil and smoke. In some of the examples there are traces of a metal pin around which the wick was twisted.

In addition to these, in several churches are to be found lamp-niches. Some have chimneys or flues, which pass upwards, in some cases passing into the chimneys of fireplaces. Others have conical hollows in the heads or roofs, in order to catch the soot, and prevent it passing out into the church.

Now, although these lamps and cressets had their religious signification, yet this religious signification was an afterthought. The origin of them lay in the necessity of there being in every place a central light, from which light could at any time be borrowed; and the reason why this central light was put in the church was to dissociate it from the heathen ideas attached formerly to it. As it was, the good people of the Middle Ages were not quite satisfied with the central church fire, and they had recourse in times of emergency to others—and as the Church deemed them—unholy fires. When a plague and murrain appeared among cattle, then they lighted need-fires, from two pieces of dry wood, and drove the cattle between the flames, believing that this new flame was wholesome to the purging away of the disease. For kindling the need-fires the employment of flint and steel was forbidden. The fire was only efficacious when extracted in prehistoric fashion, out of wood. The lighting of these need-fires was forbidden by the Church in the eighth century. What shows that this need-fire was distinctly heathen is that in the Church new fire was obtained at Easter annually by striking flint and steel together. It was supposed that the old fire in a twelvemonth had got exhausted, or perhaps that all light expired with Christ, and that new fire must be obtained. Accordingly the priest solemnly struck new fire out of flint and steel. But fire from flint and steel was a novelty; and the people, Pagan at heart, had no confidence in it, and in time of adversity went back to the need-fire kindled in the time-honoured way from wood by friction, before this new-fangled way of drawing it out of stone and iron was invented.

The curious festival of the Car of Fire observed on Easter Eve every year at Florence carries us back to a remote period when fire was a sacred and mysterious thing. As is well known, in the Eastern Church, also in the Roman Catholic Church, all fires are extinguished before Easter; and in the Cathedral, the Bishop, on Easter morning, strikes new fire, blesses it, and all the hearths in the city receive the new fire from this blessed spark. It is vulgarly supposed that the old fire has got worn out, and has lost its full vigour by use throughout the year, and that the new fire is full of restless and youthful energy. There can be little doubt that this idea goes back to a remote and Pagan time, and the Church accepted what was a common custom, and gave it, or tried to give it, a new and Christian idea, connecting it with the resurrection of Him who is the Light of the World. The same custom of striking and blessing new fire exists in many parts of the West as well as the East, and is sanctioned by the Roman Church. But nowhere does this ancient usage assume so quaint and picturesque a form as at Florence. There, however, the primitive significance is completely forgotten, and the people have endeavoured to explain the ceremony which I will now describe in various mutually contradictory ways.

On Easter Eve, four magnificent white oxen, their huge horns wreathed with flowers, and with garlands about them, as though they were being conveyed to sacrifice, draw a huge car, painted black, some twenty-five feet high, pyramidal in shape, and crowned with a mural coronet, into the piazza before the west doors of the white marble cathedral. The car is itself wreathed with flowers to its highest pinnacle, and with the flowers various fireworks are interspersed. As soon as this great trophy is in place, and the oxen unyoked, the west doors of the cathedral are thrown open, and a rope is strained from the top of the car to a pillar that is erected in front of the high altar, a distance of some two hundred yards. On this cord is seen perched a white dove, composed of some white substance, probably plaster. For two hours before the event of the day takes place the great piazza and the nave of the vast cathedral are crowded. Villagers from all the country round have arrived; but there are also present plenty of townsfolk, and strangers from foreign lands. At half-past eleven, the archbishop and all his clergy come in procession down the body of the church, pass out of the west doors, and make the circuit of the cathedral. Before twelve o'clock strikes they are again in their places in the choir. At the stroke of noon the newly-blessed fire is applied to a train of gunpowder at the foot of the pillar. In another moment the pigeon skims down the nave, pouring out a shower of fire, sweeps out of the west door of the cathedral, reaches the trophy in the square, sets fire to a fusee there, then turns and flies back along the rope, still discharging a rain of fire, till it has reached its pillar before the altar, and there is still.

Fig. 32.—THE CARRO, FLORENCE.

But in the meantime the fusee at the car has set fire to various squibs and petards and crackers there, and the whole structure is speedily enveloped in fire and smoke, from which explosions issue every few moments. As soon as the last firework has expired, the white oxen are again yoked to the car, and it is drawn away.

The flight of the dove is watched by the peasants with breathless anxiety, for the course it takes indicates, in their idea, the sort of weather that is likely to ensue during the year. If the bird moves slowly, halts, then goes on again, halts, and is sluggish in its flight, they conclude the year will be tempestuous and the harvest bad. If the dove skims along to the car and back without a hitch, they calculate on a splendid summer and autumn, on a rich yield of corn, and overflowing presses of grapes.

And now for the legends whereby the people explain this curious custom. According to one, a certain Florentine named Pazzino went to Jerusalem in the twelfth century, kindled a torch there at the Holy Sepulchre on Easter Eve, and resolved to bring this same sacred fire with him back to Florence. But as he rode along, the wind blew in his face and well-nigh extinguished his torch, so he sat his steed with his face to the tail, screening the flame with his body, and so rode all the way home! The people along his route, seeing him thus ride reversed, shouted out, "Pazzi! Pazzi!" ("O fool! fool!") and that name of "fool" he and his family assumed; and the family is still represented in Florence.

There is another version of the story; one Pazzino, seeing the Holy Sepulchre in the hands of the infidels, broke off as much of it as he could carry to convey home to his dear Florence. As he was pursued by the Saracens, he reversed the shoes of his horse to avoid being tracked. On reaching Florence it was resolved that the new Easter fire should always be kindled on the stone of the Holy Sepulchre he had brought home. In honour of his achievement, moreover, the municipality ordered that the ceremony of the Car of Fire and the fiery dove should be maintained every year. For many centuries the expenses were borne by the Pazzi family; but of late years they have been relieved of these by the municipality.

The third version of the story is, that Pazzino was a knight with Godfrey de Bouillon in the first Crusade, and that he was the first of the besiegers to mount the walls and plant on them the banner of the cross. Moreover, he sent the tidings of the recovery of the Holy Sepulchre home to Florence by a carrier-pigeon, and thus the news reached Florence long before it could have arrived in any other way.

Such are the principal legends connected with this curious ceremony, and we are constrained to say that we believe that one is as fabulous as another. The explanation of the custom is really this.

The rite of striking the new fire was observed at Florence, as elsewhere, from an early date, but the *communication* of the new fire from the newly-ignited candle was both a long affair, and occasioned noise, struggle and inconvenience. Accordingly—partly to save the church from being the scene of an unseemly scramble, and partly to make the communication of the fire an easy matter to a large number of persons at once—an ingenious contrivance was made, whereby a dove should carry the flame from the choir of the cathedral, above the reach of the people, who therefore could not scuffle and scramble for it, to the market-place outside, where it ignited a bonfire, to which all the people could apply their candles and torches. After a while the real intention was forgotten, and the bonfire was converted into a great exhibition of fireworks in the daytime.

The whole ceremony has a somewhat childish character, but then it dates back to a period when all men were children; and it serves, if rightly understood, to link us with the past, and enables us to measure the distance we have trodden since those ages when fire was one of the most difficult things to be re-acquired, if once lost, and the preservation of fire and the striking of fire were matters of extreme importance, and were after a while reserved to a sacred class.[22]

VI.
Umbrellas.

Some years ago I happened to be at that most picturesque old city of Würzburg on a showery May market-day. The window of my hotel commanded the square. The moment that the first sprinkle came over the busy scene of market women and chafferers, the whole square suddenly flowered like a vast garden. Every woman at her stall expanded an enormous umbrella, and these umbrellas were of every dye—crimson, blue, green, chocolate, and—yes, there was even one of marigold yellow, under which the huckstress crouched as beneath a mighty inverted eschscholtzia. Nor were these umbrellas all *selfs*, as horticulturists describe monotoned pansies; for some were surrounded with a perfect rainbow of coloured lines as a border; and others were wreathed about with a pattern of many-hued flowers. Presently, out came the May sun, and, *presto*, every umbrella was closed and folded and laid aside: the flower garden had resolved itself into a swarm of busy marketers.

On reaching Innsbruck, I lighted on an umbrella-maker's shop under one of the arcades near the Golden Roof of Frederick with the Empty Pockets. I saw suspended before the vault in which the man dwelt or did business, umbrellas the exact reproductions of what I had seen at Würzburg—red, green, brown, blue, even white—lined with pink, like mushrooms: and for the sum of about fifteen shillings I became the happy possessor of one of these articles, which I proceed to describe. The covering was of a brilliant red, and imprinted round it was a wreath of flowers and foliage, white, yellow, blue, and green; around the ferule also was a smaller wreath similar in colour and character. This cover was stretched on canes, such canes as are well known in schools; and the canes were distended by twisted brass strainers, rising out of a sliding tube of elaborately hammered brass, through which passed the stick of the umbrella. The whole, when expanded, measured nearly five feet, and was not extraordinarily heavy, nothing like the weight of a gig-umbrella. Walking under it was like walking about in a tent, taking the tent with one; and walking under it in the rain filled one with sanguine hopes that the day was about to mend, so surrounded was one with a warm and cheerful glow. On a hot climb over a pass, when I spread this shelter above my head against the sun, I felt that I must appear to the shepherds on the high pastures like a migratory Alpine rose.

I met with no inconvenience whatever from my umbrella till I reached Heidelberg on my way home, and innocently walked with it under my arm in the Castle gardens on Sunday afternoon. Then I found that it provoked attention and excited astonishment. Such an umbrella had its social level, and that level was the market-place, not the Castle gardens; it was sufferable as spread over an old woman vending *sauerkraut*, but not as carried furled in the hand of a respectably dressed gentleman. So much comment did my umbrella occasion that it annoyed me, spoiled the pleasure of my walk, and I accepted the offer of a friend to relieve me of it. He took my umbrella and thrust it up his back under his coat, and with crossed arms to the rear, hugged it to his spine. But even so it was not to escape observation, for the black handle, crooked, appeared below his coat, a fact to which I was aroused as I dropped behind my friend, by the exclamations of a nursemaid: "*Ach Tausend!* the Herr has a curly tail!" and then of a Professor, who, beckoning some students to him, said: "Let us catch him—the Missing Link, *homo caudatus*."

On reaching England, the great scarlet-crimson (it was neither exactly one nor exactly the other) umbrella was consigned to the stand in the hall. Those were not the days when ladies spread red parasols above their bonnets, and had sunshades to match their gowns: in those days all parasols were brown or black; consequently the innovation of a red umbrella would be too great, too startling for me to attempt. But one morning—it was that on which the Duke and Duchess of Edinburgh made their entry into London after their marriage—I started early to drive to the station and go to town and join the sightseers. It may be in the recollection of those who were out that day that snow fell. Early in the morning in the country there was a good deal of snow, so much, that I thought I might safely take my Tyrolese umbrella to cover me in my gig. I intended to furl it before I reached the station and such places where men do congregate. It was remarkable that although the snow spoiled the picturesque effect of the procession in Regent's Street by making the redcoats draw on their overcoats, it induced me to unfurl my marvellous red travelling tent—which is an instance, may be, of the compensation there is in nature.

As I drove along, I chanced on an umbrella-maker, trudging through the snow, head down, with a bundle of his manufacture under his arm. He neither saw nor heard the dogcart till it was close on him, when the driver shouted to him to stand aside. Then he started back, looked up, and I saw the change of expression in the man's face, as his eyes took in the apparition above him of the expanded red umbrella, flower-wreathed and brass-mounted. The face had been inanimate; then, a wild enthusiasm or astonishment kindled it, and down into the snow at his feet fell the umbrellas he was carrying. I drove on, but looked back at intervals, and as long as he was in sight, I saw him standing in the road, with eyes and mouth open, hands expanded and every finger distended, and his umbrellas, uncollected, scattered about him in the snow.

These reminiscences of my remarkable umbrella lead me to say something of umbrellas in general.

I hardly think that the true origin, development, and, shall I say, degradation of the umbrella, is generally known. Yet it deserves to be known, for it supplies a graphic and striking condensation of vast social changes.

The umbrella comes to us from the East, from nations living under a burning sun, to whom shade is therefore agreeable. We can understand how the giving of shade came easily to be regarded as a symbol of majesty. In the apocryphal book of Baruch occurs the passage, "We shall live under the shadow of Nebucodonosor, king of Babylon, and under the shadow of Balthasar, his son." Primitively, kings gave audience and delivered judgment seated under trees, not only because of the comfort of the shade, but also because of the symbolism. So, when Ethelbert, King of Kent, received St. Augustine, he was seated under an oak; and Wagner is quite right when, in the opening scene in *Lohengrin*, he makes King Pepin hold his court enthroned under a tree.

But when sovereigns took to receiving suitors and dispensing justice indoors, they transferred with them to within the symbol of the tree. Phylarchus, in describing the luxury of Alexander, says that the Persian kings gave audience under plane trees or vines made of gold and hung with emeralds, but that the magnificence of the throne of Alexander surpassed theirs. Curtius relates how the kings of India had golden vines erected in their judgment halls so as to overspread their thrones. The throne of Cyrus was over-canopied by a golden vine of seven branches. Firdusi describes a similar throne-tree at the festival given by Kai Khosru:

> "A tree was erected, many-branched,
> Bending over the throne with its head:
> Of silver the trunk, but the branches of gold;
> The buds and the blossoms were rubies;
> The fruit was of sapphire and cornelian stone;
> And the foliage all was of emerald."

From the East, the idea or fashion was transplanted to Byzantium, and the emperors there had similar trees erected above their thrones overshadowing them. William of Rubruquis describes a great silver tree in the Palace of the Khan of the Tartars, in 1253, of which leaves and fruit, as well as branches, were of silver. But kings went about, and wherever they went their majesty surrounded them; and consequently, with the double motive of comfort and of symbolism, the umbrella was invented as a portable canopy or tree over the head of the sovereign.

The Greeks noticed and disapproved of the use of the umbrella.[23] Xenophon says that the Persians were so effeminate that they could not content themselves in summer with the shade afforded by trees and rocks, but that they employed portable contrivances for producing artificial shade. But when he says this, he most certainly refers to the kings, for they alone had the right to use umbrellas.

On Assyrian and Persepolitan reliefs we have an eunuch behind the sovereign holding an umbrella over him when walking, or when riding in his chariot, or when seated; on a bas-relief of Assur-bani-pal, however, the king is figured reclining under an overshadowing vine, which is probably artificial. Firdusi says of Minutscher: "A silken umbrella afforded shade to his head."

M. de la Loubière, envoy extraordinary from the French King in 1687 and 1688 to the King of Siam, says in his narrative that the use of the umbrella was granted by the sovereign to certain highly honoured subjects. An umbrella with several rings of very wide expansion was the prerogative of the king alone, but to certain nobles was granted by princely condescension the right to have their heads and faces screened from the sun by smaller shades. In his quaint old French, M. de la Loubière says that in the audience-chamber of the king:—"Pour tout meuble il n'y a que trois para-sols, un devant la fenêtre, á neuf ronds, et deux á sept ronds aux deux côtéz de la fenêtre. Le para-sol est en ce Pais là, ce que le Dais est en celui-ci"— that is to say, a mark of the highest power.

The Mahratta princes had the title of "Lords of the Umbrella." The chàta of these princes is large and heavy, and requires a special attendant to hold it, in whose custody this symbol of sovereignty reposes.

In Ava it seems to have been part of the royal title that the sovereign was "King of the White Elephant and Lord of Twenty-four Umbrellas." In 1855 the King of Burmah directed a letter to the Marquis of Dalhousie in which he styles himself "His glorious and most excellent Majesty, reigning over the umbrella-wearing princes of the East."

Among the Arabs the umbrella is a mark of distinction. Niebuhr says that it is a privilege confined to princes of the blood to use an umbrella.[24]

In the East the umbrella has come to be regarded as connected with royalty as much as the crown and the throne; and among the Buddhists it has remained so. Four feet from the throne of the Great Mogul, as described by Tavernier, were two spread umbrellas of red velvet fringed with pearls, the sticks of which were wreathed with pearls. Du Halde says that in the Imperial palace at Pekin there were umbrellas always ready for the Emperor; and when he rode out, a canopy was borne on two sticks over his head to shade him and his horse. Of Sultan Mohammed Aladdin we are told that he adopted insignia of majesty hitherto used in India and Persia and unknown in Islam; among these was a canopy or umbrella held over his head when he went abroad. Of one Sultan's umbrella we are told that it was of yellow embroidered with gold and surmounted by a silver dove.

But as the umbrella was the symbol of majesty held over the king's head, it behoved the royal palace to imitate the same, and by its structure show to all that it was the seat of majesty. Thus came into use the cupola or dome, and what was given to the king's house was given also to the temples. In Perret and Chapui's conjectural reconstruction of the temple of Belus, near Babylon, above the seven stages of the mighty pyramid, is the shrine of the god surmounted by a dome. In all likelihood this really was the apex of the pyramid; the dome was a structural umbrella held over the supreme god.

The great hall of audience of the Byzantine emperors was surmounted by a cupola. Two Councils of the Church, in 680 and 692, were held in it, and obtained their designation *in Trullo* from this fact. From the royal palace the cupola passed to the church, as the crown of the House of the King of Kings; and a dome was erected over the church of the Holy Sepulchre by Constantine, and over the church of the Eternal Wisdom by Justinian. But it had already been employed as the crown of a temple, not only in the Pantheon at Rome, but in the Tholos, the temple of Marnas or Dagon at Gaza.

The great dome or umbrella by no means excluded the lesser one beneath it, and kings' thrones under cupolas were also over-canopied by structures of wood, or marble, or metal. Such a *baldacchino* is seen over the sun-god in a bas-relief at Sippar. It became common, and when of wood or metal, was sculptured, or when of textile work, was embroidered with leaf and flower-work, retaining a reminiscence of the original tree beneath which the king sat and held court. It also passed to the church, and became a subsidiary umbrella over the altar. Paul the Silentiary in the sixth century describes that in the Church of St. Sophia at Constantinople as a dome resting on four silver pillars. Constantine erected much the same sort of domed covering above the tomb of the Apostles in Rome.

In the catacombs, the vaulted chapels and the over-arched recessed tombs are all attributable to the same idea; nor has the original notion been lost in them, for they are frescoed over with vines, bays, and other foliage. The most beautiful instance is also the earliest, the squire crypt in the cemetery of Prætextatus, which dates from the second century. Here the entire vault is covered with trailing tendrils and leaves with birds perched on them. A couple of centuries later the original idea was gone, and we find, instead of a growing tree, only bunches and sprigs of flowers.

So!—the umbrellas that pass in the rain under the shadow of the mighty dome of St. Paul's are its poor relations, and my flower-wreathed *regenschirm* preserves in its leafage a reminiscence of the original tree; and the old German woman sits and vends carrots under what was once the prerogative of the sovereign. Is this not a token that sovereignty has passed from the despot to the democracy?[25]

VII.
Dolls.

A white marble sarcophagus occupies the centre of one of the rooms on the basement of the Capitoline Museum in Rome. The cover has been taken off and a sheet of glass fastened over the coffin, so that one can look in. The sarcophagus contains the bones and dust of a little girl. Her ornaments, the flowers that wreathed the poor little head, are all there, and by the side is the child's wooden doll, precisely like the dolls made and sold to-day.

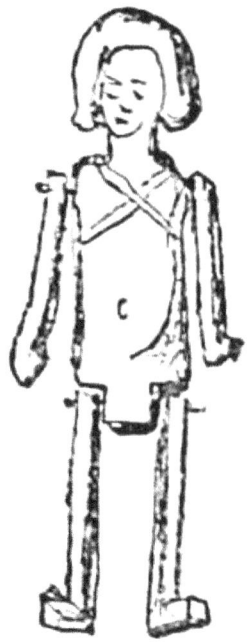

Fig. 33.—DOLL OF IVORY, FROM THE CATACOMB OF ST. AGNESE.

In the catacomb of St. Agnes one end of a passage is given up to form a museum of the objects found in the tombs of the early Christians, and among these are some very similar dolls, taken out of the graves of Christian children. It was very natural that the parents, whether Pagan or Christian, should put the toys of their dear ones into the last resting-place with them, not with the idea that they would want them to play with in the world beyond the veil, but because the sight of these dolls would rouse painful thoughts, and bring tears into the eyes of the mourners whenever come across in some old cupboard or on some shelf.

Of the greatest interest to the student of mankind are the deposits some 40 ft. deep at La Laugerie on the banks of the Vézère in Dordogne. Here at the close of the glacial period lived the primeval inhabitants of France, at the time of the cave lion, reindeer, and mammoth. That race knew nothing of the potter's art. The reindeer hunter was, however, rarely endowed with the artistic faculty, and numerous sketches by him on ivory and bone remain to testify to his appreciation of beauty of animal form. One day a workman turned up a doll carved in ivory beside one of the hearths of this primeval man. He secreted and sold it, being under a bond to deliver all such finds to the proprietor of the land. A fellow-workman betrayed him, and he was obliged to pay back the money he had received and take the doll to M. de Vibraye, to whom it was due. In a rage he said, "Anyhow, he shall not have it perfect," and he knocked off the head. In the accompanying sketch the head is conjecturally restored. The arms were broken off when discovered, if there ever had been arms, which is uncertain.

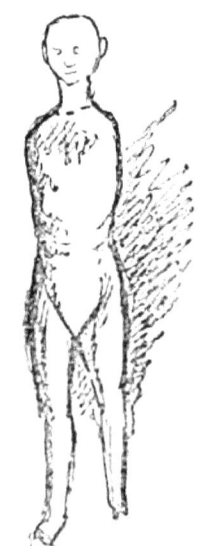

Fig. 34.—DOLL OF IVORY FROM LAUGERIE HAUTE.
(The head restored.)

Was this a child's toy or an idol of adults? Probably the former. On some of the engraved bones of the reindeer have been found sketches of singular objects which bear more resemblance to fetishes, or the images made and venerated by Ostjaks and Samojeds, than any thing else. With the savage, as with the child, that doll receives most regard which is most inartistic, for it allows greater scope for the imagination to play about it. The favourite miraculous images are invariably the rudest.

In one of the Bruges churches is a beautiful Virgin and Child in white marble, one of the few refined and beautiful things that Michael Angelo's hand turned out. But this lovely group does not attract worshippers, who will be found clustered about, offering their candles, hanging up silver hearts about a little monstrosity with a black face, and neither shape nor limbs.

Whosoever has little children of his own can learn a great deal from them relative to the early stages of civilisation of mankind. Every race of men that has not been given revelation from above has passed through a period of intellectual and spiritual infancy, and though men grew to be adults, they never grew out of the thoughts of a child relative to what was beyond their immediate sensible appreciation.

I knew a case of a woman of fifty who insisted that a certain river changed the colour of its water as it flowed in one place under the shadow of a wood, there it turned black, in another part of its course it was white. To the intelligent mind it was obvious enough that the water remained unaltered, but that it looked dark where the shadows cut off the light from the sky. No amount of reasoning could convince the woman that the water itself did not change its colour from black to white. She thought as a child, and was incapable of thinking otherwise.

Now observe a little child playing with a doll. It does not regard the doll as a symbol, a representation of a man or babe, it treats it as a creature endowed with an individuality and a life of its own. It talks to it, it feeds it, it puts it to bed, it conjures up a whole world of history connected with it. It believes the doll to be sensible to pain, and will cry to see it beaten. The doll is to it as real a person as one of its playmates.

Fig. 35.—MIRACULOUS IMAGE AT HAL, BELGIUM.

Now take a savage and his idol. The idol to him is precisely what the doll is to the child. It thinks, it eats, it suffers, it is happy. It requires clothes, it is subject to the same passions as the savage. When a heathen people has advanced to regard an image as the symbol of a deity, it has mounted to a higher intellectual plane; it has stepped from the mental condition of a child of five to that of one of twelve. If we want to see what are the thoughts of a savage, who is in the earliest stage relative to his idol, we must go to the Ostjak or Samojed on the Siberian tundra, or to the negro in Central Africa. The Greek, the Roman, the Egyptian were long past that stage when they become known to us through history and their monumental remains. Their images were symbols, and not properly idols, though there always remained among them individuals, perhaps whole strata of people, whose intellectual appreciation of the images was that of babes. This is not marvellous, for human progress is always subject to this check, that every individual born into the world enters, as to his intellectual state, in the condition of the earliest savage, and has to run through in a few years what races have taken centuries to accomplish. Where this is the case, and it is the case everywhere, there will ever be individuals, perhaps whole classes, whose mental development will suffer arrest at points lower than that attained by the general bulk of the men and women among whom they move.

Even in our own country, the most low and to us inconceivable ideas relative to God may be found among the ignorant. If I tell a story it is not to raise a laugh, but to lift a corner of the veil which covers these dull minds, to show how little they have reached the level to which we have ascended.

A middle-aged man declared to the parson of his parish that he had seen and spoken with the Almighty. He was asked what He was like. He replied that He was dressed in a black swallow-tailed coat of the very best broadcloth and wore a white tie. This was said with perfect gravity, and with intense earnestness of conviction. His highest conception of the Deity was that of a gentleman dressed for a dinner party. Anyone who has had dealings in spiritual matters with the ignorant will be able to cap such a story. This is not to be taken as laughing matter, but as a revelation of a condition of mind to us scarcely intelligible. I feel some hesitation in repeating the incident, but do so because I do not see in what other way I can make those who have not been in communication with the very ignorant understand the full depth of their ignorance.

Now let us look at the ideas that those of a low mental condition among the savage races have relative to their idols. I will take the instance of the Ostjaks and Samojeds. The latter have their *Hakes*. They are figures—sometimes only bits of root of tree or wood that have a distant resemblance to the human form, or some unusual shape. Every family has its *Hake*—sometimes has several. These are wrapped up in coloured rags, given necklaces and bangles, and a tent or apartment to themselves. They have their own sledge, the *haken-gan*, and following after a Samojed family, on its journey from one camping place to another, may be seen a load of these unsightly dolls in their sledge. If some figure out of the usual, in wood or stone, attracts general attention, and is too big to be carried about, it is regarded as the *hake* of a whole tribe. These images are provided with food. Family affairs are communicated to them, and they are supposed to rejoice with domestic joys, and lament family losses.

When their help is required, offerings are made to them, but if the desired help be not given, the *hake* gets scolded, refused his food, and sometimes is kicked out into the snow. The face of the *hake*, or what serves as face, is smeared with reindeer blood. It is the same with the Ostjaks. Their idols are dressed in scarlet, furnished with weapons, and their faces smeared with ochre. They are called *Jitjan*. "Often," says Castrén, "each of these figures has its special office. One is supposed to protect the reindeers, another to help in the fishery, another to care for the health of the family, etc. When need arrives, the figures are drawn forth and set up in a tent at the reindeer pastures, the hunting or fishing grounds. They are presented with sacrifices now and then, which consist in smearing their lips with train oil or blood, and putting before them a vessel with fish or meat."[26]

It is very much the same thing with the negro, who stands on the same intellectual level as the Siberian savage. His fetish is anything out of the way—a strangely-shaped stone or bit of bone, a bunch of feathers, a doll, anything about which his imagination may work, and his reason remain torpid.

I have watched a little boy of six play with a piece of ash twig. I drew it, and noted what his proceedings were. He had picked up this twig, and suddenly exclaimed, "I have found a horse. It is lying down. Get up, horse! Get up!" He took it to some grass to make it eat, then went with it to a pond, and made it drink. There the twig fell in, and he cried out that the horse was swimming. I picked out the twig for him. Presently, by throwing it into the air, he found that his horse could fly. Finally, he set to work to build a stable, and furnish it for his horse.

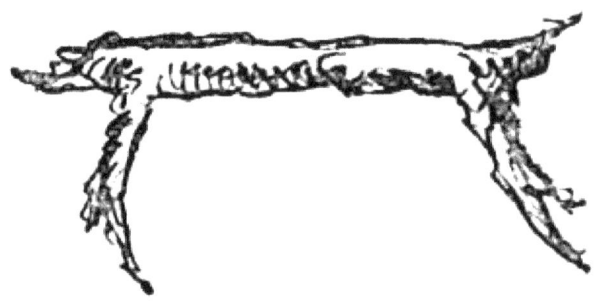

Fig. 36.—THE HORSE.

I had been reading Castrén's account of the *hakes* and *jitjan* at the time, and under my eyes a child doing with a bit of stick exactly what a Turanian nomad of full age does now, and has done for thousands of years. In two or three years this boy's mind will have expanded, and his reason have got in the saddle, and will hold in the imaginative faculty with bit and bridle, and then he will cease to see horses in ash twigs; but the wanderers on the Asiatic tundras have never got beyond the stage of an English child of six and never will.

I quote a passage from "The Beggynhof; or, City of the Single," to show how that it is possible for a tolerably-educated, religious Belgian of the present day to stand at the same point as that of a child of six, and of an Ostjak savage.

"St. Anthony is a favourite saint with the good, holy, simple-minded Beguines; but woe betide him if he refuse his powerful intercession. I once saw a poor little statuette of this domestic saint left outside on the window-sill when the snow lay deep on the ground. On inquiring why it did not occupy its place on the mantelshelf, I was told that the saint had been refractory; that the Beguine who occupied that room had been very patient and forbearing for some days, but that, finding gentleness had no effect in obtaining what she wanted, she now thought herself justified in trying what effect punishment would have, so she had turned the effigy of the rebellious saint out into the snow, and sat with her back towards it, that her patron might understand she did not intend to address him again until he granted her his protection and influence."[27] Precisely in like manner, when Germanicus died, did the rabble of Rome pelt the temples and statues of the gods with mud and stones, because they had failed to hear their prayers for the recovery of their beloved prince.

We all of us pass through this stage of intellectual and spiritual growth, except a few who never get beyond it. It is said of the negro that as a child he is clever and bright, but that he never attains the mental condition of an European of fifteen. But there are men and women among us who, in certain matters, never get beyond the condition of mind of a child of six. We may be shocked at this, but we cannot help it; they are so constituted—something in their cranial structure, or some natural deficiency in mental vigour is the occasion of this. In religious matters they cannot get beyond Fetishism; and if we deny them that, we deny them all religious comfort and worship. Sometimes, through some accident, a leg or an arm gets diseased, whereas the rest of the body grows; so is it with the mind—certain faculties get diseased, perhaps the reasoning power, and then the imagination runs riot.

To an ordinary cultured Pagan of Rome, or Greece, or Egypt, idolatry was impossible. The gods, figured in marble and bronze, were to them symbols and nothing else, precisely as to us the letters of the alphabet are symbols of certain sounds, and the pictographic characters of cuneiform and hieroglyphic writing were anciently symbols of certain ideas. So also idolatry is absolutely impossible to anyone who has gone through the elements of modern education. Religious statues and pictures are historic representations of personages and events in the sacred story, but to look upon them with the eyes of an Ostjak or a child of six is a psychological impossibility, except only for such as are mentally stunted like the Beguine of Ghent. It is, therefore, without the smallest scruple that we can employ imagery in our churches, knowing that the possibility of misusing it is gone past reversion to it in nine hundred and ninety-nine persons out of a thousand, and that the thousandth person who would misuse it is incapable of any other religious exercise, and it were better that he had some religious conceptions, however low these were, than none at all.

To draw this moral has not been my object in penning this article, but to direct the attention of the intelligent to the nursery, and show them how that the elements for the study of primitive culture, the means of following the development of ideas in man are to be found wherever there are little children.

VIII.
Revivals.

Of the three factors that go to make up man—body, intellect, and the spiritual faculty, the last has been allowed somewhat to fall into neglect in the present age, when special stress has been laid on the education and development of the intellect. Nevertheless it is a factor that must not be ignored, and it is one that is likely to revenge itself for neglect by abnormal action.

In the Middle Ages it was the reverse; under the preponderating influence of the Church, the spiritual faculty was cultivated to extreme of mysticism, and the intellect on one side, and the body on the other, hardly received sufficient recognition. When an ascetic would neither think out a problem nor keep himself clean, he exhibited a monstrosity, not as repulsive, but as certainly a monstrosity, as one of the gladiators depicted on the pavement of the Baths of Caracalla—this latter, a man cultivated to the highest point of animal strength and physical activity. It is probable that a purely intellectual man without idealism, without religiosity, is as much a monster as either of the other, though not in the nineteenth century as repugnant to us as they are.

A religion that is good for anything must not only be one that is intelligible and reasonable, but must satisfy the spiritual cravings, and also exercise moral control over the animal nature. At the same time, it is liable to undue stress in each direction; it may become a mere theological speculation, mere mysticism, or resolve itself into exterior formalism. Whenever it manifests a preponderating tendency in one or other of these directions—the element in man that is not given its adequate scope will revolt, and fling itself into an opposite scale.

The function of the reason in religion is to act as the balance wheel of the spirit. Reason is not the mainspring, not the motive power of religion; it is its controlling, moderating faculty.

Throughout the history of mankind we are coming continually upon phenomena of a spiritual nature, outbursts of the spiritual faculty in strange and often in very repulsive manifestations, and it may not be amiss to look at some of these and to learn what is their real nature.

Among the primitive races which at this day represent the earliest phases of psychological development, the savage man has a vague apprehension of the existence of a spiritual world, haunted by the souls of the dead which have not been absorbed into the universal spirit from which they emanated. He has no definite belief, he has only an apprehension. In the spiritual world, the existence of which he suspects, there is no system; concerning it he has no doctrine. Its existence implies no responsibilities.

Even the idea of an all-pervading spirit is inchoate. All that man is confident about is that he is surrounded by and subject to the influences of spirits, now beneficent, then malevolent, always capricious, that have to be humoured and propitiated, and that allow themselves to be consulted.

There is but one, so to speak, natural mode of holding intercourse with the spirits, and that is by ecstasy, whether natural or superinduced by narcotics. The man who falls into hysterics, the man who is cataleptic, is the natural priest. An hysterical, a cataleptic condition, is not understood, and just as the unusual and contorted bit of wood or stone receives reverence as a fetish, so does the man subject to unusual fits become a priest. To him the man of less nervous organism applies when he desires to hold intercourse with the unseen world. Incantation, whereby the hysterical work themselves into hysteria, and religious rite are one. The Shaman or Medicine-man is the only priest.

Indeed, there is not a people, at a low stage of mental and moral development, among which this phase of religion is not found, before the spirit world coagulates into distinct beings, the rudiments of a theology appear, the priesthood emerges as a caste, and worship is fixed in ceremonial observance.

As man advances in the scale of general culture, and thinks more of the unseen world, his reason or fancy, or reason and fancy acting together, become creative; in the protoplastic, nebulous spirit-world points of light appear, the light is divided from the darkness, and the spiritual entities take rank, and assume characteristics. Religion enters on the polytheistic phase.

At the same time the moral sense has advanced; it has seen that there is some relation between the two worlds determined by good and bad. An ethic code is evolved, imposed on man by the superior beings in the world unseen.

But whilst some of the more gifted in a generation attain to this religious and moral conception, there remain others, at the same time, unable to rise, who still occupy the same low level as the earlier men, who are conscious of spiritual forces, but unable to differentiate them, who are lost in a vague dream, incapable of accepting a theologic system, and unwilling to submit to moral restraint. Such men will always turn away from a definite creed, view a priestly caste with suspicion, and kick against an ethical code. To them the Schaman is still the only priest, and delirious ecstasy the only sacrament that unites the worlds. Their psychic development is so rudimentary, that they are ready to accept as consecrated whatever utterance is vented, whatever act is performed in the transport of temporary delirium.

Before proceeding any further with the account of the growth of religion, it will be well here to give an account of Schamanism as it at present exists. For this I will quote a description given by Lieutenant Matjuschin who accompanied Baron Wrangel on his Polar Expedition in 1820-3. Lieutenant Matjuschin visited a Tungu Schaman near the Lena, in 1820.

"In the midst of the gurte (hut) burnt a fire, round which was laid a circle of black sheepskins. On this the Schaman paced, uttering his incantations in an undertone. His black, long, coarse hair nearly covered his dark-red face; from under his bushy eyebrows gleamed a pair of glowing bloodshot eyes. His kirtle of skins was hung with amulets, thongs, chains, bells, and scraps of metal. In his right hand he held his magic drum, like a tambourine, in his left an unstrung bow. By degrees the flame died away; he cast himself on the ground; after five minutes he broke out into a plaintive muffled sound like the moans of several voices. The fire was fanned into a blaze again. The Schaman sprang up, planted his bow on the earth, rested his brow on the upper end, and ran at a rapidly increasing pace round the bow. Suddenly he halted, made signs with his hands in the air, grasped his drum, played a sort of melody on it, leaped and twisted his body into strange contortions, and turned his head about so rapidly that it seemed to us more like a ball attached to the trunk by a string. All at once he fell rigid on the ground; two men whetted great knives over him, he uttered his mournful tones, and moved slowly and convulsively. He was forced upright, and he was as one unconscious, only with a slight quiver in his body; his eyes stared wildly and fixedly out of his head, his face was covered with blood, which poured out with sweat incessantly from his pores. At last, leaning on the bow, he swung the tambourine hastily, clattering over his head, then let it fall to earth. Now he was fully inspired. He stood motionless with lifeless eyes and face; neither the questions put to him, nor the rapid unconsidered answers he gave, produced the slightest alteration in his frozen features. He replied to the queries, of the majority of which he can have had no comprehension, in an oracular style, but with great firmness of assurance. Matjuschin asked how long our journey would last? Answer, 'Over three years.' 'Would we effect much?' 'More than was expected at home.' 'Should we all keep our health?' 'All but you; but you will not be really ill?' (Matjuschin suffered for a long time with a wound in the throat.) 'How is Lieutenant Anjou?' 'He is three days distant from Bulun, where he has taken refuge, having barely saved his life from a frightful storm on the Lena.' (This was afterwards found to be true.) Many answers were so vague and poetical as to be unintelligible. When we had done questioning him, the Schaman fell down and remained a quarter of an hour on the ground suffering from violent convulsions. 'The devils are departing,' said the Tungu, and opened the door. Then the man awoke as out of a deep sleep, looked about in a bewildered manner, and seemed unconscious of what had taken place.

"At another place a Schaman went into ecstasies. The daughter of the house, a Jakutin, became white, then red, then the bloody sweat broke out, and she fell unconscious on the ground. Matjuschin ordered the Schaman to desist; as he did not, he flung him out of the house, but he continued his leaps and contortions outside in the snow. The girl lay stiff, the lower part of her body swelled, she had cramps, shrieked, wrung her hands, leaped and sang unintelligible words; at last she fell asleep, and when she woke after an hour, knew nothing of what had happened. Her father told us she often had these ecstasies, foretold the future, and sang in the Lamutisch and Tungu languages, which she did not know."

Matjutschin remarks on what he saw: "The Schamans have been represented as being mere gross deceivers; no doubt this is true of many of them, but the history of others is very different. Born with ardent imaginations and excitable nerves, they grow up amidst a general belief in the supernatural. The youth receives strong impressions and desires to obtain communication with the invisible world. No one teaches him how to do so. A true Schaman is not a cool and ordinary deceiver, but a psychological phenomenon."

These hysterical transports are infectious. Several cases have been known where a Schaman has begun his operations, that onlookers have been convulsed, have communicated their agitation to others, and it has run through an entire settlement, all becoming frantic, shouting, rolling on the ground, with nervous jerks of the head and spasms of the body.

We find precisely analogous practices everywhere among men on the same psychological platform as Lapps, Ostjaks, and Tungus. Sometimes medicinal plants and drugs are used to provoke intoxication or excite dreams.

Madness, epilepsy, catalepsy, hysteria, in fact all nervous maladies are at present little understood by science, and among rude nations, where there is no science, are not understood at all, and are regarded with superstitious terror. The violence of the patient, the fancies that possess him, his incoherent cries, the distortion of his body, the alteration in his features, all seem to point out that he has fallen under the domination of a foreign power, and such a person is said to be *possessed*. His actions, his words, are no longer his own, but those of the spirit that occupies his body. There was not of old, nor is there still among savages, any sharp distinction between good spirits and bad. All spirits are those of the dead. It is only by those who have advanced to a higher stage that these are classified as angels or devils. In Baron Wrangel's "North Polar Travels," already quoted, is another significant passage which illustrates this point. He says that in Northern Siberia an epidemic disease called the Mirak appears, which, according to the universal belief of the people, proceeds from the ghost of a dead sorceress entering into and tormenting the patient. But Wrangel says, "The Mirak appears to me to be only an extreme form of hysteria; the persons attacked are chiefly women."

Our word *mania* traces back to the period when the madman was supposed to be possessed by the *manes*, the spirit of some dead man; but such an idea was already abandoned by the classic Roman, who gave the word to us.

As already said, it was inevitable that Schamanism should co-exist along with an organised religion, for only one portion of a people would have made sufficient progress to be able to receive a dogmatic faith and accept a formulated worship. There would always remain a substratum of ignorance and unintelligence which would have recourse to diviners and dealers with familiar spirits, that is to Schamans or medicine-men. And now we can understand the true position of the Witch of Endor. The faith of the Jewish people had taken shape; it had its monotheistic creed, its altars, and its priesthood, but the religious development of the people was not on a level with the scheme of Mosaism. The law was formal, unspiritual—that is to say, unsensational—to those to whom the only religion that was acceptable was one of vague spiritualism and ecstatic hallucination. Saul himself was one of these. As long as all went well with him he adhered to the authorised religion, but the moment he was in real distress and alarm he had recourse to the baser, proscribed system, level with his own low spiritual perceptions.

All the denunciations in the Old Testament against witchcraft are properly denunciations not of devil worship, but of a relapse from the highly organised faith, to the inchoate form of religion suitable only for savages, from which the Divine Revelation had lifted the sons of Israel. We find precisely the same condition among the Greeks. They had their temples, their priests, their mythology. But this was beyond the spiritual range of some, and these had recourse to the Goetoi, true Schamans, that took their title from the cries they uttered. These Goetoi were, in fact, the successors of the medicine-men of pre-historic Hellas. They were looked upon with mistrust and some fear by the superior, cultured classes, and laws were passed, but always evaded, prohibiting these men from exercising their functions, and the people from having recourse to them.

Superstition has been called the Shadow of Religion. It may be so regarded, as it always dogs its steps; but a more exact and philosophic view of superstition is to regard it as the protoplasm of belief, co-existing alongside with fully articulated religion, as the jelly-fish floats in the same wave where the vertebrate-fish swims. Superstition is the pap of religion to those incapable of digesting and assimilating a solidified creed. To those low in the psychic scale there is a consciousness of spirit; but spirit must be vague, and the means of holding communion with spirit must be something that appeals to their coarse, uneducated fancy, as hysteric convulsions or maniacal ravings.

The Gospel was preached to Jew and Gentile, and a change came over the face of the religious world. Religion was carried into an infinitely higher sphere. Christianity stood above classic Paganism, as classic Paganism stood above Schamanism.

Let us take a passage from the history of the Church in Apostolic times, and we shall see the reappearance of the same phenomenon.

During the course of his second missionary journey, St. Paul came to Corinth, and abode there eighteen months, during which time he laboured to spread the Gospel. He addressed himself first to the Jews residing in Corinth, but roused so great an opposition that he turned to the Greeks, and succeeded so well in gathering about him a crowd of persons who made profession of conviction, that the Jews seized and dragged him before Gallio, the Roman proconsul, accusing him of opposition to the law of Moses. But the Governor put the whole matter from him, as one out of his jurisdiction, if not beneath his notice. Shortly after St. Paul departed to Syria by ship.

It is worth considering the quality of the converts made at Corinth, that we may understand what followed. Corinth, the capital of Achaia, was noted for its wealth and luxury. It was the place for the performance of the Isthmean games, in which boxing, horse-racing, and musical contests formed the great attraction. It was the Newmarket of Greece, and swarmed with those doubtful characters, of low intellect and depraved morals, who generally congregate about the race-course, the boxing-ring, and the music-hall. The heathen orator, Dio Chrysostom, who lived at the same time as St. Paul, says of Corinth that it was verily the most licentious of all the cities that ever were, and that ever had been.

It was to the people of such a city that St. Paul addressed himself, and amongst whom he met with a certain amount of success. He tells us himself to what class the bulk of his converts belonged. There were "not many wise men after the flesh," that is, very few of the philosophers, the only representatives of a higher life and clear intelligence, the only men who struggled after a knowledge of God, and for pure morality. They stood aloof. There were also "not many mighty," few in authority; "not many noble," few of the respectable citizens. In fact, he got his converts from the riff-raff of an utterly vicious town. We must bear this in mind.

A community of believers gathered from among the inhabitants of Corinth must have presented phenomena deserving special attention. Surrounded by the prevailing immorality, open, flagrant, stalking the streets, they had ceased from earliest infancy to blush at evil sights, and words, and thoughts. They were tainted to the heart's core. At the same time they were an excitable people, with high-strung nervous temperaments, such as are found in a nursery of the arts, where the sense of physical not of moral beauty is cultivated.

Such persons were ready, for the sake of its novelty, to embrace the new religion preached in their midst. They ran after the new preacher as they ran to hear a new singer; they took up his doctrine as they took up a new philosophy, for the sake of its newness. They rushed into the Church as they elbowed their way into the theatre. As to realising the purity, the self-denial that Christianity requires—of that they had not the faintest idea.

The profession of Christianity subdued these converts for a while—for a few months; but though regenerate in baptism, the old "phronema sarkos" remained like a sleeping leopard waiting its time to awake, stretch itself, and seek its prey. Regeneration is not a magic spell; it is an initiation, not an act. St. Paul was in Corinth eighteen months only, and in this short time it was impossible for him to establish the Church on firm foundations. Besides, he was an initiator and not by any means an organiser.

He had not been long gone before the natural result of an indiscriminate conversion made itself apparent, and St. Paul had to write to the young Church at Corinth a letter which has been lost or suppressed. This was followed by a second, and that by a third, and we have got only the two latter. Probably, the Church of Corinth thought it best to put the first in the fire and not publish its shame. But the second and third—the first and second, as we call them—throw a tolerably clear light on the state of this Church.

There were dissensions in it, and no wonder; then scandal, and, again,—no wonder. Of the dissensions I need not speak.

First among the scandals came the Love Feasts. The feast was instituted in order that all the faithful might meet, and eat and drink together, the rich contributing the provisions and sitting down with the poor. It is not to be confounded with the Holy Eucharist, which was something quite distinct. The Love Feast took place at night, the Eucharist in the early morning.

However excellent in intention the institution might be, in a very short time it was abused. The well-to-do brought food and wine with them, and ate and drank by themselves, apart from the slaves and the members whom poverty prevented from contributing. The poor were compelled to look hungrily on, while the rich brethren, having more than sufficed, indulged to excess. One was hungry, and another was drunken.

It is not difficult to trace the origin of these Love Feasts; they were a local adaptation from the heathen ceremonial of the Temple of Aphrodite.

The Greeks had mysteries in their principal temples, into which the devout were initiated. Baptism was one of the initiatory acts. Then the neophytes were taught certain secret doctrines which they were forbidden to reveal to the profane without. After that they partook together of a sacred feast, and then ensued ecstatic raptures, hysterical ravings, and orgies of a licentious character in those shrines dedicated to the goddess of love.

The newly converted Christians of Corinth were desirous of getting as much excitement out of their new religion as they could. So they treated Christian baptism as an initiation into Christian mysteries; they instituted the Love Feast as a close reproduction of the banquet with which they were familiar in the Temple of Aphrodite, and then followed a condition of disorder very little more decent than the heathen orgies.

St. Paul notes three abuses, into which these Corinthians fell, all three borrowed from the heathen mysteries. They revelled at the Love Feasts, they fell into moral disorder, and they gave way to hysterical ravings. The third abuse St. Paul was a little puzzled at, and he dealt with it more leniently than with the drunkenness and debauchery of his converts. He was prepared to humour the wild exhibition, perhaps in hopes that by degrees the converts, as they mended their morals, would mend in this particular also. The outburst of incoherent ravings to which he referred was much the same as what had occurred in the heathen mysteries, and the same phenomena are met with to the present day among North American Indians and negroes. We have seen a Schaman in the same state in Siberia. These Corinthians, some tipsy with the wine they had drunk in excess, others half starved, but frenzied by their easily-wrought-on religious feelings, jabbered disconnected, unintelligible words. They raved, fell into cataleptic fits, and made a scene of confusion and uproar such as is hardly to be found out of the wards of Bedlam.

In the heathen temples women were placed over cracks in the rock, whence exhaled intoxicating vapours, and becoming giddy, they uttered oracular sentences, which were generally nonsense, and could, therefore, be interpreted to mean anything. The apostle now met with the outbreak of a phenomenon among his converts very similar, which he could not understand, and did not know in what manner to treat. He contented himself with giving rules for its direction. He struck at the root of the spiritual disturbances when he insisted on a moral reformation. Till that was effected, there would be no abatement of these perplexing and indecent manifestations. Where there were incoherent ravings, there "an interpreter" was to be set in the assemblies to make what sense he could out of the unintelligible noises.

The discipline to which the Corinthians were subjected by St. Paul brought them to some sort of order for awhile, but it is not to be expected that, with the lofty standard of life set before them, there would not be found a considerable number who would kick at it.

St. Paul, in his polemics against the Judaisers, had written with heat against the law, and had exalted the freedom of the Gospel. He had not supposed it necessary to nicely discriminate between the ceremonial obligations and the moral commands of the law. Accordingly a good many of his converts took the matter into their own hands, and he was surprised and confounded to find a party fully prepared to take his strongest words *au pied de la lettre*, to roll moral and ceremonial commands into one bundle, and throw all overboard.

Accordingly we find that the early Church was infested with a multitude of Evangelicals, professing themselves to be disciples of St. Paul, appealing to his words as their justification, and casting all morality to the winds.

In the following ages we find exactly the same sort of scenes as those that startled St. Paul at Corinth settling into an acknowledged institution, and ending in such orgies, that the heathen were almost justified in regarding Christianity as a religious nuisance, and a danger to common morality. The accounts we have of the assemblies of the followers of Valentine, Mark, Carpocrates, Epiphanes, and Isidore, of the Ophites and Antitactites, present us with pictures of religious revivals ending in the orgies of satyrs.

The empire, under Constantine, became Christian. Then the Church, no longer persecuted, spread throughout the world with a definite creed, an organised priesthood, a fixed mode of worship, and a rigid moral code.

Then, as heretofore, in the early Church, in heathen Rome and Greece, there were those unable to receive a religion so perfect or so defined. They must have something vague and rudimentary, something that did not require too much of them, that did not lay upon them too many restrictions. These men sought what suited them in various forms of heresy, or in the secret performance of Pagan rites, the heresies all forms of negation, the Paganism altogether gross and elementary. All these forms of revolt were reversions to the earliest protoplasmic type. It is not my purpose to trace the history of these relapses throughout the Middle Ages, for I am not writing a history of heresy; my object is simply to note the fact that Spiritualism or Schamanism constantly appears in the history of religion, varying its name but few of its characteristics; sometimes becoming grossly immoral, sometimes decent, but always whilst professing almost ascetic virtue with a tendency to licentiousness.

As soon as Christianity became established, at once all the gods of the heathen became devils, and their worship the worship of devils. "Idolatry," said Eusebius, in the *Præparatio Evangelica*, "does not consist in the adoration of good spirits, but in that of those which are evil and perverse."[28] The Christian emperors forbade the sacrifices to the gods, as sacrifices to devils. In 426, Theodosius II. ordered every temple to be destroyed. Those who clung to the old religion were driven to worship on mountains and in the depths of forests. In 423, he had issued an injunction against the sacrifices, on this very ground, that they were made to devils.

What took place in Italy or Greece, took place elsewhere in later days, when the barbarians became Christians, or, at least, were made nominal

Christians, under Christian Frank emperors. The *Indiculus superstitionum et Paganiarum* of the Council of Leptines in Hainault, in the eighth century, shows us Paganism completely converted into witchcraft. Those who were addicted to it went to retired huts (*casulæ*) in places formerly held sacred (*fana*); there they offered sacrifices to Jupiter, Mercury, or some other god; they took auguries, drew lots, called up spirits, made little images of linen and flour, and carried them about the country, precisely as Sulpicius Severus says was done by the Gauls in the time of St. Martin. Pope Gregory III. condemned those who made sacrifices to fountains and trees, used divinations, exercised magical rites, in honour of Belus and Janus, "according to the customs of the Pagans," and he anathematised all those who took part in diabolical rites, and gave worship to devils. Finally the Capitularies of Charles the Great and his successors armed the secular power against all these remnants of idolatry.

At about the same period, the seventh century, Camin the Wise, Abbot of Hy (Iona), tells us that the like superstitions prevailed in Ireland.

But, before this, the Council of Ancyra, in 341, had issued a decree, which has, indeed, been called in question, but which was embodied in the "Canon Episcopi," by which the bishops were required to exercise vigilant supervision over magical practices, and especially to excommunicate certain impious females, who, blinded by the devil, imagined themselves riding through the air in company with Hecate and Herodias—Herodias is no other than Hruoda, a Lombard goddess, the same as the Saxon Ostara.[29] The injunction was repeated by the Synod of Agde, in 506, which, with other decrees of the sixth and seventh centuries, represents witchcraft as a Pagan delusion. Magic and heresy were one. Heresy was a turning away from the truth, and magic was its ritual. Enmity to orthodoxy implied enmity to God, and enmity to God alliance with the devil.

The charges which had been brought by heathens against early Christians were now, under altered circumstances, launched by Christians against heretics and witches. The hideous description of Christianity given by Cœcilius, in Minutius Felix, as a secret and desperate faction leagued against God and man, and celebrating the foulest nocturnal rites, became the type of accusations levelled by orthodox Christians against their dissenting brethren; and, as the charge of Cœcilius was justified by the conduct of a portion of the Christian converts, so was the charge of the orthodox against the schismatics in mediæval times justified by the conduct of some of them. The Cathari, Manichæans, Paulicians, Patarines, Albigenses, were all heretics so far that they reverted to heathenism, and to its most simple form of Schamanism, and some of the congregations sank into the grossest immorality.

The writers on witchcraft who theoretically worked out its criminal details—Eumericus, Nider, Bernhard of Como, and Jacquier—spoke of it as "Secta et hæresis maleficorum," it was a heresy, one of the several forms in which lapse from the faith took. Balduinus identified Waldenses with witches.

In 1484, James Sprenger and Henry Justitor, appointed inquisitors for Upper Germany, obtained the celebrated bull of Innocent VIII., which, though far from being the origin of witch prosecutions, acted with signal effect in promoting their subsequent activity. Sprenger followed it up with his well-known treatise called "Malleus Maleficarum," as a guide to judicial theory and practice.

No object is gained by dwelling on the details of an epidemic which, for three centuries, devastated Europe, destroying so many lives. Yet two particulars challenge inquiry and remark: one, the strange uniformity of the offence as elicited by confession; the other, the curious analogy which is found to exist between the rites practised by the witches at their gatherings and those of the heretics of earlier times, Pagan and semi-Christian. The uniformity in the confession of the witches has excited surprise, and has been variously accounted for—some supposing that there must have been an external reality in the way of profane imposture, a remnant of heathen practice; others referring it to morbid subjectivity in the accused, caused by melancholy and hypochondria.

That there was some objective reality, I can hardly doubt; not only are the confessions of those accused curiously alike in their account of the ceremonies of the Sabbath, when they assembled, but we know that human nature is always the same, and it is inconceivable that there should have been a cessation at any period of those gatherings of men and women who found the only satisfaction for their religious cravings in vague spiritualism.

One may say boldly that Europe was half Pagan in the Middle Ages; all the old superstitions lived, but under a new disguise. The religions of Gaul, of Germany, of Great Britain, of the Scandinavian and the Slavonic lands, the mythologies of Greece and of Rome, lived on in a crowd of legends, which modern erudition delights in collecting and tracing back to their sources. These legends, more numerous in the lands occupied by Teutonic peoples, are almost always of Pagan stuff, embroidered over with Christian ideas. Not only so, but the very names of the old gods remain; they no longer remain as the names of gods held high in heaven, but of devils cast down to earth. With us the Deuce signifies Satan, and is in common usage in the mouth as an oath, but he takes his name from the Dusii, the night genii of the Kelts. Old Nick again is Hnikr, an honourable designation of Wuotan, the supreme god of the Anglo-Saxons, who gives his name to Wednesday.

So, also, we use the word Bogie, Bogart, as a designation of an evil spirit, and Bug is the name of a night-tormenting insect. It is well-known that in an old English Bible the verse in Ps. xci. runs, "He shall deliver thee from the Bug that walketh in darkness," that is, from the Hobgoblin. The

Norsemen and Danes brought this name with them to England. Bog is in Slavonic God. Biel-bog is the White God, Czerni-bog is the Black God of the Slavs.

The Northmen had formerly come across Slavs on the Continent, and they, the worshippers of Odin, scorned the gods of the Slavs as devils, and called all unclean spirits—Bogs or Bogies. And now, also, the Supreme God of the Norsemen, Hnikr, has become our Old Nick.

This being so, it will be seen at once how the votaries of the dethroned god came to be regarded as devil-worshippers, and how that in time, when the old religion with its myths and theogony was long dead, those who still clung to an hysterical religion, with love-feasts, dances, and ecstasies, came to believe themselves to be devil-worshippers.

The Reformation caused such a disturbance of religious ideas, incited to such revolt against all that had been held sacred in the past, that it is only natural that those whose religion had been one of pure spiritualism, of ecstasy and hysteric raving, should believe that their day had come. But after the first explosion, the Reformers set to work to consolidate their several systems into dogmatic shape; they drew up Institutes, Confessions, Articles, and agreed only in this, to put down Mysticism as severely as they had dealt with Catholicism. And they had good cause to come to this resolution, for on all sides the Mystics were breaking forth into the wildest excesses. In Münster they had set up a Kingdom of Salem, from which every element of common decency was expelled, and which knew no law save the revelations accorded to the prophets.

The "spiritually minded," that is to say, the unintelligent, hysterically disposed, did not at all relish the form given to belief, and the discipline of Divine service framed by the Reformers. They founded sects on all sides following the old lines of the Markosites and Cathari.

Bishop Barlow, one of those who helped to draw up the English Prayer-book, was himself an eye-witness of the proceedings of some of these sects, and he describes them in words we do not care to quote.[30]

England, Germany, Switzerland, Scandinavia, were overrun with these sectaries, with their love-feasts, raptures, and license. It was the old story again of the revolt of the spiritual faculty against the reason, a story that will be told over and over again as long as man lives on the earth, and religion is dogmatic and exercises moral restraint.

One essential condition was always present in order to produce its effect in these sectarian meetings. The intellect must remain inactive, the emotions must be excited, and the sentiment of vague fear must be specially appealed to and powerfully wrought upon. It was this condition which determined the success alike of the revivalist meetings of the Mystics, and the revelries of the witches. This condition it was that provoked the orgies at Corinth among St. Paul's converts, and the scenes in the assemblies of the Carpocratites. It was this condition which roused the attendants on the assemblies of the Goeti, of the Dionysian revellers, and of the Schamans and the medicine men.

These meetings always took place at night. There is reason to believe that during each day there is a normal alteration in the functions of the intellectual and emotional parts of the brain; that during the sunlight the perceptive faculties and the reflective are chiefly active; and that these, reposing during the night, permit the feelings to be mostly dominant; and it is well-known that general and simultaneous activity, both of the intellect and of the emotions, is unnatural; that thought and feeling are antagonistic to each other. Prayer meetings and witches' assemblies alike began after dark and were often continued till the small hours of the morning. Ignorant men and women, and the youth of both sexes, were crowded together to partake in some mysterious spiritual rite. The quiescence of the observant and reflective faculties was facilitated, the imagination goaded and stimulated until it conjured up conceptions of hell and visions of devils with a vividness approaching reality; then came cries, tremblings, fallings on the ground, and raptures.

During Wesley's preaching at Bristol, "one after another," we are told, "sank to the earth." Men and women by "scores were sometimes strewed on the ground at once, insensible as dead men." During a Methodist revival in Cornwall, 4000 people, it was computed, fell into convulsions. "They remained during this condition so abstracted from every earthly thought, that they stayed two and sometimes three days and nights together in the chapels, agitated at the time by spasmodic movements, and taking neither repose nor refreshment. The symptoms followed each other usually as follows:—A sense of faintness and oppression, shrieks as if in the agony of death, convulsions of the muscles of the eyelids—the eyes being fixed and staring—and of the muscles of the neck, trunk, and arms, sobbing respiration, tremors, and general agitation, and all sorts of strange gestures. When the exhaustion came on, patients usually fainted and remained in a stiff and motionless state until their recovery."[31]

Now let the reader turn back to the account of the Tungu Schaman, at the beginning of this article. Is it not obvious that we have here precisely the same phenomenon?

While at Newcastle, Wesley investigated the physical effects that resulted from his preaching. "He found, first, that all persons who had been thus affected were in perfect health, and had not before been subject to convulsions of any kind." Secondly, that they were affected suddenly. Thirdly, that they usually fell on the ground, lost their strength, and were afflicted with spasms. "Some thought a great weight lay upon them, some said they were quite choked, and found it difficult to breathe." Wesley believed these phenomena were of diabolic origin. One section of Methodists, in Cornwall and Wales, was seized with a dancing or jumping mania. Because David danced before the ark, these fanatics concluded that jumping and dancing must form an acceptable form of service. The practice became epidemic. Each devotee would caper for hours, till, completely exhausted, he or she fell insensible.

During a great Presbyterian revival, which passed over Kentucky and Tennessee in the beginning of this century, persons swooned away and lay as dead on the ground for a quarter of an hour; this "falling exercise" was succeeded by that of the "jerks." A Backwoods preacher who has left us his valuable biography, says:—

"A new exercise broke out among us, called the *jerks*, which was overwhelming in its effects upon the bodies and minds of the people. No matter whether they were saints or sinners, they would be taken under a warm song or sermon, and seized with a convulsive jerking all over, which they could not by any possibility avoid, and the more they resisted, the more they jerked. I have seen more than five hundred persons jerking at one time in my large congregations. Most usually persons taken with the jerks would rise up and dance. Some would run, but could not get away. To see those proud young gentlemen, and young ladies dressed in their silks, jewelry, and prunella, from top to toe take the jerks, would often excite my risibilities. The first jerk or so, you would see their fine bonnets, caps, and combs fly; and so sudden would be the jerking of the head that their long, loose hair would crack almost as loud as a waggoner's whip."[32]

Another revivalist in Kentucky says; "While preaching, we have after a smooth and gentle course of expression suddenly changed our voice and language, expressing something awful and alarming, and instantly some dozen or twenty persons, or more, would simultaneously be jerked forward, where we were sitting, and with a suppressed noise once or twice, somewhat like the barking of a dog. One young woman went round like a top, we think, at least fifty times in a minute, and continued without interruption for at least an hour, and one young woman danced in her pew for twenty or thirty minutes with her eyes shut and her countenance calm, and then fell into convulsions; some ran with amazing swiftness, some imitated the motion of playing on a fiddle, others barked like dogs."

Surely we have here a scene precisely identical in character with that described by Dr. Hecker as having broke out in Germany in 1374. He says: "It was called the dance of St. John or of St. Vitus, on account of the Bacchantic leaps by which it was characterised. The dancers, appearing to have lost all control over their senses, continued dancing, regardless of the bystanders, for hours together in wild delirium, until at length they fell to the ground in a state of exhaustion.... While dancing they neither saw nor heard, being insensible to external impressions through the senses, but were haunted by visions, their fancies conjuring up spirits whose names they shrieked out."[33]

It has happened in some cases, especially in that of women, that they have tried to tear off their clothes, and this explains the account given by those who had attended the Witches' Sabbath, that many present were stark naked. We know that some of the wilder congregations of the Hussites developed their fanaticism in this form. So did the Anabaptists in Amsterdam.

We will now take a case or two from the Roman Communion. Hysteria, as we might suppose, would be likely to manifest itself in the monastic orders. St. Joseph of Cupertino was one Christmas Eve in church, when the pifferari began to play their carols. Joseph, who was a Franciscan friar, carried away by religious emotion, began to dance in the midst of the choir, and then, with a howl, he took a flying leap and lighted on the high altar. He was then vested in a gorgeous cope, conducting the service. The carollers were amazed, no less than the friars; and their amazement was increased when they saw him jump from the altar on to the pulpit ledge, fifteen feet above the ground. One day he went into the convent choir of the Sisters of St. Clara, at Cupertino. When the nuns began to sing, Joseph, unable to restrain his emotion, ran across the chancel, caught the old confessor of the convent in his arms, and danced with him before the altar. Then he span himself about like a teetotum, with the confessor clinging to his hands, and his legs flying out horizontally.

St. Christina, The Wonderful, a Belgian virgin, used to go into fits when her religious emotions were worked upon, put her head between her feet, bending her spine backwards, and roll round the room or church like a ball.

St. Peter of Alcantara in his fervours used to strip himself naked. He would jump, curled up like a ball, high into the air, and in and out at the church door. "What was going on in his soul all this while," says his biographer, "it is not given to mortals to declare."

The numerous cases of possession in the sixteenth and seventeenth centuries were nothing but hysterical disorders, the symptoms precisely those of Methodist revivals, Witches' Sabbaths, Paulinian orgies, and Schamanism.

It is worthy of note that the witches were always a prey to extreme exhaustion after they had attended their Sabbaths, a feature that is invariable after spiritual raptures.

In Sweden a religious revival took place in 1842-3, which swept over the country, affecting great numbers of children. Boys and girls, only eight years of age, were inspired to preach the Gospel and go about in bands singing hymns. In the province of Skaraburg, where the epidemic was least extensive, it numbered, at least, 3000 victims. The patients had "quaking fits," dropped down, became unconscious, had trances, saw visions, and preached when in an ecstatic state. Not two centuries before, a similar epidemic had passed over Sweden, affecting the children, but it then took a slightly different complexion: it was an epidemic of witchcraft. In 1669-70, the children declared that they were transported nightly to the Blockula, and their condition afterwards was one of complete prostration.

A Commission was appointed to examine into the matter, public prayers and humiliations were ordered, and a great number of women and children were executed for their guilt in having attended these meetings on the Blockula.

Into the details of the Witch-Sabbaths I have not entered; it is unnecessary. My object has been to show that in all likelihood there were such gatherings, that they took the place of assemblies of Pagan origin, which were analogous to the assemblies of the spiritual Pauline heretics in the early Church; that modern revivals are not derived from these, but are analogous exhibitions, and that all are alike manifestations of hysteria, superinduced by a love of the sensational, a vague credulity, and an absolute stagnation of the intellectual powers.

We are in the age of compulsory education; in our Board Schools religious teaching is reduced to the thinnest gruel, absolutely tasteless, and wholly unnutritious. We are straining, perhaps over-straining, the mental faculties, and making no provision for the co-ordinate development of the spiritual powers in the soul. The result will be, not that we shall kill the spiritual faculty, but that we shall drive it in—and it will break forth inevitably in extraordinary and outrageous manifestations. It must do so—just as a check to the free action of the pores superinduces fever. We shall have a sporadic fever of wild mysticism bursting forth, in the place of healthy religion. The spiritual element in man will rebel against compression, will insist on not being ignored. We are now suffering from the nuisance of the Salvation Army. But the Salvation Army is a comparatively innocuous form of reaction, or is comparatively innocuous just at present. We do not know but that it may herald other and worse forms of spiritual excitement, or that it may not itself develop in an Antinomian direction. We have no guarantee. There is a law in these manifestations that is constant. They all begin in ecstatic raptures and with a high moral aim, and all inevitably fall into laxity if not license in morality. The moral sense becomes inevitably blunted. It ceases to speak and work when man takes his ecstatic thrills and visions— which are veritable hallucinations—as the guide of his conduct, in place of the still small voice of conscience, instructed by the written, revealed law.

IX.
Broadside Ballads.

"I love a ballad in print, a' life," said Mopsa, in the "Winter's Tale," and the clown confessed to the same liking. "I love a ballad but even too well; if it be doleful matter merrily set down, or a very pleasant thing indeed, and sung lamentably."

Fig. 37.—BALLAD SINGER, FROM A BROADSIDE.

In 1653, Dorothy Osborne tells Sir William Temple that she has received from her brother a ballad "much older than my 'Lord of Lorne,' and she sends it on to him." Would that she had told us more about it. And then she writes, "The heat of the day is spent in reading or working, and about six or seven o'clock I walk out into a common that lies hard by the house, where a great many young wenches keep sheep and cows, and sit in the shade singing of ballads. I go to them and compare their voices and beauties to some ancient shepherdesses that I have read of, and find a vast difference there; but, trust me, I think these are as innocent as those could be. I talk to them, and find they want nothing to make them the happiest people in the world but the knowledge that they are so."

Walton in his "Complete Angler," printed in the very same year in which Dorothy Osborne wrote to her lover of the singing peasant girls, says: "I entered into the next field, and a second pleasure entertained me: 'twas a handsome milk-maid, that had cast away all care, and sung like a nightingale; her voice was good, and the ditty fitted for it; 'twas that smooth song which was made by Kit Marlow, now at least fifty years ago; and the milk-maid's mother sung an answer to it, which was made by Sir Walter Raleigh in his younger dayes."

We know what the song was, "Come, live with me and be my love."

The mother says to Walton, "If you will but speak the word, I will make you a good sillabub, and then you may sit down in a hay-cock and eat it, and Maudlin shall sit by and sing you the good old song of the Hunting in Chevy Chase, or some other good ballad, for she hath good store of them: Maudlin hath a notable memory."

But ballad-singing was not confined to milk-maids and clowns, for Walton proposes to spend a pleasant evening with his brother, Peter, and his friends, "to tell tales, or sing ballads, or make a catch, or find some harmless sport to content us."

It is a somewhat sad fact—fact it is, that the ballad is at its last gasp among us. It has gone through several phases, and it has now reached the last, when it disappears altogether.

The ballad was anciently a story set to music, and music to which the feet could move in dance. The *ballet* is the dance to which the *ballad* was sung. It was not always danced to, but it always could be danced to. It was of great length, but not too long for light hearts or light feet on a threshing-floor. The ballad was accommodated to the exigencies of the dance, by being given a burden, or *bourdon*, a drone that was sung by the young men, when no bagpipe was there. This burden appears in numerous ballads, and has usually no reference to the story told by the singers, and when printed is set in italics. In the scene in the "Winter's Tale," already quoted, the servant alludes to these burdens, "He has the prettiest love-songs for maids—with such delicate burdens of 'dildos and fadings.'"

Thus:—

> "There was a lady in the North country,
> *Lay the bent to the bonny broom,*
> And she had lovely daughters three,
> *Fa, la la la; fa, la la la ra re.*"

or:—

> "There were three sisters fair and bright,
> *Jennifer, Gentle, and Rosemaree,*
> And they three loved one valiant knight,
> *As the doo (dove) flies over the mulberry tree."*

In the first edition of Playford's "Dancing Master," in 1650-1, nearly every air can be proved to have been that of a song or ballad of earlier date than the book. Of these only a few have the words preserved, and we cannot be sure that the words of those we have got were the original, as ballads were continually being written afresh.

It was not till about 1690 that tunes were composed expressly for dancing, and in the later editions of the "Dancing Master," 1715 and 1728, about half the airs given are old ballad tunes. The other half, newly composed dance tunes, had no traditional words set to them, and none were composed to fit them.

In the old English romance of "Tom of Reading," printed before 1600, we have an instance of the way in which a ballad came to be turned into a dance. Tom Dove was an Exeter clothier passionately fond of music. William of Worcester loved wine, Sutton of Salisbury loved merry tales, Simon of Southampton "got him into the kitchen and to the pottage and then to a venison pasty."

Now a ballad was composed relative to Tom of Exeter:—

> "Welcome to town, Tom Dove, Tom Dove,
> The merriest man alive.
> Thy company still we love, we love,
> God grant thee well to thrive.
> And never will we depart from thee
> For better or worse, my joy!
> For thou shalt still have our good-will,
> God's blessing on my sweet boy."

And the author adds, "This song went up and down through the whole country, and at length became a dance among the common sort."

The old heroic ballad was a *geste*, and the singer was a gestour. Chaucer speaks of—

> "Jestours that tellen tales
> Both of seeping and of game."

The tales of game were stories calculated to provoke laughter, in which very often little respect was paid to decency; sometimes, however, they were satirical. These tales of game were much more popular than those of weeping, and the gestour, whose powers were mainly employed in scenes of conviviality, finding by experience that the long lays of ancient paladins were less attractive than short and idle tales productive of mirth, accommodated himself to the prevailing coarse taste, and the consequence was that nine of the pieces conceived in a light vein have been preserved to every one of the other.

In the "Rime of Sir Thopas," Chaucer speaks of—

> "Minestrales
> And gestours for to tellen tales,
> Of romaunces that ben reales,
> Of popes and of cardinales
> And eke of love-longing."

Here we have the historic geste and the light and ribald tale. When Chaucer recited the Ballad of Sir Thopas, conceived after the fashion of the old romances, the host interrupted him and said—

> "This may well be rime—dogerel,
> Mine eres aken of thy drafty speche."

We heartily wish that Chaucer had finished the tale. The host merely repeated the general objection to the heroic ballad, and showed the common preference for the ribald tales. The author of the "Vision of Piers the Ploughman," complains that the passion for songs and ballads was so strong that men attended to these to the neglect of more serious and of sacred matters.

> "I cannot parfitly my paternoster, as the priest it singeth,
> But I can ryme of Roben Hode, of Randolf erl of Chester,
> But of our Lord and our Lady I learn nothing at all;
> I am occupied every day, holy daye and other, with idle tales at the ale."

The degradation in the meaning of the names once given to minstrels of various classes tells its own sad tale. The *ryband* has lent his name to ribaldry; the *scurra* to whatever is scurrilous; the *gestour*, who sang the *gestes* of heroes, became the jester, the mere buffoon; the *joculator* degenerated into a joker; and the *jongleur* into a juggler.

A few men of taste and of reverence for the past stood up for the old heroic ballads, which, indeed, contained the history of the past, mixed with much mythical matter. So the great Charles, says his scribe, Eginhard, "commanded that the barbarous and most ancient song in which the acts and wars of the old kings were sung should be written down and committed to memory." And our own Alfred, says Asser, "did not fail to recite himself and urge on others, the recitation by heart of the Saxon songs." But the English ballad found no favour with the Norman conquerors, who readily received the Provençal troubadour. The old heroic ballad lingered on, and was killed, not so much by the ridicule of Chaucer as by the impatience of the English character, which will not endure the long-drawn tale, and asks in preference what is pithy and pointed.

Of song and ballad there were many kinds, characterised rather by the instrument to which it was sung, than by the nature of the song itself; or perhaps we may say most justly that certain topics and certain kinds of composition suited certain instruments, and were, therefore, accommodated to them.

In the "Romans de Brut" we have a list of some of these:

> "Molt ot a la cort jugleors,
> Chanteors, estrumanteors;
> Molt poissiez oir chançons,
> Rotruanges et noviaz sons
> Vieleures, lais, et notes,
> Lais de vieles, lais de rotes,
> Lais de harpe et de fretiax."

Here we have the juggler, the chanter, and the strummer. What the *strumentum*[34] was we do not exactly know, but it was clearly a stringed instrument that was twanged, and it has left its reminiscence in our language,—every child strums before it can play a piano. There exists an old table of civic laws for Marseilles of the date 1381, in which all playing of minstrel and jongleur,—in a word, all strumming was disallowed in the streets without a license.

To return to the passage quoted from the "Romans de Brut," we have among the chançons, those on the rote, and those on the vielle, those on the harp and those on the fret, (*i.e.* flute).[35] The rote was a pierced board, over which strings were drawn, and it could be played with both hands, one above, the other below, through the hole. The vielle was a hurdy-gurdy.

A healthier taste existed in Scotland than in England, and the old heroic ballads were never completely killed out there. In England they had been expelled the court, and banished from the hall long before they disappeared from the alehouse and the cottage. The milk-maids sang them; the nurses sang them; the shepherds sang them; but not the cultured ladies and gentlemen of the Elizabethan period. The musicians of that period set their faces against ballad airs, and introduced the motette and madrigal, in which elaborate part-singing taxed the skill of the performers. But the common people loved the simple melodious ballads. Miles Coverdale, in his "Address unto the Christian Reader," in 1538, which he prefixed to his "Goastly Psalms," laments it. "Wolde God that our mynstrels had none other thynge to play upon, neither our carters and pluomen other thynge to whistle upon, save psalmes, hymns, and such godly songes. And if women at the rockes (distaff), and spinnynge at the wheles, had none other songes to pass their tyme withal than such as Moses' sister ... songe before them, they should be better occupied than with, *Hey nonny nonny,—Hey trolly lolly*, and such like fantasies."

Laneham, in 1575, thus describes his evening amusements: "Sometimes I foot it with dancing; now with my gittern, and else with my cittern, then at the virginals (ye know nothing comes amiss to me); then carol I up a song withal; that by and by they come flocking about me like bees to honey; and ever they cry, 'Another, good Laneham, another!'"

In the great agitation of minds caused by the Reformation, the itinerant minstrels were an element of danger to the Crown, for they kept alive the popular feeling against the changes in religion, and the despotic measures of the Sovereign. Moreover, an immense number of ballads were printed, having a religious or political character, were set to the old ballad airs, and sung in place of the traditional lays, and then hawked by the singers. Accordingly, in 1543, an Act was passed "for the advancement of true religion," and it recites that, forasmuch as certain froward persons have taken upon them to print "ballads, rhymes, etc., subtilly and craftily to instruct His Highness' people untruly, for the reformation whereof His Majesty considereth it most requisite to purge the realm of all such books, ballads, rhymes, and songs." The Act contains a list of exceptions; but it is noticeable that no ballads of any description were excepted.

Fig. 38.—BALLAD SINGERS, FROM A BROADSIDE.

In the reign of Queen Elizabeth another Act was passed, in 1597, against "minstrels wandering abroad," by virtue of which they were to be whipped, put in the stocks, and imprisoned, if caught going from place to place with their ballads.

Then came the period of Puritan domination under the Commonwealth, when every engine was set to work to suppress popular music and ballad singing, and to sour the English character. The first Act levelled against them and stage players was in 1642. In the following year a tract was issued complaining that this measure had been ineffective, in which the writer says, "Our musike that was held so delectable and precious that they scorned to come to a tavern under twenty shillings salary for two hours, now wander with their instruments under their cloaks (I mean such as have any), to all houses of good fellowship, saluting every room where there is company with, *Will you have any musike, gentlemen?*" But even the license to go round the country was to be denied the poor wretches. In 1648 Captain Bertham was appointed Provost Marshall, "with power to seize upon all ballad-singers, and to suppress stage-plays." The third Parliament of Cromwell struck the heaviest blow of all. It enacted that any minstrel or ballad-singer who was caught singing, or making music in any alehouse or tavern, or was found to have asked anyone to hear him sing or play, was to be haled before the nearest magistrate, whipped and imprisoned.

With the Restoration came a better time for ballad-singing; but the old romantic ballad was almost dead, and though many of the ancient melodies remained, to them new ballads were set. Of these vast numbers poured from the press. The printed ballad which supplanted the traditional ballad was very poor in quality. It turned on some moral or religious topic; it satirised some fashion of the day; it recorded in jingling rhymes some fire, earthquake, flood, or other accident. Above all, it narrated the story of a murder. Now for the first time did the vulgar assassin stand forward as the hero of English poetry and romance.

Many an old song or ballad was parodied. Thus the famous song of "The Hunt is up," was converted into a political ballad in 1537; and a man named John Hogon was arrested for singing it. "An Old Woman Clothed in Grey" was the tune to which all England rang at the Restoration, with the words, "Let Oliver now be forgotten." "Grim King of the Ghosts" was made use of for "The Protestants' Joy," a ballad on the coronation of King William and Queen Mary; and "Hey, then, up go we!" served, with parodied words against the Rump Parliament, as the "Tories' Delight," as an anti-Papal ballad, and even as a ballad on the great frost of the winter of 1683-4.

The dissociation of the old tunes from the ballads that had given them their names, and to which they had been composed, did much to occasion the loss of our early ballads. Not only so, but with James I.'s reign there came in a fashion for recomposing the old themes in the new style; and the new editions caused the disappearance of the earlier ballad. There can be little doubt that the romantic and historic ballad, which has been happily preserved in Scotland, was common to all English-speaking people. These ballads are called Scottish, because they have been preserved in Scotland, but it is more than doubtful that they are of Scottish origin. Ballads travelled everywhere. We have in Thomas of Erceldoune's "Sir Tristram," an instance of a French metrical romance turned into a long poem in Scotland, in the thirteenth century. Many of the Scottish ballads have, as their base, myths or legends common to all the Norse people, and found in rhymes among them.

At the beginning of this century, Mr. Davis Gilbert published a collection of Cornish Christmas Carols, and subjoined a couple of samples of the ballads sung by the Cornish people. One is "The Three Knights." It begins—

> "There did three knights come from the West,
> With the high and the lily oh!
> And these three knights courted one lady,
> And the rose was so sweetly blown."

This is precisely the ballad given by Herd and others as "The Cruel Brother." One version in Scotland begins:—

> "There was three ladies play'd at the ba'
> With a hegh-ho! and lily gay;

> There came a knight and play'd o'er them a',
> And the primrose spread so sweetly."

But another version sung in Scotland begins—

> "There was three ladies in a ha',
> Fine flowers i' the valley;
> There came three lords among them a',
> Hi' the red, green, and the yellow."

Now, the remarkable thing is, that there is still sung in Cornwall—or was, till quite recently—a form of the ballad with a burden like this latter. It begins—

> "There was a woman and she was a widow,
> O the red, the green, and the yellow!
> And daughters had three as the elm tree,
> The flowers they blow in the valley."

with this chorus:—

> "The harp, the lute, the fife, the flute, and the cymbal.
> Sweet goes the treble violin,
> The flowers that blow in the valley."

How is it possible that a ballad sung in two forms in Scotland, and recovered there in a fragmentary condition, should be known in very similar forms in Cornwall? To suppose that the two versions were carried from the Highlands to the Land's End, so as to have become popular, is inconceivable. It is more likely that the same English ballad found its way both north and south-west, and when it had been displaced elsewhere, remained in the extremities of the island. The burden in each case is clearly that which marked the melody. We very much wish that the Scottish airs, to which these ballads were sung, had been preserved, that they might be compared with those to which they were sung in Cornwall. The burden in each case has nothing to do with the story, but it seems to indicate that the same ballad in its two forms, to two independent airs, was carried all over Great Britain at some period unknown. The same ballad was also sung in Cheshire at the close of last century, and also in Ireland.

Another specimen given by Mr. Gilbert is that of the "Three Sisters."

> "There were three sisters fair and bright,
> Jennifer, Gentle and Rosemaree;

And they three loved one valiant knight;
As the doo (dove) flies over the mulberry tree."[36]

The same is found in broadside, in the Pepysian and other collections, and as "The Unco Knicht's Wooing" in Scotland.
Take again the ballad of "The Elfin Knight" or "The Wind hath blown my Plaid away." This is found in Scotland, but also as a broadside in the Pepysian collection; it was the subject within the memory of man of a sort of play in farmhouses in Cornwall; it is found in a more or less fragmentary condition all over England. The same ballad is found in German, in Danish, in Wend—and the story in Tyrol, in Siberia, and Thibet.
Buchan, in his "Ballads of the North of Scotland," gives the ballad of "King Malcolm and Sir Colvin," but it is based on a story told by Gervase of Tilbury, in his Otia Imperialia, and the scene is laid by him on the Gogmagog Hills in Cambridgeshire. He wrote in the 12th century, and his story is clearly taken from a ballad. So also Buchan's "Leesome Brand" is found in Danish and Swedish. And "The Cruel Sister" is discovered in Sweden and the Faroe Isles. At an early period there was a common body of ballad, where originated no one can say; the same themes were sung all over the North of Europe, and the same words, varied slightly, were sung from the Tweed to the Tamar, in the marches of Wales and in Ireland.
The greatest possible debt of gratitude is due to the Scots for having preserved these ballads when displaced and forgotten elsewhere, and it speaks volumes for the purity of Scottish taste that it appreciated what was good and beautiful, when English taste was vitiated and followed the fashion to prefer the artificial and ornate to the simple and natural expression of poetic fancy.
It has been said that about the period of James I., the fashion set in for re-writing the old ballads in the style then affected.
There is a curious illustration of this accessible.
A ballad still sung by the English peasants, and found in an imperfect condition in Catnach's broadsides, is "Henry Martyn." It is couched in true ballad metre, and runs thus—

"In merry Scotland, in merry Scotland
There lived brothers three,
They all did cast lots which of them should go
A robbing upon the salt sea.

"The lot it fell upon Henry Martyn,
The youngest of the three,
That he should go rob on the salt, salt sea,
To maintain his brothers and he.

"He had not a-sailed a long winter's night,
Nor yet a short winter's day,
Before he espied a gay merchant ship
Come sailing along that way.

"Oh when that she came to Henry Martyn,
Oh prithee, now let me go!
Oh no! oh no! but that will I not,
I never that will do.

"Stand off! stand off! said he, God wot,
And you shall not pass by me.
For I am a robber upon the salt seas,
To maintain my brothers and me.

"How far? how far? cries Henry Martyn,
How far do you make it? says he,
For I am a robber upon the salt seas,
To maintain my brothers and me.

"They merrily fought for three long hours,
They fought for hours full three.
At last a deep wound got Henry Martyn,
And down by the mast fell he.

"'Twas a broadside to a broadside then,
And a rain and a hail of blows.
But the salt, salt sea ran in, ran in;
To the bottom then she goes.

"Bad news! bad news for old England;
Bad news has come to the town,
For a rich merchant vessel is cast away,
And all her brave seamen drown.

"Bad news! bad news through London street,
Bad news has come to the King,
For all the brave lives of his mariners lost,
That sunk in the watery main."

Now there is sad confusion here. The ballad as it now exists is a mere fragment. Clearly the "bad news" belongs to an earlier portion of the ballad, and it induces the King to send against the pirate and to sink his vessel. This "Henry Martyn" is, in fact, Andrew Barton. In 1476, a Portuguese squadron seized a richly laden vessel, commanded by John Barton, in consequence of which letters of reprisal were granted to Andrew, Robert, and John Barton, sons of John, and these were renewed in 1506. The King of Portugal remonstrated against reprisals for so old an offence, but he had put himself in the wrong four years before, by refusing to deal with a herald sent by the Scottish King for the arrangement of the matter in dispute. Hall, in his Chronicle, says: "In June, 1511, the King (Henry VIII.) being at Leicester, tidings were brought him that Andrew Barton, a Scottish man, and a pirate of the sea, did rob every nation, and so stopped the King's streams that no merchants almost could pass, and when he took the Englishmen's goods, he said they were Portingale's goods, and thus he haunted and robbed at every haven's mouth. The King, moved greatly with this crafty pirate, sent Sir Edward Howard, Lord Admiral of England, and Lord Thomas Howard, son and heir to the Earl of Surrey, in all haste to the sea, which hastily made ready two ships, and without any more abode, took the sea, and by chance of weather, were severed. The Lord Howard lying in the Downs, perceived when Andrew blew his whistle to encourage the men, yet, for all that, the Lord Howard and his men, by clean strength, entered the main deck; then the Englishmen entered on all sides, and the Scots fought sore on the hatches, but, in conclusion, Andrew was taken, which was so sore wounded that he died there; then all the remainder of the Scots were taken with their ship, called the *Lion*."

Buchanan, about twenty years after Hall—*i.e.*, in 1582—also tells the story. Barton he calls Breton with further details. He says that Andrew Breton, though several times wounded, and with one leg broken by a cannon ball, seized a drum and beat a charge to inspirit his men to fight, until breath and life failed.

Now a ballad relative to Sir Andrew Barton has been given by Percy; it is found among the Douce, the Pepysian, the Roxburghe, the Bagford, and the Wood collection of old English ballads. In the Percy MS. the ballad consists of eighty-two stanzas, but there is something lost between the thirty-fifth and the next. It begins:—

> "As itt beffell in Midsummer-time
> When birds sing sweetlye on every tree,
> Our noble king, King Henry the Eighth,
> Over the river Thames past he."

Another version is in the black letter collection. It begins:—

> "When Flora, with her fragrant flowers,
> Bedeckt the earth so firm and gay,
> And Neptune, with his dainty showers,
> Came to present the month of May,
>
> "King Henry would a progress ride;
> Over the river Thames past he,
> Upon a mountain top also
> Did walk, some pleasure for to see."

The first is a recomposition of the earlier ballad in the reign of James I. It makes a historical blunder. It supposes that Lord Charles Howard, who was not born till twenty-five years after the death of Andrew Barton, was sent against the pirate. The memory of the admiral who served against the Armada had eclipsed the fame of the earlier high admiral. The fact of this historic error existing in the ballad marks it as a late composition.

The second ballad is a still later recast, probably of the reign of Charles II. These two later versions would be all that we have, had not the popular memory held to the earliest and original ballad—because associated with a remarkably fine melody. Unhappily, it has retained but a few of the stanzas. The Robin Hood ballads most fortunately escaped remodelling, and they retain the fresh character of the ancient ballad.

Ravenscroft preserved some ballads in his "Deuteromelia," 1609. One begins:—

> "Yonder comes a courteous knight
> Lustily raking over the lay.
> He was full 'ware of a bonny lasse,
> As she came wandering over the way.
> Then she sang, downe a down a down,
> Hey down derry."

Another is "John Dory":—

> "As it fell on a hole day
> And upon a hole tide,
> John Dory bought him an ambling nag,
> Ambling nag to Paris for to ride."

Another:—

> "Who liveth so merry in all the land

> As doth the poor widow that selleth sand,
> And ever she singeth as I can guess,
> Will you buy my sand, my sand, mistress?"

Also:—

> "The Flye she sat in the shamble row,
> And shambled with her heels, I trow,
> And then came Sir Cranion
> With legs so long and many a one."

A few—but only a few, unspoiled ballads have found their way into print in broadsides. Such are, "The Baffled Knight," "The Knight and the Shepherd's Daughter," "Lord Thomas and the fair Eleanor," "Barbara Allen," "The Bailiff's Daughter of Islington," "The Brown Girl." They are miserably few, but they are all that remain to us of the ballad poetry of England, except what has been preserved to us by the Scotch, who knew better than ourselves what was good, and had a finer poetic sense.

Fig. 39.—WOMAN AT HER SPINNING WHEEL, FROM A BROADSIDE.

Moreover, our English ballad collectors never went to the right sources. There were to be had black and white letter broadsides, more or less scarce, and they set their booksellers to work to gather for them the drifting sheets, and fondly thought that they were collecting the ballad poetry of England. They were collecting make-shifts, the wretched stuff which had ousted the old ballad poetry. It occurred to none of them to go to the people. What would have been the result had Motherwell, Kinloch, Buchan, and Herd set to work in the same fashion? There is to be found in the British Museum a volume of Scottish Broadside Ballads printed at Aberdeen, and Glasgow, and Edinburgh. What do these sheet ballads contain? As great rubbish as do the English broadsides? Herd, Motherwell, and Buchan had more sense than our Ritson, Phillips, and Evans; they sat at the feet of the shepherds, listened beside the wheels of the old spinners, sat at the tavern table and over the peat fires with the peasants, and collected orally. Percy went to his MS. folio, Ritson to his booksellers, and passed over the great living wellspring of traditional poetry. Now it is too late. The utmost that can be gleaned is fragments. But enough does remain either in MS. or in black letter broadside, or in allusion and quotation by our early dramatists, to show that we in England had a mass of ballad poetry, one in kind and merit with the Scottish.

The first collection of scattered ballads and songs in a garland was made in the reign of James I., by Thomas Delony and Richard Johnson, and from that time forward these little assemblages of fugitive pieces were issued from the press. They rarely contain much that is good; they are stuffed with recent compositions. Everyone knew the traditional ballads, and it was not thought worth while reprinting them. A new ballad had to be entered at Stationers' Hall, and composer as well as publisher reaped a profit from the sale, as a novelty.

The old tunes remained after that the words to which they had been wedded were forgotten; and it may be said that in the majority of cases the music is all that does remain to us of the old ballad song of England.

This is the sort of balderdash that was substituted by a degraded taste for the swinging musical poetry of the minstrel epoch—

> "In searching ancient chronicles
> It was my chance to finde
> A story worth the writing out
> In my conceit and mind," etc.

or:—

> "Of two constant lovers, as I understand,
> Were born near Appleby, in Westmoreland;
> The lad's name Anthony, Constance the lass;
> To sea they both went, and great dangers did pass."

or:—

> "I reade in ancient times of yore,
> That men of worthy calling
> Built almeshouses and spittles store,
> Which now are all downfalling," etc.

Compare the following with such beginnings as these:—

> "In summer-time, when leaves grow green,
> And blossoms bedecke the tree,
> King Edward wold a hunting ryde,
> Some pastime for to see."

or:—

> "There came a bird out o' a bush,
> On water for to dine;
> An' sicking sair, says the King's dochter,
> O wae's this heart o' mine," etc.

or:—

> "There was a pretty shepherd boy
> That lived upon a hill,
> He laid aside his bag o' pipes
> And then he slept his fill."

or:—

> "O! blow away, ye mountain breezes,
> Blow the winds, heigh-ho!
> And clear away the morning kisses,
> Blow the winds, heigh-ho!" etc.

The ring of the latter is fresh and pleasant; the former have no ring at all. The first articles are manufactured in a garret by a publisher's poetaster, the latter have sprung spontaneously from the hearts of the people in the merry month of May.

Of black-letter printed ballads, the earliest we have are, "The Nut-brown Maid," which was discovered in a book of customs, dues, etc., published at Antwerp, about 1502, and "The Ballade of the Scottish King," written by John Skelton, poet laureate to King Henry VIII., and of the date 1513. This was found within the binding of an old book that was knocking about on the floor of a garret in a farmhouse at Whaddon, in Dorset. Mr. Arber's Transcripts of the entries in Stationers' Hall give us the list of ballads issued from the press, with their dates.

The list begins in the year 1557. We will take a few extracts only.

1588, 4th March. John Wolfe obtained leave to print three ballads; one was, "Goe from my window, goe." Now this no longer exists as a ballad, but as a folk-tale, in which occur snatches of rhyme, with a certain melody attached to them; and this air, with the snatches of rhyme, has been preserved. Both are printed by Mr. Chappell in his "Popular Music of the Olden Time." What the subject of the ballad was the writer learned from a blacksmith, who told him that he was in a village inn about 1860, when a very old man came in, and standing by the fire, recited and sang the following story:—

"Two men courted a pretty maid; the one was rich, the other was poor; and the rich man was old, but the poor man she loved; he was young. Her father forced her to marry the rich man, but still she loved the poor man; and sometimes he came under her window and tapped, and when the husband was away she let him in.

"So passed a twelvemonth and a day, and she had a little child.

"Then one night the lover came under the window, thinking her goodman was from home. With his tapping the husband woke, and asked what the sound was. She said an ivy leaf was caught in a cobweb, and fluttered against the pane. Then the lover began to call, and her husband asked what that sound was. She said the owls were hooting in the night. But fearing lest her lover should continue to call and tap, she began to sing, as she rocked the cradle:—

> "'Begone, begone, my Willy, my Billy!
> Begone, my love and my dear.
> O the wind, and O the rain,
> They have sent him back again,
> So thou can'st not have a lodging here.'

"Again the lover tapped, and the husband asked what that meant. She said it was a flittermouse that had flown against the pane. Then she sang:—

> "'Begone, begone, my Willy, my Billy!
> Begone, my love and my dear.
>
> O the weather is so warm,
> It will never do thee harm,
> And thou can'st not have a lodging here.'

"Then the lover began to call a third time, and the husband asked what it was. She said it was the whistling of the wind among the trees, and she sang:—

>"'Begone, begone, my Willy, my Billy!
>Begone, my love and my dear.
>O the wind is in the West,
>And the cuckoo's in his nest,
>So thou can'st not have a lodging here.'

"Again the lover tapped. Then she sprang out of bed, threw open the casement, and sang:—

>"'Begone, begone, my Willy, you silly;
>Begone, you fool, yet my dear.
>O the devil's in the man,
>And he can not understan'
>That he cannot have a lodging here.'"

The melody was arranged for Queen Elizabeth, and is in her Virginal Book. In Beaumont and Fletcher's "Knight of the Burning Pestle," old Merrythought says,

>"Go from my window, love, go;
>Go from my window, my dear.
>The wind and the rain
>Will drive you back again;
>You cannot be lodged here.
>
>"Begone, begone, my juggy, my puggy;
>Begone, my love, my dear.
>
>The weather is warm;
>'Twill do thee no harm;
>Thou can'st not be lodged here."

It is again quoted in Fletcher's "Monsieur Thomas," and again in "The Tamer Tamed."

Almost certainly this was originally a ballad. But the ballad tale has been lost, and only scraps of rhyme were committed to writing.

1588, 26th Sept. John Wolfe had license to print "Peggy's Complaint for the Death of her Willye."[37]

9th Nov. Thomas Orwyn had license to print "Martyn said to his man, Who is the foole now?"

This has been preserved for us, with its tune, by Ravenscroft, in his "Deuteromelia."

> "Martyn said to his man, fie man, fie O!
> Who's the fool now?
> Martyn said to his man, fill the cup and I the can,
> Thou hast well drunken, man,
> Who's the fool now?
>
> "I see a sheep sheering come, fie man, fie O!
> And a cuckold blow his horn.
>
> "I see a man in the moon
> Clouting St. Peter's shoon.
>
> "I see a hare chase a hound
> Twenty miles above the ground.
>
> "I see a goose ring a hog,
> And a snayle that did bite a dog.
>
> "I see a mouse catch a cat,
> And the cheese to eat a rat."

1591, 27th August. Robert Bourne obtained license to print a ballad on "A combat between a man and his wife for the breeches." This has been often re-written.

1592, 5th Jan. Richard Jones, "The Valliant Acts of Guy of Warwick," to the tune of "Was ever man soe tost (lost) in love?" The ballad of Guy is lost. The tune we have.

1592, 18th Jan. H. Kyrkham, "The crowe she sitteth upon a wall:" "Please one and please all." The former is, perhaps, the original of "The crow sat in a pear-tree." "Please one and please all" has been preserved.

1592, 21st July. John Danter, "The soules good morrowe."

1592, 28th July. H Kyrkham, "The Nightingale's Good-night."

1593, 1st Oct. Stephen Peel, "Betwixt life and death," to the tune of "Have with you into the country."

1594, 16th Oct. John Danter, "Jones' ale is new." This is sung to the present day in village taverns. One verse is roared forth with special emphasis. It is that of the mason:—

> "He dashed his hammer against the wall;
> He hoped both tower and church would fall;
> For Joan's ale is new, my boys,
> For Joan's ale is new."

1594, 16th Oct. E. White, "The Devil of Devonshire and William of the West, his Sonne." This is lost.

1595, 14th Jan. Thomas Creede, "The Saylor's Joye," to the tune of "Heigh-ho! hollidaie." Both ballad and air lost.

1595, 24th Feb. Thomas Creede, The first part of "The Merchante's Daughter of Bristole." This we have, but it is a recast in the sixteenth century of a far earlier ballad.

1595, 15th Oct. Thomas Millington, "The Norfolk Gentleman, his Will and Testament, and howe he committed the keeping of his children to his owne brother." This—"The Babes in the Wood," we have, as well as the melody.

1595, 15th Oct. W. Blackwall, "The Prowde Mayde of Plymouthe." Lost.

1603, 11th June. Wm. White, "A Sweet Maie Flower;" "The Ladie's Fall;" "The Bryde's Buriell;" "The Spanish Ladie's Love;" "The Lover's Promises to his Beloved;" "The Fayre Lady Constance of Cleveland and of her Disloyal Knight."

We have "The Lady's Fall" and the two that follow. "A Sweet Mayflower" is probably a real loss, as also the ballad of the Lady Constance and her disloyal knight. This will suffice to show how interesting are these records, and also how much has perished, as well as how much is preserved. It must not, however, be lost to mind that these were all new ballads, and were serving to displace the earlier and better ballads.[38]

Every accident, every murder, every battle was turned into doggerel and printed as a new ballad. Fourpence was the cost of a license.

In Beaumont and Fletcher's "Philastes," Megra threatens the King—

> "By all those gods you swore by, and as many
> More of mine own—
> The princess, your daughter, shall stand by me
> On walls, and sung in ballads."

She refers to the manner in which every bit of court scandal was converted into rhythmic jingle, and also to the custom of pasting the ballads on the walls. The least acquaintance with the old black-letter ballads will make the reader understand the allusion to the two figures heading the broadside, in rude woodcut, standing side by side.

A large proportion of the black-letter ballads were of moral and religious import. In Beaumont and Fletcher's "The Coxcomb," the tinker refers to these, when he finds poor Viola wandering in the streets at night, and listens to her doleful words. He says:—

"What's this? a prayer or a homily, or a ballad of good counsel?"

If we compare the black-letter issues of the sixteenth century with the snatches of ballads that come to us through the playwrights, we find that they do not wholly agree.
The dramatists made their characters sing the folk-ballads, the same that are described in "A Defence for Milksmaydes" in 1563.

"They rise in the morning to hear the larke sing,
And welcome with balletts the somer's coming.

In going to milking, or coming away,
They sing merry balletts, or storeys they say.
Their mouth is as pure and as white as their milk;
—You can not say that of your velvett and silke."

So the mad jailor's daughter in Fletcher's and Shakespeare's "The Two Noble Kinsmen."

She says: "Is not this a fine song?"
Brother. "Oh, a very fine one!"
Daughter. "I can say twenty more, I can sing *The Broom* and *Bonny Robin*."

And she begins to troll "Oh fair! oh sweet!" etc.
Unhappily the authors of this play did not write out the song, as it was too well known to require transcription, and now it is lost. So also are those she sings in another scene.

"The George alow came from the South,
From the Coast of Barbary-a!
And there we met with brave gallants of war,
By one, by two, by three-a!

"Well hail'd, well hail'd, you jolly gallants!
And whither now are you bound-a?
Or let me have your company

Till I come to the Sound-a!"

This sounds as though a part of the "Henry Martyn" (Andrew Barton) already given. Another of the mad girl's songs is:—

"There were three fools fell out about an howlet.
The one said 'twas an owl;
The other said nay.
The third he said it was a hawk,
And her bells were cut away."

So also with some of the songs and ballads of Ophelia. They were too well known to be printed, and now they are irrecoverably gone.
We have lost nearly the whole of our earliest ballad poetry, and only a tithe of that which took its place has come down to us.
"Our earliest ballads," says the editor of Percy's folio, "though highly popular in the Elizabethan age, were yet never collected into any collections, save in Garlands, till the year 1723. They wandered up and down the country without even sheepskins or goatskins to protect them; they flew about like the birds of the air, and sung songs dear to the hearts of the common people—songs whose power was sometimes confessed by the higher classes, but not so thoroughly appreciated as to conduce them to exert themselves for their preservation."
In the reign of Queen Anne and through the early Hanoverian period, sheets of copperplate were issued with engraved songs and ballads, together with their music. Among them may be found a few—but only a very few—of the old favourites. Most are compositions of Arne, Carey, Berg, Dunn, etc., and the words are quite unsuited to hold the attention of the peasantry. Hardly any of these found their way into broadsides and garlands, and none can now be heard by the cottage fire or in the village ale-house.
In 1808, John Catnach of Newcastle settled in London, and began to print broadsides. He was quickly followed by others in London and in country towns. Catnach kept a number of ballad-mongers in his pay, who either composed verses for him or swept up such traditional ballads as they chanced to hear. They were paid half-a-crown for a copy, whether original or adulterate. If one of these poetasters chanced to hear an ancient ballad, he added to it some of his own verses, so as to be able to call it his property, and then disposed of it to one of the broadside publishers.

If these men had been sent round the country to collect from cottages and village hostelries, in the way in which Wardour Street Jews send about into every part of England to pick up old oak, then a great amount of our traditional ballad poetry might have been recovered. It was not too late in the first ten or twenty years of this century. But this was not done. These pot-poets loafed about in the low London public-houses, where it was only by the rarest chance that a country man, fresh from the fields, and woods, and downs, with his memory laden with the fragrance of the rustic music, was to be found. Moreover, these fellows were overweening in their opinion of their own powers. They had neither taste, nor ear, nor genius. They poured forth floods of atrocious rhymes, and of utter balderdash, as was required, as an occasion offered, and as they stood in need of half-crowns. Consequently the broadside "white-letter" ballad no more represents the folk ballad of the English people than does the black-letter ballad.

Who that has a sprinkling of grey on his head does not remember the ballad-singer at a fair, with his or her yards of verse for sale? The ballad-seller, who vended his broadsheets, did much to corrupt the taste of the peasant. He had begun to read, and he read the ha'penny broadside, and learned by heart what he had bought; then he set it to some fine old melody as ancient as the Wars of the Roses, and sang it; and what is unfortunate, discarded the old words for the sake of the vile stuff composed by the half-tipsy, wholly-stupid band, in the pay of Ryle, Catnach, Harkness of Preston, Williams of Portsea, Snidall of Manchester, etc.

Mr. Hindley, in his "History of the Catnach Press," 1886, gives an amusing account of his acquaintance with John Morgan, the last surviving of Catnach's poets:—"Mr. John Morgan, full of bows and scrapes, was ushered into our presence. 'Take a seat, sir.' 'Yes, sir, and thank you too,' he replied, at the same time sitting down, and then very carefully depositing his somewhat dilapidated hat under—far under—the chair. We then inquired whether he would have anything to eat, or have a cup of coffee. No! it was a little too early for eating, and coffee did not agree with him. Or, a drop of good 'Old Tom,' we somewhat significantly suggested. Mr. John Morgan would very much like to have a little drop of gin, for it was a nasty, raw, cold morning. In answer to our inquiry whether he would prefer hot or cold water, elected to have it neat, if it made no difference to us.

"Mr. John Morgan, at our suggestion, having 'wet the other eye,' *i.e.*, taken the second glass, the real business commenced thus:—'We have been informed that you were acquainted with, and used to write for, the late James Catnach, who formerly lived in Seven Dials, and that you can give us much information that we require towards perfecting a work we have in hand, treating on street literature.' ... Here Mr. Morgan expressed his willingness to give all the information he could on the subject, and leave it to our generosity to pay him what we pleased, and adding that he had no doubt that we should not fall out on that score. Mr. Morgan talked and took gin. Mr. Morgan got warm—warmer, and warmer,—and very entertaining. We continued to talk and take notes, and Mr. Morgan talked and took gin, until he emulated the little old woman who sold 'Hot Codlings,' for of her it is related that, 'The glass she filled, and the bottle she shrunk, And this little old woman in the end got—'

"At last it became very manifest that we should not be able to get any more information out of Mr. John Morgan on that day, so proposed for him to call again on the morrow morning. Then having presented him with a portrait of Her Most Gracious Majesty, set in gold, we endeavoured to see him downstairs, which, we observed, were very crooked; Mr. Morgan thought they were very old and funny ones....

"At length the wishful morrow came, also ten of the clock, the hour appointed, but not so Mr. John Morgan, nor did he call at any hour during the day. But soon after eleven o'clock the next day he made his appearance; but being so stupidly drunk we gave him some money and told him to call again tomorrow. And he did, but still so muddled that we could make nothing out of him, and so curtly dismissed him."

Here are specimens of the sort of stuff turned out for Catnach by John Morgan and the like. The first is on the birth of the Princess Royal.

> "Of course you've heard the welcome news,
> Or you must be a gaby,
> That England's glorious queen has got
> At last a little baby.
>
> "A boy we wanted—'tis a girl!
> Thus all our hopes that were
> To have an heir unto the Throne
> Are all *thrown to the air*."

Here is a ballad on a policeman of the old style when the new regulations came in, in 1829:—

> "Upon his beat he stood to take a last farewell
> Of his lantern and his little box wherein he oft did dwell.
> He listen'd to the clock, so familiar to his ear,
> And with the tail of his drab coat he wiped away a tear.
>
> "Beside that watchhouse door a girl was standing close,
> Who held a pocket handkerchief, with which she blew her nose.
> She rated well the policeman, which made poor Charley queer,
> Who once more took his old drab coat to wipe away a tear.

"He turn'd and left the spot; O do not deem him weak;
A sly old chap this Charley was, though tears were on his cheek.
Go watch the lads in Fetterlane, where oft you've made them fear;
The hand, you know, that takes a bribe, can wipe away a tear."

Here is one stanza by a composer with whom the writer of this article made acquaintance:—

"Pale was the light of the Pole-axe star,
When breakers would hide them so near.
But Love is the ocean of hunters far,
And convoys him to darkness so drear.
Then sad at the door of my love I lay,
Slumbering the six months all away."

Horace sang something about lying exposed to the cold and rain at the door of his beloved, and vowed he would not do it again. There is certainly a distance of something beside two thousand years between Horace and the gentleman who wrote the above lines.

There is a really astonishing poem entitled "The Lights of Asheaton," which, happily, everyone can purchase for a ha'penny. It is the composition of a recent Irish poet of the same class as Mr. John Morgan, and is a dissuasive against Protestantism. What the "Lights" of Asheaton are does not transpire. It opens thus:—

"You Muses now aid me in admonishing Paganism,
The new Lights of Asheaton, whose fate I do deplore.
From innocence and reason they are led to condemnation,
Their fate they've violated, the occasion of their woe."

After some wonderful lines that we hardly like to quote, as savouring of irreverence—though that was far from the poet's intention—he assures us:—

"Waters will decrease most amazing to behold,
No fanatic dissenter, no solvidian (*sic*) cripple,
Dare them to dissemble, the truths for to relinquish,
For the enthusiast will tremble at the splendors of the Pope."

The sheet of broadside ballad that is passing away deserves a little attention before it disappears. It reveals to us the quality of song that commended itself to the uneducated. It shows us how the song proper has steadily displaced the ballad proper. It is surprising for what it contains, as well as for what it omits. Apparently in the latter part of this century the sole claim to admission is that words—no matter what they be—should be associated to a taking air. We find on the broadsheets old favourites of our youth—songs by Balfe, and Shield, and Hudson; but the Poet Laureate is unrepresented; even Dibdin finds but grudging admission. When we look at the stuff that is home-made, we find that it consists of two sorts of production—one, the ancient ballad in the last condition of wreck, cast up in fragments; and the other, of old themes worked up over and over again by men without a spark of poetic fire in their hearts. A century or two hence we shall have this rubbish collected and produced as the folk song of the English peasantry, just as we have had the black-letter ballads raked together and given to the world as the ballad poetry of the ancient English.

The broadside ballad is at its last gasp. Every publisher in the country who was wont to issue these ephemerides has discontinued doing so for thirty or forty years. In London, in place of a score of publishers of these leaves, there are but three—Mr. Fortey, of Seven Dials; Mr. Such, of the Boro'; and Mr. Taylor, of Bethnal Green. As the broadside dies, it becomes purer. There are ballads in some of the early issues of a gross and disgusting nature. These have all had the knife applied to them, and nothing issues from the press of Mr. Fortey, Mr. Such, and Mr. Taylor which is offensive to good morals. Mr. Such, happily, has all his broadsides numbered, and publishes a catalogue of them; some of the earlier sheets are, however, exhausted, and have not been reprinted.

It is but a matter of a few years and the broadside will be as extinct as the Mammoth and the Dodo, only to be found in the libraries of collectors. Already sheets that fetched a ha'penny thirty years ago are cut down the middle, and each half fetches a shilling. The garlands are worth more than their weight in gold. Let him that is wise collect whilst he may.

X.
Riddles.

There is a curious little work, the contents of which are said to have been collected by Hans Sachs, the Nuremberg cobbler and master-singer, in 1517. This curious book was reprinted several times in the seventeenth and early part of the eighteenth century, but it is now somewhat scarce. It was issued without place of publication or publisher's name, in small form without cover. The book pretends to have been prepared by Hans Sachs for his private use, that he might make merriment among his friends, when drinking, and they were tired of his songs. It does not contain any anecdotes; it is made up of a collection of riddles more or less good, some coarse, and some profane; but the age was not squeamish. The title under which the little work was issued was, *Useful Table-talk, or Something for all; that is the Happy Thoughts, good and bad, expelling Melancholy and cheering Spirits, of Hilarius Wish-wash, Master-tiler at Kielenhausen.* The book consists of just a hundred pages, of which a quarter are consumed by prefaces, introductions, etc., and about thirteen filled with postscript and index. The humours of the book are somewhat curious; for instance, in the preliminary index of subjects it gives—"IX. The reason why this book of Table-talk was so late in being published." When we turn to the place indicated for the reason, we find a blank. There is no such reason. There is a fulsome and absurd dedication to the "Honourable and Knightly Tileburner" who lives "By the icy ocean near Moscow, in Lapland, one mile below Podolia and three miles above it."

Although we are not told in the place indicated why the little collection was not issued immediately after the death of Hans Sachs, nor among his works, we learn the reason elsewhere, in the preface, where we are told that the jokes it contained were so good that a rivalry ensued among them as to precedence, and till this was settled, it was impossible to get the book printed. The collection contains in all one hundred and ninety-six riddles; among them is that which gives the date of the book, and that in a chronogram: "When was this book of Table-talk drawn up? *Answer.* In IetzIg taVsenD fIInff hVnDert sIbenzehenDen Iahr" (1517).

Here are some of the conundrums.—*Question.* After Adam had eaten the forbidden fruit, did he stand or sit down?—*Ans.* Neither; he fell.

Ques. Two shepherds were pasturing their flocks. Said one to the other: "Give me one of your sheep, then I shall have twice as many sheep as you."—"Not so," replied the second herdsman: "give me one of yours, and then we shall have equal flocks." How many sheep had each?—*Ans.* One had seven, the other five. If the first took a sheep out of the flock of the second, he had eight, the other four; if the contrary, each had six.

Ques. What is four times six?—*Ans.* 6666.
Ques. What does a goose do when standing on one leg?—*Ans.* Holds up the other!
Ques. When did carpenters first proclaim themselves to be intolerable dawdles?—*Ans.* When building the Ark—they took a hundred years over it.
Ques. What sort of law is military law?—*Ans.* Can(n)on law.
Some of the riddles have survived in the jocular mouth to the present day; for instance, who does not know this?—*Ques.* What smells most in an apothecary's shop?—*Ans.* The nose. There is one conundrum which surprises us. The story was wont to be told by Bishop Wilberforce that he had asked a child in Sunday School why the angels ascended and descended on Jacob's ladder, whereupon the child replied that they did so because they were moulting, and could not fly. But this appears in Hans Sachs' book, and is evidently a very ancient joke indeed.

In this collection also appears the riddle: "Which is heaviest, a pound of lead or a pound of feathers?" which everyone knows, but with an addition, which is an improvement. After the answer, "Each weighs a pound, and they are equal in weight," the questioner says further: "Not so—try in water. The pound of feathers will float, and the pound of lead will sink."

Ques. How can you carry a jug of water in your hands on a broiling summer day, in the full blaze of the sun, so that the water shall not get hotter?—*Ans.* Let the water be boiling when you fill the jug.
Ques. How can a farmer prevent the mice from stealing his corn?—*Ans.* By giving them his corn.
Ques. A certain man left a penny by his will to be divided equally among his fifty relatives, each to have as much as the other, and each to be quite contented with what he got, and not envy any of the other legatees. How did the executor comply with this testamentary disposition?—*Ans.* He bought a packet of fifty tin-tacks with the penny, and hammered one into the back of each of the legatees.

There is another very curious old German collection of riddles called *Æsopus Epulans*; but that contains anecdotes as well and a great deal of very interesting matter. This is a much larger volume, and is the commonplace book of a party of priests who used to meet at each other's houses to smoke, and drink, argue, and joke. One of the members took down the particulars of conversation at each meeting, and published it. A most curious and amusing volume it is. Some of the conundrums the old parsons asked each other were the same as those in Hans Sachs' collection; they had become traditional. We may safely say that none were better, and some were, if possible, more pointless. They have all much the same character:

they resemble faintly the popular conundrum of the type so widely spread, and so much affected still by nurses and by the labouring class, and which so often begins with "London Bridge is broken down," or, "As I went over London Bridge." These are very ancient. We have analogous riddles among those which Oriental tradition puts into the mouth of the Queen of Sheba when she "proved Solomon with hard questions." Mr. Kemble published for the Ælfric Society a collection of questions and answers that exist in Anglo-Saxon as a conversation between Solomon and Saturn, and numerous versions existed in the Middle Ages of the dialogue between Solomon and—as the answerer was often called—Markulf. But these questions only partially correspond with our idea of riddles.

A more remarkable collection is that in the Icelandic *Herverar Saga*, where the King Heidrek boasts of his power to solve all riddles. Then Odin visits him in disguise as a blind man, and propounds to the king some hard questions. Of these there are sixty-four. We will give a few specimens. *Ques.* What was that drink I drank yesterday, which was neither spring water, nor wine, nor mead, nor ale?—*Ans.* The dew of heaven. *Ques.* What dead lungs did I see blowing to war?—*Ans.* A blacksmith's bellows whilst a sword was being forged. *Ques.* What did I see outside a great man's door, head downwards, feet heavenwards?—*Ans.* An onion.

These riddles are all in verse, and the replies also in verse. The end was that Odin asked Heidrek what he, Odin, whispered into the ear of Baldur before he was burned on his funeral pyre. Thereupon Heidrek drew his sword and cut at his questioner, shouting: "None can answer that but yourself!" Odin had just time to transform himself into an eagle; but the sword shore off his tail, and eagles ever after have had short tails.

The Sphinx will recur to the recollection of the reader, who tore to pieces those who could not answer its riddles. At last Creon, King of Thebes, offered his sister, Jocasta, to anyone who could solve the enigmas propounded by the Sphinx. Œdipus ventured, and when asked by the monster, "What animal is four-footed in the morning, two-footed at noon, and three-footed in the evening?" answered: "Man, who as a babe crawls, and as an old man leans on a crutch." The Sphinx was so distressed at hearing its riddle solved, that it precipitated itself from a precipice and was dashed to pieces.

The Persian hero, Sal, who was brought up by the gigantic bird Simorg, appears before Mentuscher, Schah of Iran. The latter, forewarned that Sal will be a danger to him, endeavours to get rid of him. However, he first tests him with hard questions. If he answers these, he is to be allowed to live. The first question is: "There stand twelve cypresses in a ring, and each bears thirty boughs." Sal replies, "These are the twelve months, each of which has thirty days." Another question is—"There were two horses, one black, the other clear as crystal." "They are Day and Night," replied Sal.

In English and Scottish Ballads a whole class has reference to the importance of riddle answering.

A girl is engaged to a young man who dies. He returns from the grave and insists on her fulfilling her engagement to him and following him to the land of the dead. She consents on one condition, that he will answer her riddles, or else she pleads to be spared, and the dead lover agrees on condition that she shall answer some riddles he sets. Such is a ballad which was formerly enacted in the farmhouses in Cornwall. The girl sits on her bed and sighs for her dead lover. He reappears and insists on her following him. Then she sets him tasks, and he sets her tasks.

Those he sets her are:—

> "Thou must buy me, my lady, a cambrick shirt
> Whilst every grove rings with a merry antine (antienne = anthem),
> And stitch it without any needle work,
> O, and thou shalt be a true love of mine.
>
> "And thou must wash it in yonder well
> Where never a drop of water fell.
>
> "And thou must hang it upon a white thorn
> That never has blossomed since Adam was born."

Those she sets him are:—

> "Thou must buy for me an acre of land
> Between the salt ocean and the yellow sand.
>
> "Thou must plough it over with a horse's horn,
> And sow it all over with one pepper corn.
>
> "Thou must reap it too with a piece of leather,
> And bind the sheaf with a peacock's feather."

"In all stories of this kind," says Mr. Child, in his monumental work on English Ballads, "the person upon whom a task is imposed stands acquitted if another of no less difficulty is desired, which must be performed first."

An early form of this story is preserved in the *Gesta Romanorum*. A king resolved not to marry a wife till he could find the cleverest of women. At length a poor maid was brought to him, and he made trial of her sagacity. He sent her a bit of linen three inches square, and promised to marry her, if out of it she could make him a shirt. She stipulated in reply that he should send her a vessel in which she could work. We have here only a mutilated fragment of the series of tasks set. In an old English ballad in the Pepysian library, an Elfin knight visits a pretty maid, and demands her in marriage.

> "'Thou must shape a sark to me
> Without any cut or heme,' quoth he.
> 'Thou must shape it knife-and-sheerless
> And also sue it needle-threadless.'"

She replies:—

> "I have an aiker of good ley-land
> Which lyeth low by yon sea-strand.
> For thou must car it with thy horn,
> So thou must sow it with thy corn,
> And bigg a cart of stone and lyme.
> Robin Redbreast he must trail it hame,
> Thou must barn it in a mouse-holl,
> And thrash it into thy shoes sole.
> And thou must winnow it in thy looff,
> And also sech it in thy glove.
> For thou must bring it over the sea,
> And thou must bring it dry home to me."

As the Elfin knight cannot fulfil these tasks, the girl is not obliged to follow him to Elfin Land. There is another song, known in a fragmentary condition all through England:—

> "Cold blows the wind to-night, sweetheart,
> Cold are the drops of rain.
> The very first love that ever I had
> In greenwood he was slain."

The maiden being engaged to the dead man can obtain no release from him till he restores to her her freedom. She goes and sits on his grave and weeps.

> "A twelvemonth and a day being up,
> The ghost began to speak;
> Why sit you here by my grave side
> From dusk till dawning break?"

She replies:—

> "O think upon the garden, love,
> Where you and I did walk;
> The fairest flower that blossomed there
> Is withered on its stalk."

The ghost says:—

> "What is it that you want of me,
> And will not let me sleep?
> Your salten tears they trickle down
> My winding sheet to steep."

She replies that she has come to return his kisses to him, so as to be off with her engagement. To this the dead man replies:—

> "Cold are my lips in death, sweetheart,
> My breath is earthy strong,
> If you do touch my clay-cold lips,
> Your time will not be long."

Then comes a divergence in the various forms the ballad assumes. Its most common form is for the ghost to insist on her coming into his grave, unless she can perform certain tasks:—

> "Go fetch me a light from dungeon deep,
> Wring water from a stone,
> And likewise milk from a maiden's breast
> Which never babe hath none."

She strikes a spark from a flint, she squeezes an icicle, and she compresses the stalk of a dandelion or "Johnswort." So she accomplishes the tasks set her.
Then the ghost exclaims:—

> "Now if you had not done these things,
> If you had not done all three,
> I'd tear you as the withered leaves
> Are torn from off the tree."

And the maiden, released from her bond, sings:—

> "Now I have mourned upon his grave
> A twelvemonth and a day,

> I'll set my sail before the wind
> To waft me far away."

Another ballad of the same class is that of the knight who betrays a maiden, and refuses to marry her unless she can answer certain riddles. These are:—

> "What is louder than a horn?
> And what is sharper than a thorn?
> What is broader than the way?
> And what is deeper than the sea?"

The answers are:—

> "Thunder is louder than a horn,
> And hunger is sharper than a thorn,
> Love is broader than the way,
> And hell is deeper than the sea."

Now these ballads and a crowd of folk tales that bear on the same point show plainly enough that there was a time when quite as certainly as there were contests of arms, so contests of wit were gone through for great ends, sometimes with life at stake. That was a period when there was a struggle between man and man, and the fittest survived; but this fittest was not always the strongest animal, but the man of keenest wit. I do not know how else to explain the universality of these legends. The riddle is an amusement at the present day. It was an amusement at a Greek banquet, as we learn from Plutarch. But in a pre-historic period—in a mythic epoch—it was something very grave. He or she who could not solve a riddle, or a succession of riddles, forfeited life or honour.

There are two of the earliest extant rhymes of the Norse people which hinge on the same idea, and in them the gods themselves have their existence or honour at stake. These are the Vafthrudnis Mâl and the Alvis Mâl, in the Elder Edda.

In the first of these Odin the god and mythical ancestor of the Scandinavian race visits the Jute, the giant Vafthrudnir, representative of the large-sized pre-historic race which occupied Scandinavia, Great Britain, and Gaul. They go through a contest of wit. He who is defeated in this trial of skill has to lose his life.

Vafthrudnir asks:—

> "Tell me, Gagnrad,
> Since on the floor thou wilt

> Prove thy proficiency,
> How is the horse called
> That draws each day
> Forth over mankind?"

Odin, who has called himself Gagnrad, replies:—

> "Skinfaxi he is named
> That the bright day draws
> Forth over mankind.
> Of horses is he highest esteemed
> Amidst the Reid-Goths,
> Light ever streams from that horse's mane."

Next comes the question relative to the black horse of night. Then as to the stream that divides the Jutes from the Æsir (the Scandinavians). Then as to the name of the plain on which the great final fight will take place, in which the light of the gods will be quenched. And so on. The giant is overcome. This song is interesting because it is a poetic representation of an historic event, the conquest of the Jute by the Scandinavian, not so much by force of arms, as by superior mental sagacity.

The other song in the Edda is the prototype of all the Elfin Knight and analogous ballads in which a being of the under world, now an elf, then a devil, then a dead man, seeks to win to himself a maiden of the upper world, and of the dominant race.

The dwarf Alvis, who lives under the earth and under stones, *i.e.*, in a beehive hut, a representative of the pre-historic, small, short-headed, metal-working race, has somehow extorted a promise from the god Thorr, that he will give him his daughter, the "fair-bright, snow-white maiden." Thorr shrinks from doing this, but is reminded of his promise. We do not know the particulars, but in all probability the dwarf Alvis had fashioned for him his hammer, and had received the promise in return. Thorr at last yields, but only on condition that Alvis shall solve a series of riddles, or rather answer a number of questions as to the various names given to sun, moon, wind, sky, etc.

The last question asked is:—

> "Tell me, Alvis,
> How beer is called
> Which the sons of men
> Drink in all worlds."

Alvis answers:—

> "*Ale* is it called by men,
> By the Æsir *Beer*,
> By the Vans *Veig*,
> By the Jotuns *Hreina lögi*;
> In Hell it is *meed*,
> The sons of Sutung call it *sumbl*."

Then the sun rises—and as it has risen before all the questions are answered, Alvis loses his bride.
Precisely so in the Cornish version of the Elfin-Knight. Unable to accomplish the task, the dead man is caught by the sunrise, and says:—

> "The breath of the morning is raw and cold,
> The wind is blowing on forest and down,
> And I must return to the churchyard mould,
> And the wind it shaketh the acorns down."

It is deserving of note that in all these early accounts of riddle-setting, the *forfeit* is either life or honour. We have instances of riddle-setting as a test before marriage, or what is the same thing, the setting difficult tasks to be accomplished—something to prove the wit of the young woman. Unless she were "up to mark" in wit, she was held to be unfit for the marriage proposed. In one folk tale a girl is given straw to spin into gold, grains to collect and count. In Cupid and Psyche, the fair seeker after her divine lover is set tasks by Venus, without the accomplishment of which she cannot win him. In many a tale a prince is set tasks, without the accomplishment of which he cannot be accepted as lover for the daughter and heiress of a king.

In the saga of Ragnar Lodbrog, the King bids Aslaug come to him clothed yet naked, accompanied yet alone, fed yet empty. She complies by casting off her garments but covering herself with her golden hair that flows to her feet, taking with her a dog only, and chewing a blade of garlic. Satisfied with her wit, Ragnar marries her. She became by him the mother of five sons, one of whom was the ancestor of Harald Fairhair, who made Norway into one realm under his sceptre. Aslaug was the daughter of Sigurd and Brunhild, made familiar to us through Wagner's "Ring of the Nibelungen."

The forfeits of a child's game of the present day, to stand in the corner on one leg, to call up the chimney, to kiss everyone in the room—are the faintest ghostly reminiscences of the terrible forfeit, which, in the mythic age of mankind, had to be paid by the man or woman who became liable through lack of shrewdness in the great contest of wit. The man who did not solve the riddle lost his life. The woman who failed to answer the questions had to leave her race, suffer social death, and pass over to the realm of the conquered race.

I repeat it, it is quite impossible to explain the stories of riddle-setting which appear as a matter of most serious import as they come to us out of a remote antiquity, and from every part of Europe and Asia, unless we hold that there were in a pre-historic age these contests of wit for the highest stakes, just as there were holm-gangs, duels, like those of David and Goliath, of the Horatii and Curiatii, of Herakles and Geryon.

But the existence of the riddle and of the forfeit attaching to inability to answer the riddle, does not, we may be sure, begin with such cases as the contest of Odin and Vafthrudnir, Thorr and Alvis, Œdipus and Sphinx. As it appears thus in myth, it is a survival of a still earlier condition of affairs.

At the present day throughout Europe, nurses ask children riddles, and very often a forfeit attaches to inability to answer them. This points to the riddle as a means of education of the young mind, but also as a test of its powers. In legend and myth it does not appear as educative, but as a test of mental power. How came it to be a test?

We know that among certain races in a primitive, even in a cultivated condition, the feeble and halt children are cast forth to perish. It was so with the Greeks and Romans, it was so with the Norse, it has been so in every ancient race. I cannot but suspect, from the many indications given by tradition, that the riddle was employed at one time as a brain test. That not only were the physically weak cast out, but also the mentally incapable.

The most startling reminiscence of the old ordeal of brains is that of the Wartburg Contest in 1206 or 1207, under the Landgrave Hermann. The poem of the "Kriec von Wartburg" was not indeed composed till a century later, but that only makes it the more astonishing. It represents the minnesingers under the Landgrave contesting in song and riddle, and those who are defeated forfeit *life*. Christian knights and ladies could look on at a tourney in the lists with life at stake, and Christian knights and ladies in the fourteenth century thought it by no means a monstrous thing that he who could not answer a riddle should submit his neck to the executioner's sword. Such a condition of ideas is only conceivable as a heritage from a past when men had to show that they had an intellectual as well as a physical qualification to live among their fellow-men.

The riddle has gone into an infinity of forms. A German writer[39] sets to work to analyse its various manifestations. There is the numerical riddle, the conundrum, the logogryph, the charade, the rebus, the picture puzzle, the epigram, and so forth. Its last transformation is the novel of the type of Wilkie Collins' "Moonstone," in which the brain of the reader is kept in tension throughout, and the imagination at work to discover the solution of the question—Who stole the moonstone? A German poet, who cannot have thought much on the matter, says:—

> "The riddle, charade, and all of that ilk,
> Are the bacon and beans of small brains."

But the riddle and the forfeit have had to do with the development of mankind, the killing out of the witless, and the survival of the intelligent. As the young were tested whether strong enough to live and by brute force to hold their own, so, apparently, at a remote period in man's history the brains of the young were passed through ordeal, and those who lacked readiness were also cast out as profitless.

That was the first stage—and that is one which we conjecture that man passed through; we have no direct evidence that it was so. Then came the second, in which a trial of strength or of wit determined great issues. Lastly, the riddle degenerated into a mere pastime. But as a pastime it remains to us a monument of great interest and of great antiquity. In every railway station in Germany is a measure. He who is below that mark is unprofitable for Fatherland and rejected from military service. The riddle was this mark before history dawned. Only such as were mentally capable of solving a simple question were considered worthy to be enrolled in the family or tribe. As in Germany at the present day, the lad who cannot pass the examination loses all chance of the short military service to which the man of culture is entitled, and is subjected to the long service of a common country lout, and the fact of his failure closes to him all professions, so was it in the primeval world. He who could not pass through his examination in riddles was condemned, if not to lose his life, at least to lose caste, and the consciousness that each lad must pass through this mental test served to sharpen intelligences, and so conduced to the advancement of mankind.

XI.
The Gallows.

Among our national institutions there is one—the gallows—to the roots of which, in a remote past, antiquarians have, to the best of my knowledge, not dug, and which they have not laid bare. Possibly this omission is due to the fact that it is not an institution of which we are proud; possibly also to the fact that it is an institution which we keep as clear from touching as we well can.

Nevertheless, the origin and original signification of the gallows are too curious to be neglected. The origin is, moreover, so remote that unless it were pointed out it would be wholly unsuspected.

In France and in Germany the wheel has occupied the place in the history of crime which the gibbet has taken with us; and the wheel, as I shall presently show, has as old and significant an origin.

We know pretty exactly the date of the introduction of this institution into our island; we owe it, along with our ale and our constitutional government, to the Anglo-Saxon invaders.

There were no gallows in Britain under the Celts. The kingdom of Kent was founded in 449, and it was then that the gallows first made their appearance among us; and from the Isle of Thanet spread over the whole land.

The great god of the conquering races, who invaded Britain and subdued the Britons, was Woden, who has given his name to Wednesday; and this god with one eye had a double aspect. He was god of the air, the wind, and he was also god of the sun. According to the etymology of his name, he was the god of the gale, and the source of all breath; but his one fiery eye was most certainly the sun; and he was represented holding a wheel of gold, and that golden wheel symbolised the sun. The Gauls also had a sun god, representations of whom holding a wheel have been discovered in France in considerable numbers; and, unquestionably, when Goths, Burgundians, and Franks invaded Gaul, or swept over it, their sun god and the Gallic wheel-bearing god were identified.

But those who thought of and adored Woden as god of the wind thought nothing of the wheel. Woden was a cruel deity, who demanded sacrifices; and the sacrifices he required were human.

In the Elder Edda, a collection of very ancient songs relating to the Norse gods and heroes, who were the same as the gods and heroes of our Anglo-Saxon forefathers, is one mysterious poem, supposed to be sung by Odin

(Woden) himself as he hangs in the world-tree, a self-immolated victim, between heaven and earth for nine nights.

> "I knew that I hung
> In the wind-rocked tree
> Nine whole nights,
>
> Wounded with a spear;
> And to Odin offered
> Myself to myself,
> On that tree,
> Of which no one knows
> From what root it springs."

As he thus hangs, himself the sacrifice offered to himself as god, he composes a song of twice nine runes, and the result of the twelfth is:—

> "If on a tree I see
> A corpse swinging by a halter,
> I can so grave runes
> And them write
> That that man shall with me
> Walk and converse."

That is to say, every victim hung on a tree becomes one of Odin's band, with whom he rides in the storm blast over the earth.

Unfortunately, the myth connected with this curious poem is not preserved; but we can gather so much from it, that Odin was said to have immolated himself to himself by hanging in the world-tree, and that thenceforth he claimed all men who had been hung as members of his band.

In one of the early Norse sagas we have a story about a king called Vikarr, who desired to dedicate himself to the god, and so he had a gallows erected before his palace, and got a friend to fasten a halter round his neck and hang him on the gallows. Another tells of a woman who, to gain her husband's love, hung her son to the god to obtain his assistance so as to brew a good vat of ale. At Lethra, in Denmark, every nine years ninety-nine men, and as many horses, were hung in honour of the god; and at Upsala numerous human victims swung by the neck about the image of Odin. After their great victory over the Romans the Cymbri and Teutons hung all their captives as a thank-offering to their gods; and after the slaughter of the legions of Varus the horses of the Romans were found hung on the trees on the scene of defeat.

Indeed, one of the names of Odin was the Hanging God, either because he hung himself, or because he had victims hung to him.

The world-tree, the great tree in which he hung, the tree which supports heaven and earth, was called Yggdrasil, which means Ogre's horse, for one of the names of Odin was Yggr or Ogre, to express his love of human sacrifices; and all the old nursery tales and rhymes concerning ogres have reference to this great god of the English people. Jack mounts the beanstalk, and above the clouds enters the land of the Ogre, with his one eye, who devours men. Jack the Giant Killer, who lives in Cornwall, represents the British Christian fighting against the Pagan Saxon, impersonated as the great man-eating ogre.

> "Fee-fo-fum, I smell the blood of an Englishman.
> Whether he be alive, or whether he be dead,
> I'll grind his bones to make my bread."

In this again we have a reference to Woden or Odin, who was also called the Miller; for the mutter or roll of the thunder was supposed to be the working of his quern, grinding up his human victims for his meal.

Originally, victims were either freewill offerings, or were chosen from among the best in the land. So we hear of a Norse king every ten years sacrificing one of his sons, and of the Swedes, in time of famine, sacrificing their king, but it became general to offer the prisoners taken in war, and when these lacked, to sacrifice those who lay in prison condemned for crimes.

In one of the Norse sagas, we are told of a king's daughter that, on hearing of the death of her father in battle, she went to the valley dedicated to the gods and there hung herself. Her father, having died in battle, went to Walhalla to Odin, and her only chance of being with him in the spirit world was to hang herself to the honour of Odin, who would then receive her among his elect, and so associate her with her father. If she were to die in her bed, she would go down to the nether world of Hela.

It is curious that in the West of England there are fields, generally situated in lonely spots, that go by the name of gallows'-traps, and the popular saying concerning them is that whoever sets foot in them is predestined to die on the gibbet. The probable origin of this superstition is that these were actual traps for the unwary, in which to catch victims for sacrifice.

In certain districts a parcel of land was set apart to the god, and it was agreed that whosoever set foot on it should be sacrificed. Usually this was a stranger, unaware of the sacredness of the ground he trod. He was seized and hung to Woden. We cannot say for certain that this is the origin of the gallows-traps, but it is the most probable explanation of their origin, and of the superstitious dread of them still existing among the people.

In France and Germany the wheel was used as the instrument of death as frequently as the gallows; those executed on the wheel were set upon poles, the wheel horizontal, and their broken limbs intertwined among the spokes. Originally they were thus put to death as oblations to the sun-god, whose symbol was the wheel. Little by little the idea of sacrifice in these executions disappeared. When Germans, Franks, and Anglo-Saxons became Christian, human sacrifices ceased as a matter of course, but as it was still necessary to put malefactors to death, the same kind of death was adjudged to them as before Christianity was professed. The gradual process whereby human sacrifices were changed in the classic world is well known to us. At first every victim was a freewill offering, and even a beast was obliged to appear so. To make the ox seem to consent to its despatch, drops of oil or water were put into its ears, that it might nod and shake its head. Prisoners taken in war, then criminals, were substituted for persons voluntarily devoting themselves to death to the honour of the gods. When it came to the execution of criminals, the idea of sacrifice readily evaporated.

One remarkable fact remains to be noticed. In all religions the sacrifice becomes identified with the god to whom it is offered, and partakes of his powers.

Whether this be a mere confusion of ideas, or whether there is some logical process at the bottom, we will not stop to consider, but it remains a fact everywhere. The victim is always thought to become invested with some of the attributes of the god.

Now a whole series of superstitions exists connected with men hung; and an executioner till of late years derived a small revenue from the sale of the cord, or other articles connected with the criminal who had been hung, and these relics were preserved, not out of a morbid love of horrors, but out of a real belief that they were beneficial, that they brought with them protection against accidents and ailments. I remember, not ten years ago, being shown by a woman, by no means in the lowest walks of life, a small object in a frame. This she said was a bit of the skin of a certain famous murderer, for which she had given a guinea.

"And what on earth makes you preserve it?" I inquired.

"Oh!" replied the woman, "the house will never catch fire so long as that is in it."

The mutilation of bodies hung in chains was of frequent occurrence in former times, on account of like beliefs. The hands and feet and hair of the dead were cut off. The former were constantly taken by thieves and burglars, who believed that the hand of the man hung would enable him to open any lock, and enter any house with immunity.

The plunder of the gallows was sought in the first days of Christianity in England by those who were still Pagans at heart, and desired to put themselves under the protection of the old gallows god, Woden, but the original meaning of this robbery of the dead soon faded away, and the practice remained without explanation.

Our word gallows is compound. The old word is *galz*, and gallows means the *low* or mound of the gibbet, and we speak of the gallow-tree, or the wood on the gibbet hill. When we remember that the gallows on which Odin hung is called Ogre's horse, it is interesting to note a popular riddle asked children in Yorkshire. "What is the horse that is ridden that never was foaled, and rid with a bridle that never had bit?" The answer is—The Gallows. A German name for it is the raven's stone, not only, perhaps, because ravens come to it, but because the raven was the sacred bird of Odin.

Now let us turn to the wheel.

On the Continent, in Germany and in France, breaking on the wheel was a customary mode of execution. The victim was stretched on the wheel, and with a bar of iron his limbs were broken, and then a blow was dealt him across the breast. After that the wheel was set up on a tall pole, with the dead man on it, and left to become the prey to the ravens.

This was a survival of human sacrifices to the sun-god, as hanging is a survival of human sacrifices to the wind-god.

Fig. 40.—THE SUN-GOD, AFTER GAIDOZ.

With regard to the solar-wheel, a great deal of very interesting information has been collected by M. Gaidoz.[40] He points out that in the museums of France there are a good many monuments that represent the sun-wheel along with the thunderbolt as the symbol of Jupiter, that is to say, the old Gaulish solar-god identified with the Roman deity, Jupiter. Gaulish warriors wore a wheel on their helmets—a wheel was a favourite symbol as a personal ornament, or perhaps as an amulet. The wheel-window in a Gothic minster derives from the solar-wheel.

Fig. 41.—ALTAR TO THE SOLAR-GOD, NIMES.

When Constantine led his legions against Maxentius, he professed to have seen a sign in the heavens, and he believed it to be a token of Christ's assistance. What he really saw was a mock-sun. He adopted and adapted the sign for his standards, and the *Labarum* of Constantine became a common Christian symbol. That there was policy in his conduct we can hardly doubt; the symbol he set up gratified the Christians in his army on one side, and the Gauls on the other. To the former it was a sign compounded of the initial letters of Christ, to the latter it was the token of the favour of their solar deity. An addition Constantine certainly made to the six-rayed wheel, but it was not one that materially affected its character.

Among the Sclavonic races in like manner the sun was worshipped, and worshipped with symbols precisely the same.

Fig. 42.—THE LABARUM.

The solar god of the Sclaves was Swanto Wit or Swato Wit, *i.e.*, Holy Light. The sun was the chief god of the Sclaves, and as the cock crows before sunrise and announces the coming day, the cock was regarded as sacred to the god, and sacrificed to it. The worship of this god consisted in circular dances, called *kolos*, and the dance was taken to represent the revolution of the planets, the constellations, the seasons about the sun. An old writer says of the dances of Swanto Wit that they were celebrated annually on the feast of St. John the Baptist, that is, on Midsummer Day. "Benches are placed in a circle, and these are leaped over by those who take part in the rite. No one is allowed to be present dressed in red. The entire month that precedes St. John's Day, the votaries are in an excited condition, and in carrying on their dances they fall a prey to nervous terrors."[41] Another writer tells us that they swung about a fiery wheel in their dances, a symbol of the solar disc.[42]

In the Bavarian highlands, where the mountain names are many of them of Sclavonic origin, and testify to a Sclavonic race having occupied the Alps, this is still customary. The midsummer dances, and the whirling of fiery wheels, are still in vogue. It is the same elsewhere. A writer on the customs of the Sclaves says: "They give each other a hand, and form a circle, whence the name of the dance, kolo = a circle, or wheel. They take three quick steps or leaps to the left, then a slow stride to the right; but when men alone dance it, after the three quick steps, they stand, and kick with the right leg into the middle of the circle. When the dance is accompanied by singing, one portion of the circle sings one strophe, and the other repeats it. The Sclave dance is most wild; and the same is found among the Carinthians and the Croats."[43] In Dalmatia and Croatia, on St. Vitus' Day the peasants dance, holding burning pieces of fragrant wood in their hands.

In the reign of Pepin, the father of Charlemagne, the Abbot Fulrad obtained the relics of St. Vitus, a boy-martyr, from Rome, and conveyed them to St. Denis. When the Abbey of New Corbey was founded in Saxony, Warin, the abbot, wrote to Hilduin of St. Denis, to entreat the gift of these relics for his church. Accordingly, in 836, they were conveyed to their new resting-place in Saxony. In 879, the monks of Corbey started on a mission to the Sclaves in Rügen and Pomerania, carrying with them a portion of the relics of St. Vitus. They erected a chapel in Rügen, which they dedicated to the saint. The attempt failed; and when, later, the Rugians were converted, the missionaries supposed that the Swanto Wit, whom they found them worshipping, was this very St. Vitus, in Sclave Swante Vit, whose relics had been laid in Rügen. When, in 1124, Otto, Bishop of Bamberg, laboured for the conversion of the Pomeranians, he took with him a figure of a cock and a silver arm that contained bones of St. Vitus. The Pomeranians reverenced the cock as a sacred being, and when Otto appeared before them, holding up the cock and the silver arm, they prostrated themselves to the cock, and he was gratified at having thus inveigled them into doing honour to the relics of St. Vitus.

Saint Wenceslas, Prince of Bohemia, in 930 destroyed the temple of Swanto Wit at Prague, and erected on its site a church to Swante Vit, *i.e.*, St. Vitus.

When Ancona was besieged by the Christian host under Waldemar I., a prophecy circulated that the city would fall into their hands on St. Vitus' Day. So it did, and Waldemar at once destroyed the temple of Swanto Wit in the city, and on its ruins erected a church to Swante Vit.

Thus it came to pass that in Sclavonic lands the *cultus* of St. Vitus usurped the worship of the sun-god. But to return to the dances. As we have seen, the solar dances held in honour of Swanto Wit were held an entire month. St. Vitus' Day falls on June 15th, very near to Midsummer Day, and as these dances continued in Christian times, and St. Vitus had taken the place of the sun-god, they acquired his name; they were called the dances of St. Vitus.

In 1370 an epidemic of chorœa broke out in Germany, especially along the valley of the Rhine. Young people of both sexes were the victims; they danced, jerked, and fell into hysterical convulsions. Those who saw them were affected in like manner. The phenomenon so much resembled the annual St. Vitus' dances that the disorder thenceforth took as its special designation, "St. Vitus' Dance."

Dancing in a circle was a piece of sacred ritual in honour of the revolving wheel of the sun. In the Bavarian highlands at Midsummer a fiery wheel is waved and rolled down the mountain sides. The same sort of rite was anciently observed at the same time in England. A monk of Winchelscombe, in the reign of Henry VI., gives an account of the popular festivals in his time. He speaks of three sorts of amusements that take place on the vigil of St. John the Baptist. One of these is the whirling of a cart wheel. Another writer of the following century, in his poem, "Regnum papisticum," gives further details. He says that the country people take an old wheel, surround it with straw, so as completely to cover it, and carry it to a height. At nightfall they set it on fire and roll it down; a monstrous sight, he adds, and one would believe that the sun was rolling down out of heaven.

Exactly the same usage is, or was, common in Belgium. In a charter, by which the Abbess of Epinal ceded a wood to the magistrates of that town in 1505, she made provision that every year, as an acknowledgment, they should furnish "The Wheel of Fortune, and the straw wherewith to cover it."

Pages might be crowded with illustrations. I must refer the curious to the treatise of M. Gaidoz. Sufficient evidence has been collected that the wheel was the sacred symbol of the sun among the Gauls, the Teutons, and the Sclaves. We can, therefore, see how that an execution on the wheel was in its original conception a sacrifice to the sun.

Long after this was forgotten the wheel remained, as has the gallows with us, as the instrument for the execution of criminals. In Germany, even in cases of decapitation, the person executed was placed on a wheel and his head on a pole, when separated from the body. The last instances of breaking on the wheel were in the first forty years of this century. The fact of the use of the wheel as a means of execution continuing so many hundreds of years after the worship of the sun-god had ceased, and of the gallows with us, for the same purpose, is a very curious and instructive illustration of the persistence of customs of which the original significance is absolutely lost.

XII.
Holes.

In the village churchyard where as a boy I often played, is a tomb, built up to the height of about five feet, with a slate slab let into the south face, on which is an inscription. In this slab is a hole, and it used to be said among the village boys that any one who looked in through this hole and knocked at the slate would see the dead man within open his eyes. Often have I and my brother peeped in and knocked, but the experiment failed, because, when the eye was applied to the hole, it excluded external light.

Fig. 43.—HOLED TOMBSTONE, BURGHEAD.
(*From Mitchell's "The Past and the Present."*)

The monument is still where it was, and is in the same condition. Whether boys still knock and look in I do not know.[44]

Curiously enough, a somewhat similar practice exists at Burghead, about nine miles from Elgin, which is described by Professor Mitchell in his "Rhind Lectures," 1880. He says: "There is a memorial slab built into the wall of the burial-ground, called the Chapel Yard, at the south-east corner; it is 35 inches high by 20 inches wide; close above it, and also built into the wall, there is a hewn lintel-like stone, 37 inches long by 1½ inches thick. On the narrow exposed face of this stone there is no sculpturing.

"The woodcut shows the position on the cradle stone (as it is called) of a cup-like hollow, which is quite round 2¼ inches in depth. This hollow has been produced by the children of Burghead, who are in the habit of striking the spot with a beachstone (which is also represented in the woodcut), and then quickly putting their ears to the place, when the sound of a rocking cradle and the crying of a child are said to be heard, as if coming from a cavern deep under ground. I am told that during last century the stone was not visited by children, but by women, who believed that they were to become mothers if they heard the rocking of the cradle and the crying of the child after tapping on the stone."

What is certainly a curious coincidence is that the pre-historic rude stone ossuaries, dolmens or cromlechs, have very frequently in like manner a hole worked in them.

Trevethy cromlech, in the parish of St. Cleer, Cornwall, has a hole perforating the capstone. The Maison des Fées at Grammont, in Hérault, has a hole bored through the head or western supporter. Another, now destroyed, was at Cahaignes, in Normandy. The covered avenue of Conflans now transferred to the fosse of the Musée, St. Germain, has not only the round hole bored in one upright, but also the stone that closed this opening.[45]

Holes in like manner have been bored in the cromlechs of Avening and Rodmarton. Those in Circassia, in Palestine, and in India, have also holes. Colonel Meadows Taylor found that 1,100 dolmens out of 2,219 in the Dekhan had these holes in them. Similar holes have been observed in the dolmens of Sardinia.

Fig. 44.—DOLMEN WITH HOLE AND PLUG, IN THE CAUCASUS
(*after Cartailhac*).

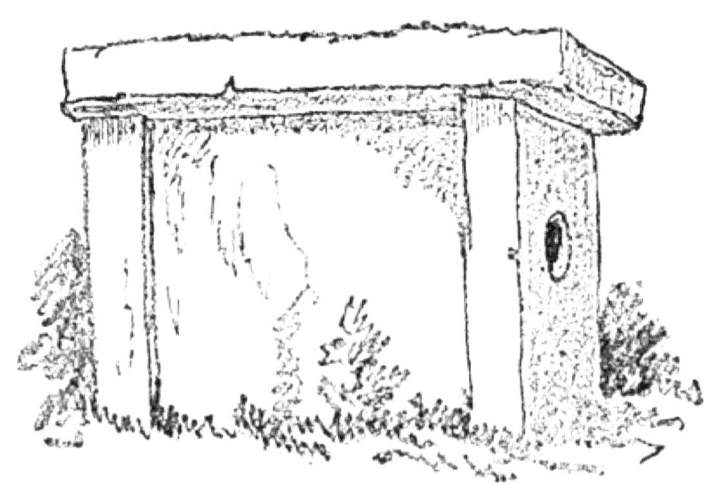

Fig. 45.—DOLMEN IN THE CRIMEA, WITH HOLE IN THE SIDE
(*after Cartailhac.*)

In a majority of cases these holes will not serve the purpose of giving admission to the interior of the monument, though in some large enough. These megalithic structures were ossuaries; often, no doubt, the dead was laid in one as he had died; but in a great many cases, always where the dead had fallen in battle at a distance from the family mausoleum, his bones were cleaned of flesh and sinew before being brought to it. The bones bear marks of the scraper that cleared them of flesh, and they are not put together in correct position. In like manner the Landgrave Ludwig, husband of St. Elizabeth, died at Otranto, in 1227; his body was boiled to get the flesh off the bones, and then the bones alone were conveyed to Germany, to be interred at Eisenach.

It has often been noticed that along with ordinary interments in barrows, incineration has been practised. This was probably another means of transporting the remains of those who had died at a distance from the family or clan burial mound.

The holes in the dolmens[46] are in many cases too small to allow of anyone crawling through to carry within the remains of the last member of the family, who had succumbed and was to be placed in the dolmen. Some other explanation must be sought.

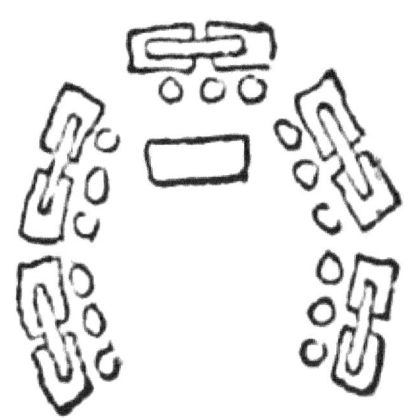

Fig. 46.—THE INNER INCOMPLETE CIRCLE, STONEHENGE, *restored.*

Now, it is remarkable that the circles of upright stones that enclose cairns and stone graves or kistvaens are rarely complete. They have been purposely made imperfect circles, with a gap or a stop in the circle; and we may ask whether the interruption in the circle has some meaning analogous to that of the hole in the stone chest.

Mr. Greenwell, in his "British Barrows," says:—"The incompleteness of these circles is so frequent a feature in their construction that it cannot be accidental. They have, moreover, been left incomplete in some cases in a way which most evidently shows a design in the operation; as, for instance, where the circle is formed of a number of stones standing apart from each other. The space between two of them has frequently been carefully built up with one large or several smaller stones. The effect of this is to break the continuity, or rather the uniformity, of the circle, and so to make it imperfect. This very remarkable feature in connection with the enclosing circles is also found to occur in the case of other remains which belong to the same period and people as the barrows. The sculptured markings engraved upon rocks, and also upon stones forming the covers of urns or cists, consist in the main of two types, cup-shaped hollows, and circles, more or less in number, surrounding in most cases a central cup. In almost every instance the circle is imperfect, its continuity being sometimes broken by a duct leading out from the central cup; at other times by the hollowed line of the circle stopping short when about to join at each end. The connection of these sculptured stones, if so they may be termed, with places of sepulture, brings them at once into close relationship with the enclosing circles of barrows, and it is scarcely possible to imagine but that the same idea, whatever that may have been, is signified by the incomplete circle in both cases."[47]

Fig. 47.—CINERARY URN WITH HOLES IN THE SIDE, FROM SALISBURY PLAIN.

The great inner ring of trilithons at Stonehenge affects the horse-shoe shape, and is, and always was, incomplete. The outer ring of trilithons is too ruinous for us to be able to state what its original condition was.

The horse-shoe, the incomplete ring, is still regarded as lucky, and a protection against witches. The enchanter who raised spirits was wont to draw a complete circle around him, and the demons raged outside this circle, but could not pass within and hurt him who had conjured them up. If he stepped outside the circle, or broke the continuity of the ring, then the spirits entered and tore him to pieces.

This probably gives us a clue to the signification of the incomplete circle. The complete circle confines a spirit within it, or protects from the entrance of spirits; an interrupted circle allows spirits to pass to and fro, gives ingress and egress.

The tomb is the house of the dead. He lives in it after some mysterious, not clearly defined fashion. And as a bee-hive hut had its door, so must the hut of the dead have its door. It would be a cruelty to the dead to imprison him; and if the circle be complete, the dolmen closed in on all sides, he could not come in and out at pleasure.

Precisely what the door is to the house, that the mouth is to man; it is the door by which the spirit comes into and goes out of man. With his first inspiration he becomes a living soul; with his last breath he expires—gives up his soul.

The story is well known of the two shepherds who sat together one summer's day. One fell asleep, and whilst he slept the other saw a bee issue from his lips and creep over a blade of grass that crossed a tiny trickle of water, then fly away among flowers. After an hour the bee returned again in the same way, and re-entered the sleeping man's mouth. Thereupon he awoke, and told his friend that in dream he had crossed a magnificent bridge over a great river, and had visited Paradise.

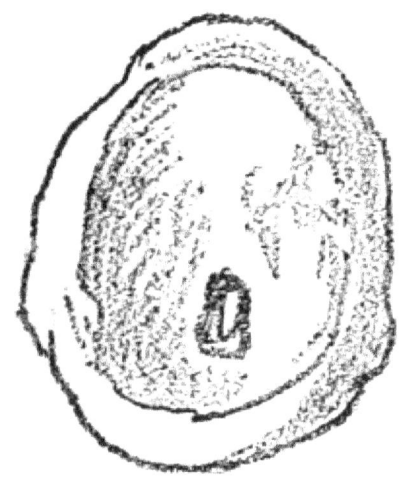

Fig. 48.—CRANIAL DISC, WITH HOLE FOR SUSPENSION.

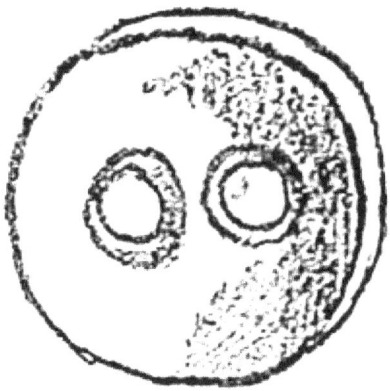

Fig. 49.—CRANIAL DISC, WITH TWO HOLES FOR SUSPENSION.

In the Caucasus, among the Abazas, when a boy dies he is put into a wooden coffin *with a hole in it*, and hung up in a tree. Bees are supposed to fly in and out at the hole, and these are taken, no doubt, to be souls visiting the boy, and the soul of the boy going in and out along with them.

I remember some years ago when a person was dying and seemed to find great difficulty in the parting of soul from body, that the nurse went to the window and opened it, whereupon the dying person heaved a sigh, and the spirit took its flight. On asking the reason of this opening of the window, the nurse answered, "You would not have the soul go up the chimney, would you?"

Mr. Rudyard Kipling, in his poem "The Gift of the Sea," refers to this belief:—

> "The widow ...
> Opened the door on the bitter shore
> To let the soul go free."

Again, it has often been noticed that holes have been knocked or bored in funeral urns containing incinerated bones. These have been made purposely, and must have had some signification. I have not myself examined such urns on the spot where discovered; but I have little hesitation in surmising that only such urns have been perforated as have had their mouths covered with another vessel inverted, or with a flat stone, and that the object of this perforation has been to make a door of ingress or egress for the spirit of the dead; that, in fact, it had the same purpose as the hole in the dolmen and the rupture of continuity in the circle.

Of a number of the smaller sized urns or vessels found in the barrows of Salisbury Plain, "a very large proportion are pierced on one side with two holes, from half an inch to two inches apart. There are exceptions with a large number of holes, but the rule is to have two holes on one side only," says Mr. Long, in his "Stonehenge and its Barrows." He proceeds to discuss their signification. The holes could not have existed for suspension, and he adopts Sir C. Colt Hoare's supposition that the perforated urns were incense vessels. But calcined bones have been found in some, and others probably served as caps to the cinerary urns. Almost certainly the people of the barrows knew nothing of incense, and the probability is that these two holes were bored as doors of egress and ingress for the spirit that still tenanted the bones.

Count d'Alviella says in his Hibbert Lectures for 1891, "Numbers of savage peoples suppose that the soul continues to inhabit the body after death, though from time to time it makes excursions into the world of the living. It therefore requires a hole if it is to escape from the enclosure. For this reason it is that, at the death of a relative, the Hottentots, the Samoyeds, the Siamese, the Fijians, and the Redskins, make a hole in the hut to allow the passage of the deceased, but close it again immediately afterwards to prevent its coming back. The Iroquois make a small hole in every tomb, and expressly declare that it is to enable the soul to go out and come in at its pleasure."

There was another usage of the men of the megalithic monuments which had, apparently, the same idea or conception of spirit as that which induced them to make holes in their dolmens.

In 1873, when the French Association for the Advancement of Science met in Congress at Lyons, Dr. Prunières produced an elliptical disc of skull which had been found by him inside a human skull that had been trepanned, and which came from a dolmen in Lozère. The disc had been cut out of a human skull by some sharp instrument at an incline. At first sight it appeared probable that this piece came from the skull in which it was discovered, but on close examination it was found that it would not fit the hole trepanned in the skull.

In the same dolmen Dr. Prunières found a second skull that had been trepanned more than once. Attention was now drawn to this remarkable phenomenon—and instances multiplied to prove that the men of the polished stone age, the men who erected Stonehenge and Carnac, were wont to cut holes in their heads.

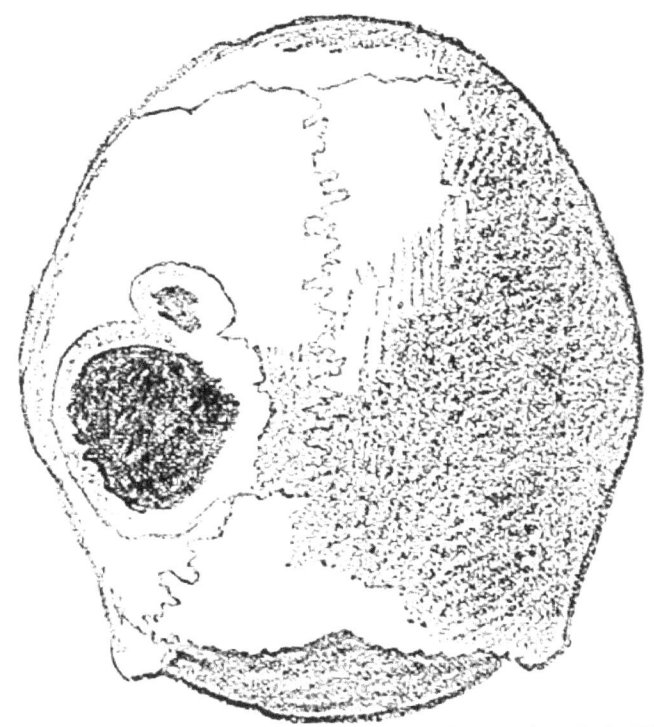

Fig. 50.—SKULL THAT HAD BEEN TWICE TREPANNED FROM A CAVE IN THE PETIT-MORIN.

Dr. Prunières especially took the matter up. He discovered in the dolmens portions of skulls, circular or elliptical, that had been pierced with holes for suspension, and had been polished by long continued wear. In the Cave de l'Homme-Mort, in Lozère, he exhumed a skull that had a surgical trepanned hole on the sagittal suture. Finally, in the great ossuary of

Beaumes Chaudes he discovered as many as sixty cranial discs. Skulls began to turn up elsewhere that had been trepanned, and all of the same epoch. They came from Sweden, Denmark, Switzerland, Bohemia, Poland, Spain, Portugal, Algeria. It was found also that trepanning skulls had been in practice among the aborigines of America. In the Peabody Museum is a skull that has had a hole cut out of it. A mound on the Devil's River yielded another. Other trepanned skulls were taken out of mounds near Lake Huron and Grape Mound. A skull found in a barrow near the River Detroit had two perforations in it. A sepulchre near Lima yielded a skull that had also been surgically treated in the same fashion. Another came from the basin of the Amazon. There is, however, a marked difference between the American holed skulls and these of the neolithic men of Europe. The American skulls have all been operated on after death, and are found only in male skulls. They were, moreover, made by means of a stone drill which was turned rapidly round. Only one circular perforation in every respect similar to these found in Europe has been noticed in America. We may, therefore, put aside the pre-historic trepannings of America as not connected directly with the subject under consideration. In Europe the majority of the cases show by evident tokens that the operations were performed during life. Of these the greatest numbers of every age and sex have been found in the dolmens of France.

In the Casa da Moura, a dolmen in Portugal, was found a skull on which the operation had been begun, but never completed. It had clearly been worked with a flint scraper. The Baron de Baye found in one of the paleolithic caves of Marne a head that had been twice trepanned.

The great majority of cases of trepanned heads show that those operated upon had lived for many years after the operation. Indeed, it cannot be said that the practice of trepanning is as yet extinct. Dr. Boulongue, in his work on Montenegro, gives a long account of this usage of the natives of the Black Mountain; they have recourse to trepanning on the smallest provocation, simply because they have headaches. He quotes numerous instances of persons who have been trepanned seven and even eight times, without this materially injuring their health.

In the same manner the Kabyles of Algeria cut holes in their heads, usually as a cure for epilepsy.

The first example of pre-historic trepanning was discovered in 1685. Montfaucon mentions it, but misunderstood it; he supposed that the man with the hole in his head had been wounded in battle, but had recovered. A second example was observed in 1816, and was also misinterpreted. A sepulchral cave had been opened at Nogent-les-Vierges, which contained two hundred skeletons. One of the skulls was found to be trepanned, and the edges of the wound showed evidence of the efforts of Nature to repair the injury. This also was supposed to be a case of wound in battle.

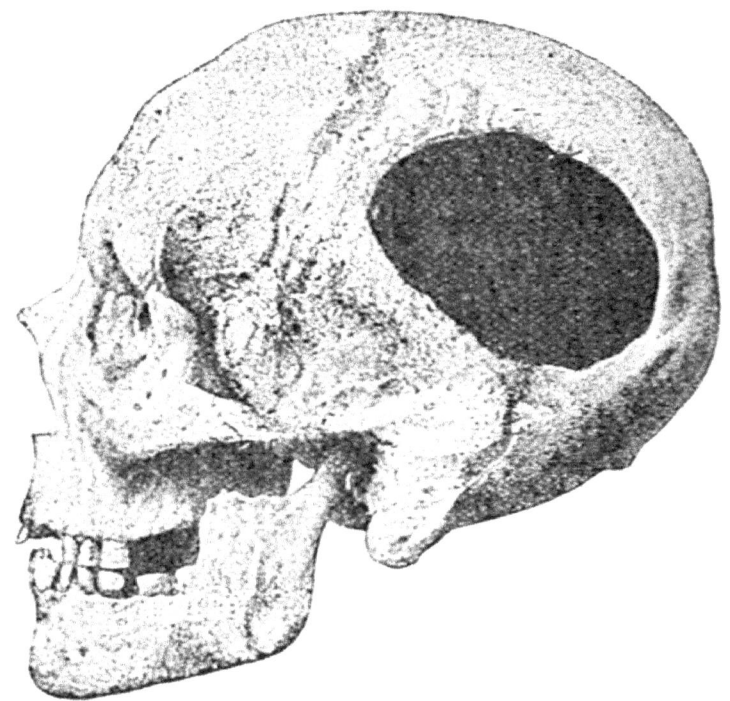

Fig. 51.—TREPANNED SKULL FROM NOGENT-LES-VIERGES (*after Cartailhac, La France Préhistorique*).

It must, however, be observed that the men thus trepanned lived in the stone age, and that no stone axe or sword could possibly gash away a slice of skull; that, moreover, the edges of the holes show that they have been laboriously worked through at an incline, the scraper held so as to make the hole convex, widest at the outer surface, and narrowing at the inner surface near the brain.

The hole in the head of the man from the Cave of l'Homme-Mort is peculiarly interesting, as it showed that he had been trepanned during life, and that Nature had done her best to smoothe the rough edges. Then, after death, a flint saw had been used, to further enlarge the hole. The marks of the two operations are quite distinct.

Now what, it may be asked, is the meaning of these holes cut in the head? Various suggestions have been offered, but the most plausible is this—that they were made in cases of epilepsy.

"The art of trepanning," says Dr. Broca, "was employed exclusively in cases of spontaneous maladies. In all likelihood the operation took place in accordance with certain ideas prevalent relative to nervous complaints, such as epilepsy, idiotcy, convulsions, mental alienations, etc. These affections, which science regards as natural, always struck the imagination of the vulgar, and were attributed to divine or demoniacal possession. Who can say whether trepanning for epilepsy—a practice now almost abandoned, but which was formerly in usage, was not adopted as a means of opening a door by which the demons possessing the patient might be allowed to escape?"[48]

We know how that even in medieval times, the evil spirit exorcised out of a man is represented as a little figure issuing from his mouth. The primitive medicine-men, supposing that the epileptic child was possessed by a spirit, cut a hole in the head, and through this hole conjured the spirit forth. Then the portion of the skull cut away obtained a superstitious value, it had been in contact with a spirit, and so was employed as an amulet. It is, however, quite possible that these discs from the heads were worn by the wives or the mothers of those from whom they were cut, out of sentiment. In some tombs, male skulls have been found stuffed with small bones of children, and not all from the same children; these skulls had been polished by friction, and seem to have been worn hung round the neck, and to have served as a sort of reticule or rather reliquary, in which the widow carried portions of the various children she had borne, who had died, packed away in their father's skull.

So much, then, for perforations in tombstones, interrupted continuity in circles, and trepanned skulls. All have the same interpretation, the opening of a means of egress for the spirit, and are precisely what the open window means now in a case of death, they are to the dead man what the door is in the house to the living man.

There is another usage of a hole that has come down to us from primeval man in a very modified form. I refer to the wedding-ring, a piece of perforated metal through which the finger is thrust. The marriage ring is a pledge of fidelity, but it must often have struck English people that it is a very one-sided arrangement when the woman has to wear the badge of being married, whereas the man wears none. The reason why the man wears no ring is probably to be sought in custom followed from the period when a man had as many wives as he liked, but the woman was debarred from belonging to more than one man.

The passing of the finger through a ring is probably a survival of the practice of passing the entire body through a ring as a symbol of covenant, of entering on new relations, a sort of regeneration into a new family or fraternity. A great number of holed stones remain among pre-historic monuments that were probably so used, for there remained a reminiscence of such usage in tradition. Wherever megalithic remains are found, there also these holed stones are found large enough for the passage of a body; sometimes only of sufficient size for the hand to be passed through.

At Boleit in Cornwall in tolerably close juxtaposition is a circle of 19 upright stones, 75 feet in diameter, "The Merry Maidens;" two menhirs, "The Pipers," respectively 15 feet and 13½ feet high; another upright stone 11 feet high, 5 barrows, and 3 holed stones.

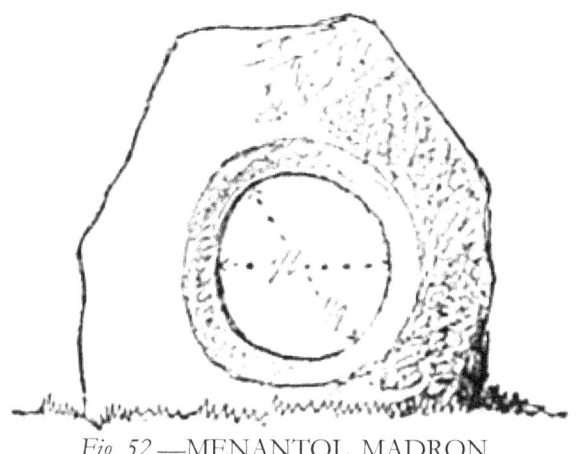

Fig. 52.—MENANTOL, MADRON.

At Tregaseal, in the same county, are four holed stones in a line, the hole in each 3¼ to 3¾ inches in diameter. At St. Buryan, near a sacred circle, is an upright slab with a hole in it 5¼ inches in diameter. Another holed stone is at Trelew in St. Buryan, the hole 5 inches in diameter. Another at St. Just, 6 inches in diameter. Another upright stone 3 feet 3 inches high at Sancreed has in it a hole 3¼ inches in diameter. But there are others far larger. The Tolven near Gweep Constantine has in it a hole 1 foot 4½ inches in diameter, and the Men-an-tol at Madron, which is near Lanyon Cromlech and Boskedrian Circle, and is itself apparently one stone in a ruined circle, has in it a hole measuring 1 foot 6 inches to 1 foot 9 inches in diameter. St. Wilfred's needle in the crypt of Ripon Minster is a hole bored in the natural rock, and girls were wont to be passed through it to prove their virtue. If they stuck in the eye of the needle they were held to be dishonest.

At Chagford in Devon again we find in connection a sacred circle, avenues, and a tolmen, or holed stone 3 feet in diameter. So also on Brimham Moor in Yorkshire; there within the memory of old men, holed stones have been used for passing children through to remove disorders. But the original purpose for which the tolmens were set up is almost certainly to furnish a means for making a covenant, for taking an oath. The woman was passed through the perforated stone before she married, as an assurance to the bridegroom that she was a pure virgin. Those entering on a covenant crawled through the hole one after another, in pledge of their having no *arrière pensée*, that they took the pledge to each other in full faith. There are several curious passages in the Icelandic sagas that illustrate this custom. The Icelanders were a very different race from the men who erected the megalithic monuments, but their Scandinavian ancestors came on the traces of the neolithic men, subdued them, and adopted many of their usages. In Iceland there are no holed stones, but the principle of passing through a hole was followed, and it assumed this curious form. A turf was cut so that it held in the ground at both ends, then it was raised in the midst, and those who entered on a covenant of brotherhood with each other crawled under the turf.

A ballad sung by the peasantry in the West of England relates how a gay trooper loved a fair damsel, and married her in military fashion:—

> "My sword it is a Damask blade,
> I bend it in a bow.
> No golden ring may here be got,
> So pass thy white hand through."

Here the hoop of steel has taken the place of the holed stone. The golden circlet has, however, become the usual substitute.

We will now consider some holes of a different description, that are not actual perforations. A custom very general in Roman Catholic countries must have struck travellers: it is that of placing cups, basins, or other concave vessels on graves. The purpose is that they may be filled with holy water—or if not with that, then with the dew of heaven. The friends, kindred, or charitable as they pass dip a little brush in the basin and sprinkle the grave with the water. This is a symbolic act, nothing more. It means that the visitor to the grave wishes well to the dead, and offers a prayer for the refreshment of the departed soul. That soul may be in purgatory, and he who sprinkles the grave knows that no drops of water thrown on the mound can slake the fire that tortures the soul, but he acts as though he thought that the soul still tenanted the body, and could be refreshed by the water thrown on his grave. I do not believe this usage to have received any formal sanction; it is a survival of a much earlier usage that has been given an altered signification. It is not a rational proceeding, but is not one particle more irrational than our putting wreaths and crosses of flowers on the graves of those we have loved. I remember a daughter planting ferns of many sorts round her mother's tomb, "because mother was so very fond of ferns." But those who thus act, when they consider, know well enough that what lies underground is the decaying husk, and that the soul, the true being, is elsewhere. Nevertheless, the mind, by force of custom and natural tendency, persists in associating soul with body after death, and the dead lady was given her ferns because they continued to give her pleasure, whilst lying in her grave, precisely as the Tartar chief is given his horse and his wives slain and laid about him in his cairn.

The original signification of the basin or cup on the tomb was that of a vessel to contain the drink supplied to the dead. The dead man continued to eat and drink in his cairn or dolmen, and the relatives supplied him with what he required.

In the British tumuli, hollows beside the dead are of common occurrence. Mr. Greenwell says: "It is of frequent occurrence to find holes, sunk below the natural surface, within the area of a barrow, and not usually in close proximity to any interment, though in some instances such has been found to be the case. Sometimes as many as four or five have been met with in a single barrow. They are of various sizes, and differ in shape, but they are generally circular, about 1½ feet in diameter, and the same in depth. In the greater number of cases they are filled with the ordinary materials of which the mound itself is composed, and contain nothing besides; but at other times pieces of animal, and much more rarely of human bones, charcoal, potsherds, and burnt earth, and stone are found in them.... It has suggested itself to me, that they may have been made as receptacles of food or of some other perishable material, and that they answered the same purpose as the vessels of pottery are supposed to have done, which are such frequent accompaniments of a burial. Their not being usually placed in close contact with the body is a fact not perhaps very consistent with this explanation of their purpose, but I am unable to offer any one more suggestion."

I differ from Mr. Greenwell in one point only—that these basins being at a distance from the body may be inconsistent with the explanation he proposes. On the contrary, I conceive that these cup-like hollows were at the circumference of the original mound, and were often replenished with food or drink. As the mound spread through the action of rain, or as other interments were made in it, and it was enlarged, these basins became buried.

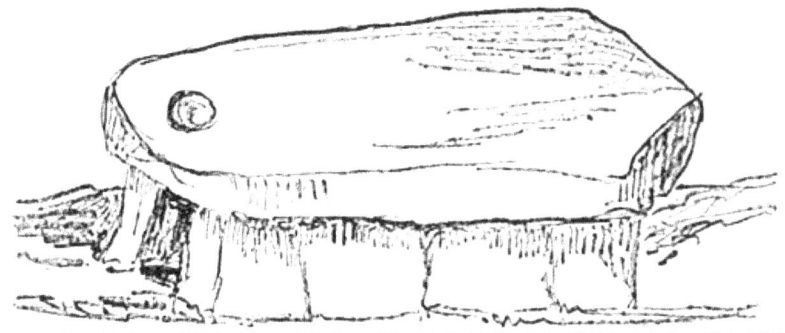

Fig. 53.—DOLMEN AT LARAMIERE (LOT), WITH CUP HOLLOW ON COVERER.

The parkin cakes baked in Yorkshire in November, the simnel or soul-mass cakes of Lancashire, the *gauffres* baked at All Souls-tide in Belgium, are all reminiscences of the food prepared and offered to the dead at All Souls, the great day of commemoration of the departed. Not only did the living eat the cakes, but they were given as well to the dead. In Belgium the idea still holds that the pancakes or *gauffres* avail the souls; but through a confusion of ideas, the ignorant suppose that the living by eating them satisfy the dead, and as these pancakes are very indigestible, it is customary to hire robust men to gorge themselves on *gauffres* so as to content the departed ones with a good meal. A has a dear deceased relative B. In order that B may be well supplied with pancake, A ought to eat a plentiful supply; but A shrinks from an attack of indigestion, which a surfeit would bring on, so he hires C to glut himself on *gauffres* in his room.

The Flemish name for these cakes are "zielen brood" or soul-bread. "At Dixmude and its neighbourhood it is said that for every cake eaten a soul is delivered from purgatory. At Furnes the same belief attaches to the little loaves called 'radetjes,' baked in every house. At Ypres the children beg in the street on the eve of All Souls for some sous wherewith 'to make cakes for the little souls in purgatory.' At Antwerp these soul-cakes are stained yellow with saffron, to represent the flames of purgatory."[49] In the North of England all idea as to the connection between these cakes and the dead is lost, but the cakes are still made. This custom is a transformation under Christian influence of the still earlier usage of putting food on the graves. When food and drink were furnished to the dead, then necessarily the dead must have their mugs and platters for the reception of their food, and the basins scooped in the soil of a barrow in all likelihood served this purpose.

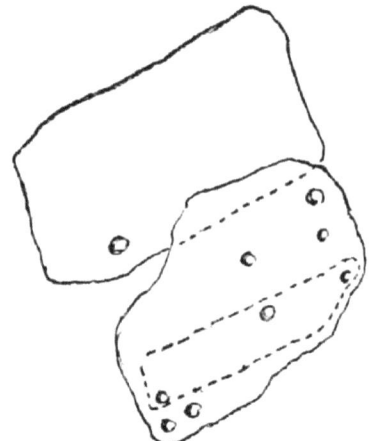

Fig. 54.—CUP-MARKINGS, CROMLECH, S. KEVERN.

In like manner there are basins cut on some of the dolmens, and other depressions that were natural were employed for the same purpose. On the coverer of a dolmen close to the railway at Assier, in the Department of Lot, is such a rock basin, natural perhaps, but if natural, then utilised for the purpose of a food or drink vessel for the dead. Another dolmen in the same department, at Laramière, has one distinctly cut by art at the eastern extremity of the covering stone. Inside dolmens and covered avenues stones have been found with cup-like hollows scooped out in them. These served the same purpose, and were in such monuments as were accessible in the interior, as, for instance, those stone basins found in the stone-vaulted tombs on the banks of the Boyne, near Drogheda, with their singular inscribed circles. Whereas such dolmens as could not be entered had the food or drink basins outside them.

"The Three Brothers of Grugith," a cromlech or dolmen at S. Kévern, in Cornwall, has eight cup-like hollows on the coverer and one in one of the uprights. They vary from 4 to 6 inches in diameter and are 1½ inches deep.

The cup-like holes found so frequently in connection with palæolithic monuments may probably be explained in this way. Originally intended as actual food receptacles or cups for drink, they came in time to be employed as a mere form, and no particular care was taken as to the position they occupied. Thus, very often an upright stone has these cup-marks on it; sometimes they are on the under surface of a covering stone. They belong to the period of the rude stone monuments. With the advent of bronze they gradually disappear. They are not found always associated with interments, though generally so, and it is probable that the stones bearing them which do not at present seem to be intended to mark the place of an interment may have done so originally.

We know that in a great number of cases a mere symbol was taken to serve the purpose of something of actual, material use. Thus, the Chinese draw little coats and hats on paper and burn them, and suppose that by this means they are transmitting actual coats and hats to their ancestors in the world of spirits. In Rome, at certain periods, statuettes were thrown into the Tiber: these were substitutes for the human sacrifices formerly offered to the river. Probably the custom of giving food and drink to the dead gradually died out among the palæolithic men, but that of making the cups for the reception of the gifts remained, and as their purpose was forgotten, the stones graven with the hollows were set up anyhow.

The question has been often raised whether the rock-basins found on granite heights are of artificial origin. It is perhaps too hastily concluded that they are produced by water and gravel rotating in the wind. No doubt a good many have this origin; but I hardly think that all are natural, and it is probable that some have been begun by art and then enlarged by nature, and also that natural basins may have been used by the palæolithic men as drink or food vessels for the gods or spirits in the wind.

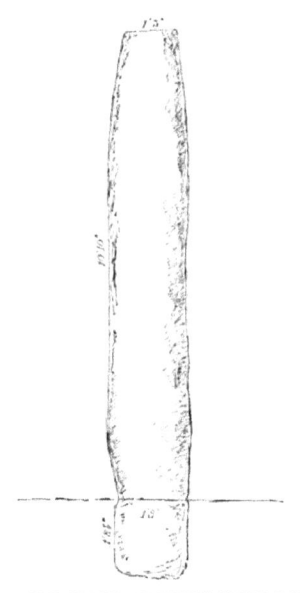

Fig. 55.—MENHIR, LEW TRENCHARD.

About twelve years ago I dug up a *menhir* that had lain for certainly three centuries under ground, and had served on one side as a wall for the "leat" or conduit of water to the manorial mill. There was no mistaking the character of the stone. It was of fine grained granite, and had been brought from a distance of some eight miles. It was unshaped at the base, and marked exactly how much of it had been sunk in the ground. It stood when re-erected 10 feet 10 inches above the surface. The singular feature in it is this. At the summit, which measures 15 inches by 12 inches, is a small cup 3 inches deep sunk in the stone, 4½ inches in diameter, and distinctly artificial. Now, that the monolith had been standing upright for a vast number of years, was shown by this fact, that the rain water, accumulating in the artificial cup, driven by the prevailing S.W. wind, had worn for itself a lip, and in its flow had cut itself a channel down the side of the stone opposite to the direction of the wind to the distance of 1 foot 6 inches.

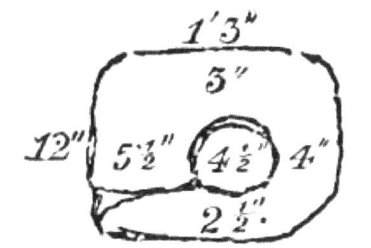

Fig. 56.—THE CUP ON THE TOP.

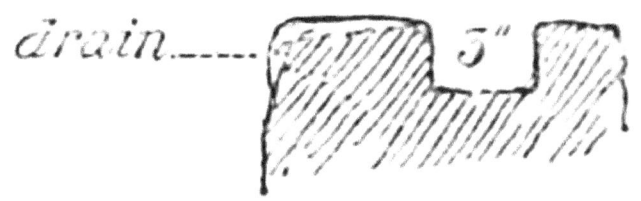

Fig. 57.—SECTION OF THE CUP.

What can this cup have been intended for? It is probable that it was a receptacle for rain water, which was to serve for the drink of the dead man above whom the monolith was erected. The Rev. W. C. Lukis, one of the highest authorities on such matters, was with me at the time of the re-erection of this monolith, and it then occurred to him that the holes at the top of so many of the Brittany menhirs, in which now crosses are planted, were not made for the reception of the bases of these crosses, but already existed in the menhirs, and were utilised in Christian times for the erection therein of crosses which sanctified the old heathen monuments. Some upright stones have the cup-hollows cut in their sides, so that nothing could rest in them; but I venture to suggest that these may be symbolic cups, carved after their use, as food and drink receptacles, had been abandoned.

Fig. 58.—THE FURROW DOWN THE SIDE.

Mr. Romilly Allen, in a paper on some sculptured rocks near Ilkley in Yorkshire,[50] that have these cup-hollows, says, "The classes of monuments on which they are found are as follows:—

1. Natural rock surfaces.
2. Isolated boulders.
3. Near ancient British (?) fortified towns and camps.
4. In connection with the lake-dwellings, underground houses, and Pictish towers.
5. On single standing stones.
6. On groups of standing stones.
7. On stone circles.
8. On cromlechs (dolmens).
9. In chambered cairns.
10. On cist-covers.
11. On urn-covers.
12. On gravestones in Christian churchyards.

} Sepulchral remains.

13. On the walls of churches themselves.

"From the fact of cup-markings being found in so many instances directly associated with sepulchral remains, I think it may fairly be inferred that they are connected in some way or other with funeral rites, either as sacred emblems or for actual use in holding small offerings or libations."

Mr. Romilly Allen is, I believe, quite right in his conjecture, which is drawn from observation of the frequency with which these cup-hollows are associated with sepulchral stones. But it must be remembered that a libation is the last form assumed by the usage of giving a drink to either the dead or to a god. The conception of a sacrifice is comparatively modern, the primitive idea in connection with the offering of a liquid is the giving of some acceptable draught to some being who is in the spirit world.

The fact, and it is a fact, that these cup-markings are found on Christian tombstones, shows how the old habit continued to find expression after the meaning which had originated it was completely lost.[51]

These singular cup-markings are found distributed over Denmark, Norway, Scotland, Ireland, England, France, Switzerland.

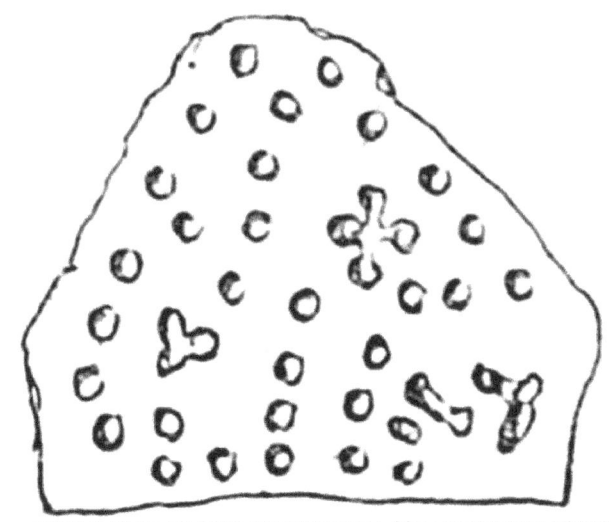

Fig. 59.—CUP-MARKINGS IN STONE AT CORRIEMONY. (*From Mitchell's "The Past and the Present."*)

All cup-hollows cannot indeed be explained as drink vessels for the dead. Those, for instance, carved in the slate at a steep incline of the cliffs near New Quay in Cornwall, and others in the perpendicular face of the rock also in the same place cannot be so interpreted, but their character is not that altogether of the cup-markings found elsewhere. The hollows are often numerous, and are irregularly distributed. Sometimes they have a channel surrounding a group. That they had some well-understood meaning to the people of the neolithic age who graved them in the rock cannot be doubted. It is said that in places grease and oil are still put into them by the ignorant peasantry as oblation; and this leads to the conclusion that, when first graven, they were intended as receptacles for offerings.

One day, in a graveyard in the west of England, I came on an old stone basin, locally termed a "Lord's measure," an ancient holy-water vessel,[52] standing under the headstone, above a mound that covered the dust of someone who had been dearly loved. The little basin was full of water, and in the water were flowers.

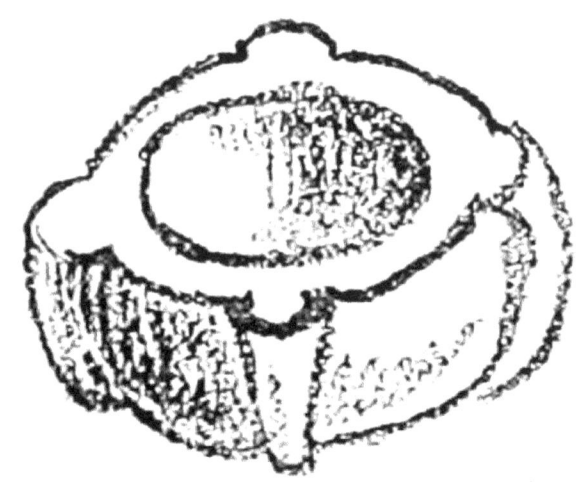

Fig. 60.—A "LORD'S MEASURE," CORNWALL.

As I stood musing over this grave, it was not wonderful that my mind should travel back through vast ages, and follow man in his various moods, influenced in his treatment of the dead by various doctrines relative to the condition of the soul.

Here was the cup for holy water, itself a possible descendant of the food-vessel for the dead. And now it is used, not to furnish the dead with drink and meat, but with flowers. And it seemed to me that man was the same in all ages, through all civilisations, and that his acts are governed much more by custom than by reason. Is it not quite as irrational to put flowers on a grave as to put on it cake or ale? Does the soul live in the green mound with the bones? Does it come out to smell and admire the roses and lilies and picotees? The putting flowers on the grave is a matter of sentiment. Quite so—and in a certain phase of man's growth in culture the food-vessel was cut in stone as a mere matter of sentiment, even when no food was put in it.

There are many of the customs of daily life which deserve to be considered, and which are to us full of interest, or ought to be so, for they tell us such a wondrous story. If I have in this little volume given a few instances, it is with the object of directing attention to the survivals of usage which had its origin in ideas long ago abandoned, and to show how much there is still to be learned from that proper study of mankind—Man.

Archæology is considered a dry pursuit, but it ceases to be dry when we find that it does not belong solely to what is dead and passed, but that it furnishes us with the interpretation of much that is still living and is not understood.

XIII.
Raising the Hat.

It is really remarkable how many customs are allowed to pass without the idea occurring as to what is their meaning. There is, for instance, no more common usage of everyday life than that of salutation by raising the hat, or touching the cap, and yet, not one person in ten thousand stops to inquire what it all means—why this little action of the hand should be accepted as a token of respect.

Raising the hat is an intermediate form; the putting up the finger to the cap is the curtailed idea of the primitive act of homage, reduced to its most meagre expression.

There is an amusing passage in Sir Francis Head's "Bubbles from the Brunnen of Nassau" on hat-lifting:

"At nearly a league from Langen-Schwalbach, I walked up to a little boy who was flying a kite on the top of a hill, in the middle of a field of oat-stubble. I said not a word to the child—scarcely looked at him; but as soon as I got close to him, the little village clod, who had never breathed anything thicker than his own mountain air, actually almost lost string, kite, and all, in an effort, quite irresistible, which he made to bow to me, and take off his hat. Again, in the middle of the forest, I saw the other day three labouring boys laughing together, each of their mouths being, if possible, wider open than the others; however, as they separated, off went their caps, and they really took leave of each other in the very same sort of manner with which I yesterday saw the Landgrave of Hesse-Homburg return a bow to a common postillion." Then Sir Francis Head goes on to moralise on courtesy, but never for a moment glances at the very curious question, "What is the meaning of this act? What was the original signification of this which is now a piece of formal expression of mutual respect?"

The raising the hat is in act similar to the subscription to a letter, "your humble servant," the recognition of being in subjection to the person saluted.

To wear a hat, a covering to the head, was a symbol of authority and power. The crown is merely the head-cover originally worn by the sovereign alone. Afterwards to cover the head signified the possession of freedom, and the slave was bare-headed. When, among the Romans, a slave was manumitted, that slave, as badge of his being thenceforth a free man, assumed the Phrygian cap. On numerous monuments, Roman masters exhibited their munificence to their slaves by engraving caps of liberty, each cap signifying a slave who had been set free.

This is the meaning of the Cap of Liberty. On the murder of Caligula, the mob hoisted Phrygian caps on poles, and ran about with them shouting that they were no longer slaves. The death of the tyrant released them from a servile position.

In mediæval Germany, the giving of a hat was a symbolic act, conveying with it feudal tenure. He who received the hat put his hand into it, as a sign that he grasped all those rights which sprang out of the authority conveyed to him by the presentation of the hat. The Pope, when creating a Cardinal, sends him a scarlet hat. The wearing the hat was allowed only to nobles and freemen—no serf might assume one. Among the Goths, the priests as well as the nobles wore the head covered.

When Gessler set a hat on a pole, it was a token that he was exercising sovereign authority. The elevation of a hat on a pole was also a summons of vassals to war, like the raising of a royal standard. In a French Court of Justice, the judges alone wear their heads covered, in token that they are in exercise of authority there. So in our own universities, the tutor or lecturer wears his square cap. So in the cathedral, a bishop was wont to have his head covered with the mitre; and in a parish church, the pastor wore a biretta. We take off our hats when entering church to testify our homage and allegiance to God; and so in old Catholic ritual, the priest and bishop removed their headgear at times, in token that they received their offices from God.

It roused the Romans to anger because the fillet of royalty was offered to Julius Cæsar. This was the merest shred of symbol—yet it meant that he alone had a right to wear a cover on his head; in other words, that all save he were vassals and serfs. That presentation by Mark Antony brought discontent to a head, and provoked the assassination of Cæsar.

Odin, the chief god of Norse mythology, is called Hekluberand, the Hood-bearer; he alone has his head covered. As god of the skies this no doubt refers to the cloud-covering, but it implies also his sovereignty. So Heckla is not only the covered mountain, but the king or chief of the mountains of Iceland.

We can now see exactly what is the meaning of doffing the cap. It implies that the person uncovering his head acknowledges himself to be the serf of the person before whom he uncovers, or at all events as his feudal inferior. How completely this is forgotten may be judged in any walk abroad we take—when we uncover to an ordinary acquaintance—or we can see it in the Landgrave of Hesse-Homburg removing his hat to the postillion. The curtsey, now almost abandoned, is the bowing of the knee in worship; so is the ordinary bend of the body; even the nod of the head is a symbolic recognition of inferiority in the social scale to the person saluted.

The head is the noblest part of man, and when he lifts his hat that covers it, he implies, or rather did imply at one time, that his head was at the disposal of the person to whom he showed this homage.

There is a curious story in an Icelandic saga of the eleventh century in illustration of this. A certain Thorstein the Fair had killed Thorgils, son of an old bonder in Iceland, named also Thorstein, but surnamed "The White," who was blind. The rule in Iceland was—a life for a life, unless the nearest relative of the fallen man chose to accept blood-money. Five years after the death of Thorgils, Thorstein the Fair came to Iceland and went at once to the house of his namesake, White Thorstein, and offered to pay blood-money for the death of Thorgils, as much as the old man thought just. "No," answered the blind bonder, "I will not bear my son in my purse." Thereupon, Fair Thorstein went to the old man and laid his head on his knees, in token that he offered him his life. White Thorstein said, "I will not have your head cut off at the neck. Moreover, it seems to me that the ears are best where they grow. But this I adjudge—that you come here, into my house, with all your possessions, and live with me in the place of my son whom you slew." And this Fair Thorstein did.

At a period when no deeds were executed in parchment, symbolic acts were gone through, which had the efficacy of a legal deed in the present day.

When Harald Haarfager undertook to subdue the petty kings of Norway, one of these kings, Hrollaug, seeing that he had not the power to withstand Harald, "went to the top of the mound on which the kings were wont to sit, and he had his throne set up thereon and seated himself upon it. Then he had a number of feather beds laid on a bench below, on which the earls were wont to be seated, and he threw himself down from the throne, and rolled on to the earls' bench, thus giving himself out to have taken on him the title and position of an earl."[53] And King Harald accepted this act as a formal renunciation of his royal title. Every head covering was a badge of nobility, from the Crown to the Cap of Maintenance, through all degrees of coronet. In 1215, Hugh, Bishop of Liège, attended the synod in the Lateran, and first he took his place on the bench wearing a mantle and tunic of scarlet, and a green cap to show he was a count, then he assumed a cap with lappets (?) *manicata*, to show he was a duke, and lastly put on his mitre and other insignia as a bishop. When Pope Julius II. conferred on Henry VIII. the title of "Defender of the Faith," he sent him as symbols of authority a sword and a cap of crimson velvet turned up with ermine.

It is probable that originally to uncover the head signified that he who bared his head acknowledged the power and authority of him whom he saluted to deal with his head as he chose. Then it came to signify, in the second place, recognition of feudal superiority. Lastly, it became a simple act of courtesy shown to anyone.

In the same way every man in France is now Monsieur, *i.e.*, my feudal lord; and every man in Germany Mein Herr; and every man in England Mr., *i.e.*, Master. The titles date from feudal times, and originally implied feudal subjection. It does so no longer. So also the title of Esquire implies a right to bear arms. The Squire in the parish was the only man in it who had his shield and crest. The Laird in a Scottish country place is the Lord, the man to whom all looked for their bread. So words and usages change their meaning, and yet are retained by habit, ages after their signification is lost.

THE END.

NOTES

[1] Sacrifices of the same kind were continued. Livy, xxii. 57: "Interim ex fatalibus libris sacrificia aliquot extraordinaria facta: inter quæ Gallus et Galla, Græcus et Græca, in Foro Boario sub terra vivi demissi sunt in locum saxo conseptum, jam ante hostiis humanis, minime Romano sacro, imbutum."

[2] Jovienus Pontanus, in the fifth Book of his History of his own Times. He died 1503.

[3] These cauldrons walled into the sides of the churches are probably the old sacrificial cauldrons of the Teutons and Norse. When heathenism was abandoned, the instrument of the old Pagan rites was planted in the church wall in token of the abolition of heathenism.

[4] There is a rare copper-plate, representing the story, published in Cologne in 1604, from a painting that used to be in the church, but which was destroyed in 1783. After her resurrection, Richmod, who was a real person, is said to have borne her husband three sons.

[5] Magdeburg, Danzig, Glückstadt, Dünkirchen, Hamburg, Nürnberg, Dresden, etc. (see Petersen: "Die Pferdeköpfe auf den Bauerhäusern," Kiel, 1860).

[6] Herodotus, iv. 103: "Enemies whom the Scythians have subdued they treat as follows: each having cut off a head, carries it home with him, then hoisting it on a long pole, he raises it above the roof of his house—and they say that these act as guardians to the household."

[7] The floreated points of metal or stone at the apex of a gable are a reminiscence of the bunch of grain offered to Odin's horse.

[8] Aigla, c. 60. An Icelandic law forbade a vessel coming within sight of the island without first removing its figure-head, lest it should frighten away the guardian spirits of the land. Thattr Thorsteins Uxafots, i.

[9] Finnboga saga, c. 34.

[10] Hood is Wood or Woden. The Wood-dove in Devon is Hood-dove, and Wood Hill in Yorkshire is Hood Hill.

[11] See numerous examples in "The Western Antiquary," November, 1881.

[12] On a discovery of horse-heads in Elsdon Church, by E. C. Robertson, Alnwick, 1882.

[13] "Sir Tristram," by Thomas of Erceldoune, ed. Sir Walter Scott, 1806, p. 153.

[14] See an interesting paper and map, by Dr. Prowse, in the Transactions of the Devon Association, 1891.

[15] Two types, the earliest, convex on both faces. The later, flat on one side, convex on the other. The earlier type (Chelles) is the same as our Drift implements. Till the two types have been found, the one superposed on the other, we cannot be assured of their sequence.

[16] In the artistic faculty. The sketches on bone of the reindeer race were not approached in beauty by any other early race.

[17] "The Past and the Present," by A. Mitchell, M.D., 1880.

[18] The author found and planned some hut circles very similar to those found in Cornwall and Down, on a height above Laruns. There was a dolmen at Buzy at the opening of the valley.

[19] Hor. Sat. ii. 8.

[20] Fornaldar Sögur. iii. p. 387.

[21] Heimskringla, i., c. 12.

[22] I have given an account of the Carro already in my book, "In Troubadour Land."

[23] Roman and Greek ladies employed parasols to shade their faces from the sun, and to keep off showers. See s. v. *Umbraculum* in Smith's Dictionary of Greek and Roman Antiquities.

[24] A good deal of information relative to umbrellas may be got out of Sangster (W.). "Umbrellas and their History." London: Cassell & Co., Ltd.

[25] The first English*man* who carried an umbrella was Jonas Hanway, who died in 1786, but it was known in England earlier. Beaumont and Fletcher allude to it in "Rule a Wife and Have a Wife":

> "Now are you glad, now is your mind at ease;
> Now you have got a shadow, an umbrella,
> To keep the scorching world's opinion
> From your fair credit."

And Ben Jonson, in "The Devil is an Ass":

> "And there she lay, flat spread as an umbrella."

Kersey in his Dictionary, 1708, describes an umbrella as a "screen commonly used by women to keep off rain."

[26] Castrén, Nordische Reisen, St. Petersburg, 1853, p. 290.

[27] "The Beggynhof," London, 1869, p. 68.

[28] Ed. Viger, IV., p. 161.

[29] So Grimm and others following him; but I am more inclined to see in Herodias, Herr-raud the Red Lord, *i.e.*, Thor.

[30] "A Dyalogue describing the orygynall ground of these Lutheran facyons," 1531. A later work on the excesses of sectaries is Featley's (D.) Dippers Dipt, 1660.

[31] Quoted in *Westminster Review*, Jan., 1860, p. 194.
[32] "Autobiography of Peter Cartwright." London, 1862 (7th ed.)
[33] "The Epidemics of the Middle Ages." London, 1859.
[34] The word is, of course, derived from *Instrumentum*.
[35] See "Fretella," in Ducange, "Fistulæ species."
[36] M. Gilbert prints, "As the dew flies," etc.; this is a mistake—"doo" is *dove*.
[37] Possibly we may have this in the still popular Cornish lament, "Have you seen my Billy coming?"
[38] On December 14, 1624, as many as 128 ballads were licensed, the names of which are given. "The Blind Beggar (of Bethnal Green);" "Maudline of Bristowe (The Merchant's Daughter of Bristol);" "Sweet Nansie I doe love thee;" "The Lady's Fall;" "My minde to me a kingdom is" (Sir Edward Dyer's famous song); "Margaret, my sweetest;" "In London dwelt a merchantman;" "I am sorry, I am sorry;" "In May when flowers springe;" "I am a poore woman and blinde;" "The Devil and the Paritor (Apparitor);" "It was a Lady's daughter;" "Roger's Will;" "Bateman (Lord);" "Bride's Good Morrow;" "The King and the Shepherd;" "As I went forth one summer's day;" "Amintas on a summer's day;" "Ah me, not to thee alone;" "Sir John Barley Corne;" "It was a youthful knight;" "Jane Shore;" "Before my face;" "George Barnwell;" "From Sluggish Sleepe;" "Down by a forrest;" "The Miller and the King;" "Chevie Chase;" "How shall we good husbands live;" "Jerusalem, my happie home;" "The King and the Tanner;" "Single life the only way;" "The Lord of Lorne;" "In the daies of old;" "I spide a Nymph trip over the plaine;" "Shakeing hay;" "Troy Toun;" "Walking of late abroad;" "Kisse and bide me welcome home;" "The chirping larke;" "John Carelesse;" "Tell me, Susan, certenly;" "Spanish Lady;" "When Arthur first in Court;" "Diana and her darlings;" "Dear love, regard my life;" "Bride's buryal;" "Shakeing of the sheets;" "A rich merchantman;" "Gilian of Bramfield;" "Fortune my Foe;" "Cripple of Cornwall;" "Whipping the catt at Abingdon;" "On yonder hill there springs;" "Upon a summertime;" "The Miser of Norfolk."
[39] Friedrich (J.B.) Geschichte des Räthsels, Dresden, 1860.
[40] "Le Dieu Gaulois du Soleil," Paris, 1886.
[41] "Scriptores rer. German. Frankof.," 1718, p. 508.
[42] "Eckhard, Monument. Jutreboc," p. 59.
[43] "Anton, Versaml. uber Sitten d. alten Slawen," II. p. 97.
[44] The date on this stone is only 1807, so that the practice must be very modern.
[45] Other dolmens with holes at Trye-le-Château, Presles, les Mauduits, in Seine et Oise; at Vic-sur-Aisne; at Bellehaye, and at Villicor—Saint Sépulcre (Oise); and others are in the Morbihan, Charente, etc.

[46] What we in England term cromlechs, the French more correctly call dolmens.

[47] The building up of part of the circle round a cairn was probably to block the way of the spirit in the direction of the village occupied by the living.

[48] Bull. de la Soc. d'anthropologie de Paris, t. ix., p. 198.

[49] Reinsberg Düringsfeld. "Trad. et Legendes de la Belgique," 1870, T. II., p. 239.

[50] Journal of the British Archæological Association, vol. xxxviii., 1882.

[51] They are found, for instance, on tombstones near Inverness.

[52] The majority of these vessels, which abound in the West of England, were unquestionably measures of corn. But all were not so; those that have rounded hollows like cups, and not square cut, were for holy water.

[53] "Heimskringla," Saga III., c. 8.

Milton Keynes UK
Ingram Content Group UK Ltd.
UKHW030906151124
451262UK00006B/966